Praise for
The Love of One

"This is a beautiful story of the healing power of love and spiritual support when Caroline's world was turned upside down."

 –*Barry Eaton,* broadcaster and author of *Afterlife* and *No Goodbyes.*

"*The Love of One* is probably the most powerful love story I have ever read. This is not a sanitised account of dealing with the illness of a loved one but a visceral journey of raw emotions. Caroline Cumming's writing style is intimate in the extreme. I felt with an overwhelming intensity every high and low of her husband's fight for survival. I shared her rage and her joy. You do not read this book, you live it and in doing so you will cherish your loved ones all the more."

 –*Anthony Peake,* consciousness researcher, speaker and author of *The Infinite Mind: The Quest to Find the Gateway to Higher Consciousness.*

"Stunning prose . . . keeps you on the edge of your seat . . . journal of what healing our fearful stories looks like and requires to be achieved . . . and of the power we have as a community when we join together with love and compassion . . . For those seeking wisdom, personal clarity and answers, or experiencing upheaval or grief, it will be a godsend. For those who love in-depth stories about people's lives, it will simply be a joy. You will be changed and potentially transformed into a better version of yourself just by reading it."

 –*Katie (Altham) Todd,* psychotherapist and bestselling author of
Who Am I? An Archetypal Quest.

"Cumming is a fantastic storyteller. One of the most extraordinary and powerful aspects of *The Love of One* is that it transports the reader so completely to be a silent companion with Caroline . . . There are precious few books that have the ability to turn a passive reader into a truly "active reader" who responds instinctively to the emotions and experiences of the book . . . A powerfully and beautifully expressed reminder to treasure those loved ones we have in our lives."

–*Dr Julie Mundy-Taylor,* Liaison Librarian, Research
Support Services, University of Newcastle.

"Spellbinding . . . (Caroline's) words connect with the reader at a deeper level, we remember our vulnerability of our shadow, and as (her) words weave their tapestry of acceptance for best outcome for 'Gordon's higher self,' we too recognise the divinity of our lives. A very powerful read."

–*Mary Atkins,* author of *Finding Your Voice* and *Losing You.*

"Absolutely brilliant! Cumming's ability to capture such authentic expression in the midst of trauma and vulnerability is both admirable and inspirational . . . you cannot help but be uplifted by the power of unconditional love, connection and the spirit of community. My heart is full after reading this book."

–*Angie Quinn,* therapist and life coach.

"Just in reading this story I felt transported into my own spirit. I would highly recommend this book to anyone . . . it takes the reader on a journey into compassion, faith, love, honesty, and the indomitable spirit of humankind."

–*Helen Gill,* intuitive and healer.

The
LOVE
of
ONE

Caroline Cumming

The
LOVE
of
ONE

A memoir of the creative power
that weaved a miracle

SIX DEGREES PUBLISHING GROUP
PORTLAND ◆ OREGON ◆ USA

The Love of One
A memoir of the creative power that weaved a miracle

Caroline Cumming

Six Degrees Publishing Group
5331 S. W. Macadam Avenue, Suite 258
Portland, OR 97239

ISBN: 978–942497-19-6
U.S. Library of Congress PCN: 2016937708
Ebook ISBN: 978-1-942497-20-2

Cover Design: James T Egan, Bookfly Design
Editor: Laurel Cohn, Laurel Cohn Editing
and Manuscript Development Services

Author's Note: This work is a memoir. Certain names, locations and identifying characteristics have been changed. Dialogue and events have been recreated from memory, and in some cases have been compressed to convey the substance of what was said or what occurred.

www.SixDegreesPublishing.com

Printed simultaneously in the United States of America, the United Kingdom, and Australia. Published in the USA.
1 3 5 7 9 10 8 6 4 2

Dedicated to my beautiful man, to all of humanity, and to the dance of the human-divine.

Contents

Preface

"Go into the forest," the voice said, breaking my reverie. My stomach tightened. I had always feared being in the forest on my own, and only ever walked there with my husband or a friend. But the clarity of the voice inside my head could not be denied.

I fidgeted in my chair, the wicker squeaking. Sitting on the verandah for many weeks now – through the golds and ochres of autumn to the bright and clean of early winter – it was as if the idea of going anywhere else was foreign.

And yet I *knew* this voice speaking to me now. It was the same one that had commanded me to "STOP! Stop everything!" after an excruciating amount of pain some months before, a pain connected with my menstruation, a pain so potent I had fainted in front of my husband and my lips turned blue. I was out cold for almost 90 seconds, and when I came to, Gordon had helped me as I crawled to the bathroom where I vomited and had diarrhea.

Hard to believe that had been almost a year after the traumas of 2012 and his coma. Being the adaptable coper I'd learned to be, I hadn't realised I'd been suffering from post-traumatic stress.

That voice had saved me. I was glad I had listened to it even though it had felt counter-intuitive to act on its instructions, what with Gordon being into his seventh month out of work, and us only having five weeks rent and living expenses in the bank with no possessions to sell if it came to it. Yes, I'd been trying to launch a new business to help things along but I knew my heart wasn't in it, and my physical energy was drained.

Heeding that voice, I retreated to the old, semi-enclosed, wooden veranda of our cottage. Held within this cocoon, I bathed in the warmth of the sun, immersed in the beauty and heady fragrance of sweet jasmine on the railing. I delighted as the butterflies danced their song and birds streaked between bare branches, and smiled as I watched the 2.30 p.m. clockwork procession of ducks waddling up from the water. I had been doing this every day, until now, until the moment the voice had announced itself and told me to go to the forest.

Trusting it, I put my jacket on and set off.

A dank mulch of leaves cushioned the way as I trod inside the silence of the eavesdropping forest. The more I walked and the more the sun filtered through in a bid to warm trunks of mahogany, bone, and silver, the more my shoulders dropped and my breathing relaxed. It was then that a sentence from out of nowhere plopped into my head and heart, followed by another one. I stopped in my tracks. Without hesitation, I knew the words marked the start of the book I was to write. The book was letting me know it was now time. Pulling the only thing from my bag that I could find – a tissue – I wrote the lines down. An hour later I was back home typing them, and more besides. The process had begun.

I wrote this book from the heart. It is a direct transmission of love, magic, miracles, and deep healing. Much of it came through in a manner similar to what happened in the forest. Many a night I would be woken by the voice, showing me a symbol to research. The voice would follow me into the toilet, telling me to change a word I had written in a chapter the day before, and so on. In queues and when driving, the voice would continue to steer this book's narrative. For almost nine months the voice and book consumed me. I gave myself to all of it. No creative energy remained for my other passions, including any other kind of writing. All I knew was this work wanted to come through and I was the one to bring it forth. Writing it became a crucial part of my healing on many levels. As you read it, I hope the same healing gifts will extend to you.

—Caroline Cumming

Introduction

THE EXPERIENCE OF SEPARATION is an illusion. Even if for a moment we buy into the idea that it is true – because sometimes it can feel so real – it is still not the whole truth. When we are asleep within this illusion, we operate from fear and mind and limited perception. We walk as if in a darkened tunnel. We can believe we are not safe. We go around needing to be in control and we believe we are in ultimate control. We hold hands with the ones we love, and we never want to let go or be let go of. We hold on for dear life. We fear loss. We believe there is an "us" or "other" *to* be lost, and our conviction is that we truly could be this thing called "alone" or "abandoned" or "unsupported". We believe that our God could have forsaken us, or that the Divine (or our mother or our father or our lover) could have abandoned us. We relate to ourselves only as the human being and the physical body, not as the intelligence or divinity that expresses itself as the human being.

This book is a messenger for the truth that we are all one. The narrative originates from a set of experiences within the illusion of separation, as well as from experiences that were beyond that illusion. In other words, it is a book of two seemingly different frequencies or vibrations. As much as it illuminates how we create the suffering and illusion of disconnection and separation in our lives – and what we need to do to heal that – it also demonstrates what it takes to open our hearts in the face of great resistance, and to find grace and strength in compassion and vulnerability. It offers inspiration about what is possible when we heed the call to be love in action, both as an individual and as a collective.

Ever since the personal events and universal themes of my story played out in 2012, the planet and humanity have mirrored heightened change, threats to what we hold dear, and more polarity amongst humans than ever before. As this period of collective transition, seeming insurmountable odds, and the meeting of shadow continues, we face the same two choices I did in the book. We can either revert to fear, judgement, control, and aggression – or know and live the truth of ourselves as love, compassion, passionate caring, and one.

However, creating change in the outer world requires each of us to heal the same wounds in our inner world, and to embrace the creative power of unconditional love for the highest good. *The Love of One* offers readers exactly that journey, told through the potency and accessibility of ordinary human beings, and a conflicted family that symbolises the largest family of all: humanity. It is a book that I believe is as pertinent for our times now, as it will be for our times yet to come. We *must* heal our sense of separation. Whilst it is likely more people around the world will continue to be brought to their knees by circumstances and chaos, this book teaches there are still choices we *can* make in that context, choices which can transform the way we live. We can meet our fears and open and thrive, even when imminent loss and our own survival appears to be in question. We can embrace the creative power of community when it focuses on being a conduit for unconditional love through prayer, intention, meditation, and surrender to the highest good. We can learn to love freely. We can gather and align with something greater than our smaller and more limited personal agenda. We can birth anew. We can create what is true to create. We can learn the dance of the human divine.

These are capacities every human being on earth can learn and live. And it is magical tales such as this one, that have a chance of delivering these ideas and instructions not just to the intellect, but right into the *heart,* where they are most needed and where they can have most impact.

That said, how you read this book is up to you. You may well find it reads *you.* What I mean by that is that the story contained within these pages is alchemical. My journey and your journey are intertwined, for we are one. Just as my shadow came up to be transmuted during my experiences, so too may yours arise within your inner or even your outer world, as you read. In the same way my heart opened, so too may yours. Like medicine and healing balm, the words of this story will work upon you the way that is needed by you, and they will land in exactly the right places.

Such is the creative power of Love.

Prologue

THE LITTLE GIRL AND HER MUMMY were on their way to the shops via the underpass. It was winter and the girl shrieked with joy as she splashed in the puddles, her excitement spilling over at being allowed to wear the new lollipop-orange gumboots that smelt of glue but which Mummy told her was PVC. As they approached the tunnel, the girl pretended she was entering the mouth of a caterpillar with a hole in his bottom. For a minute, all she could glimpse in the darkness was the glow of her own boots. She clutched onto her mummy, hurrying to keep up with the echoes of grown-up footsteps as they clopped on concrete. Adjusting to the dimness, she widened her eyes and took in the strangeness of the paint that had been sprawled across the sides of the caterpillar's belly. The stink of pee made her wrinkle her nose. A rat, scurrying out from the newspapers the caterpillar had swallowed, had her jumping in fright. She wanted to get out.

Without warning, a gust of wind blasted into the caterpillar's mouth behind her, whisking her off her feet, wrenching her from her mummy and dumping her, a yard or two away, on hands and knees that started to bleed from the grazes. For a split second she felt alone and disoriented, the breath knocked out of her, too stunned and confused to cry. Why had her mummy let go of her? The thought made her eyes fill with tears so that she could not see again. Her face crumpled and her mouth gaped as she wailed with fright and the snot streamed out of her nose. Somewhere, from within the swirls of blindness and sobbing, she heard her mummy rushing up to her and consoling her, felt the reassurance of her cuddle.

I never wore those gumboots again. Funny what your first memory can be. I was three years old yet already well on my way to making up my mind about life.

Chapter One

Day 1

9.50 a.m. – Home

O N THE MORNING OF JUNE 16TH, an egg met with its destiny in a hard and merciless crack against the cold stainless-steel rim as two agitated thumbs moved in to prise it open. Immediately exposed, the soft yolk had no option but to unceremoniously spill into the bowl that waited to receive its fall.

I watched Gordon crack a couple more as he added a knob of butter, some salt and pepper, a dash of milk and what looked like a sprinkle of unease, whisking everything to within an inch of its life until all that remained was an upset pool of lemon froth. I knew my husband well enough, after thirteen years, to realise that it was good for him to have something to do right now, even better if it was something that needed to be done. Looming over the benchtop, he moved with deliberation to the next task – the kale – as my eyes burned holes into the breadth of his back. His capable hands scooped up the thin ribbons of greens and lowered them into their pot on the stove. I snorted under my breath. Much as I loved those hands, they were made for *creating* things, for being with the earth, for caressing *me*, even – not for doing bad trades on the laptop or for typing up project reports for I.T. Nor for slamming doors in my face until they were almost off their hinges, the way he'd done hours ago when he'd bellowed his frustration.

I studied him as he covered the greens with a lid – clunk – and left them to wilt in the scalding heat while he fixed up the toast. It occurred to me he would need to change out of his track pants and T-shirt before we left. And that neither of us was speaking to each other. For his part, I knew the quietness was because he was still digesting this morning's news from the doctor, nervous of my reaction. As for me, I didn't like the starter knot of apprehension beginning to tighten in the pit of my stomach. I figured that if I stayed silent about that knot it would mean that the misgiving couldn't come out in words. And if it couldn't come out in words maybe it would stop existing altogether. Besides which, I felt more in my comfort zone by being with my irritation right now, even though something was telling me to keep a lid on that emotion too, to hold it at a mere simmer. There had been more than enough embroiling last night. Right now, we had forty-five minutes to get ready, bolt down breakfast and go. A nuisance we had needed to come all the way home first. At least we now had our health insurance cards, had been able to make the call that confirmed his eligibility for cover. The bed would be ready at 11 a.m. We needed to be there on time. *Focus.*

I turned away, leaving him to it as I paced across the room to stare at the view. Beyond the wall of window, paradise pulsed and beckoned. Today it sparkled for everybody else's pleasure, all those cockatoo-white and old-fashioned sailboats bobbing in that weekend kind of way. I squinted. Winter's sun, not content with casting its rays over the emerald headland of National Park, now streamed its way in through the glass where I stood, warming my face, tugging at me to come out and play, mistaking me for a free woman or a holidaymaker. But I was going nowhere fun today. There was no excitement on the agenda. And I was pissed off about it. Another bloody Saturday going to waste.

The scarlet streak of a King Parrot caught my eye as it flitted straight into the silvery embrace of my beloved gum tree. I held my breath enchanted, smiled at his squeaks and murmurs as he feasted on the berries amongst the leaves. The moment went, given over to the demands of my exasperation, to the thoughts that came charging in, courtesy of a legion of warriors on horseback all ready to do battle. I wanted to yell, *roar*, goddammit. All I craved was safety. Safety and security in my world, and to have a depth and truth to the connection with my man – but for Pete's sake, my man had to bloody come to the table too. Thoughts raced. *Is it too much to ask? Jesus.* I longed for my life to start returning to normality again, minus the heaviness and the unrelenting stuff-ups and drama. We'd been to hell and back in these past five years of shit hitting the fan. Why couldn't I now have ease and freedom? How on Earth could that be deemed unreasonable by him or by God or by bloody anyone? I was turning 42 in two months for Christ's sake! My biological clock had almost ticked itself out and at 57 he wasn't getting any younger either. Why this, now? Hadn't I learned my lessons – about love, about letting go, about control, about forgiveness, and true power? Hadn't I done all the damn growth that had resulted from that? What about the acceptance that I had come to, all the ways of being that had needed to go? Didn't I let fall those tired beliefs that had no longer served me? *Surely there came a point when enough was bloody enough?*

The kettle boiled and rattled in its holder, seconds away from flicking its switch. My jaw tightened. It was hard to fight the urge to explode at the world and spew at the unfairness of everything right now. I glanced over my shoulder to say something but was met only by the back of Gordon's head and the short grey hairs there that mingled with the black. I angled away again. *What's the point?*

Before I knew it, I was down the rabbit-hole of my story and anger, my arms folded against my chest as I plunged and hurtled past all the landmarks. The loss of all our money, his lies and deceit and betrayal about those dollars and how he had dispensed them; my unwitting enabling of our financial disaster; the shock and the way in which I had found out, with no income to support us; the subsequent, abrupt end to our twelve-month trip round Australia; his guilt; the months of him being out of work and looking for a job while we suffered the harassment of calls from the bank and utility companies; my attempts to set my clinic up again as a necessity, even though my heart wasn't in it. There was the return to stability only to endure a repeat of more lies and deceit over money and its misappropriation, and the loss of our savings again, including a paid-for trip to Africa; my struggle to trust him; the constancy of the hot-potato subject of us starting a family together; the conviction I had of our lives being thwarted; the strain of us camped in his mother's backyard for eighteen months as our marriage almost broke down; my spiral of rage and grief, followed by the depression that overwhelmed and swamped me. On, and on, and on down the rabbit-hole I went. When it spat me out at the other end, it was to the sounds of Gordon dishing up, chinking cutlery as he rummaged for knives and forks, and clattering pots in the sink as he ran the tap to put them in soak.

Hearing his bare feet plod the few paces over to the table, I sighed, the last steam of righteousness and exasperation misting the window as all the puffed-up fight inside my chest fizzled and swirled its leave. My shoulders sagged. Arms flopped down to my sides. I felt drained from the ride through which I'd just put myself and any sense of unfairness or injustice was now spent, a mere murmur.

"Babes, breakfast is here."

I turned. Two platefuls of green and yellow sat at the near end of the massive white table. Food made with love, though today, perhaps, more of the wretched kind. The metal legs of our chairs scraped out into the silence as we sat down, both of us oblivious to the fact that this would be the last time he would ever have scrambled eggs and sautéed kale again. How *could* we have known? I mean, you don't tend to ponder the possibility of that when you make breakfast, do you? It's not as if halfway through waiting for the toast to pop up, you ponder over how life can be turned upside down in the blink of an eye and then wonder if today will be the day it is going to happen to you. No, you don't think about these things.

Day to day, you tend to subconsciously shut down to such an idea, dismiss it, suppress it, not let it in, not *see it*. Why? Because this notion that perhaps you are not in total control – and that the mere idea of "control" is an *illusion* – is terrifying. So instead, you act out your beliefs and assume that you do know how it is in your world, you behave as if you do know what's going to happen next and what the day will bring, talk as if you are certain the weekend is indeed now going to be ruined because of an unwelcome appointment that is likely to last the day and could have been avoided. And yet all along, you deny an "inconvenient truth": that you cannot see the Big Picture, and that there is the possibility that you could get up at 8 a.m. one day, ignorant of the fact that in a few hours the Event That Changes Everything may well take place.

"I can't say as I am all that hungry. You?"

"No, not really."

"Yeah, I know, I get it."

"Mm."

"But you should eat something before you go in."

"Yeah, true."

"I mean, we don't know how long it will all take, do we? So you should eat."

A few mouthfuls passed by within the void before Gordon laid his knife and fork down and stretched his upturned arm and palm across on the table to me.

"Babes . . ." He motioned with his thick fingers for me to join him there, an exposed yet safe place where tenderness and softness and holding could meet. He nestled me, protective, stroking me again with his thumb. "Look, I'm sorry this is happening. Really, I am. But it's going to be all good you know!" He punctuated his statement with one of his trademark smiles, an exaggerated grin of optimism. My inner child needed the reassurance but wasn't convinced – didn't know for sure if she could trust the words. He squeezed my knuckles for further confirmation and my wedding and engagement rings pinched me for a second. I sighed, felt myself open up.

"Look, I'm sorry too, for my part in the row last night. I'm not angry anymore. But I *am* feeling vulnerable. If I'm honest, a bit scared. Memories of the last time you had to go in for the same thing, you know?"

"I know. I realise that."

We resumed eating, swallowing our respective mouthfuls into stomachs still stuffed with the undigested words and their acid-sloshing emotions from the night before. Outside, the kookaburras started up for the fourth time that morning, their raucous chorus spiralling and ricocheting off the lull between Gordon and me, pressing for something, demanding.

"Tell me again, exactly, word for word, what the doctor said this morning."

"It's like I said before. She ran the ECG, looked at the results, told me I was in atrial fibrillation, and that my heartbeat had gone into irregular rhythm."

"Then?"

"That I needed to get myself into hospital as soon as possible so they could flick it back with a drip or, if need be, the paddles again so that . . ."

"What about the call to the hospital?"

"Just that, after ringing Burleigh Fields, she told me I was lucky they had availability. One last bed – so long as we can get in for 11 a.m. That was it." He shovelled more food into his mouth, aware of time. "Oh yeah, and she said she didn't like the sound of my cough either. That was all."

"But what vibe did you get from her? Should we be worried? See, I *am* worried."

"Only the sense that I needed to take action and that it wasn't something I could or should dilly-dally with."

"But did she *look* concerned?" I scanned his face for any revelations that his mouth, bushy eyebrows, or gentle eyes weren't giving.

"I don't know, Babes. She just had . . . focus. You know how doctors are. Babes, please, it's going to be alright!"

"But how do you feel right now? Is your chest funny?"

"I feel alright, actually."

I couldn't help myself. Back on the ride, the words of desperation already so close to the surface now blurted free. "You should have gone to get yourself checked out with the doctor earlier this week! Not leave it so long, till now, till the weekend. I have been *asking* you all week!"

"Babes, let's not start this all up again! It is what it is!"

"But I just don't understand you! You wouldn't even leave work yesterday afternoon even though you felt 'quite unwell' as you put it. I asked you *days* ago to tune in to your intuition about going to the doctors and I can't understand for the life of me what took you so long to do that and then when you did, why your intuition just gave you an answer of 'yeah, why not, go, it can't hurt!' I mean, there is obviously a problem, so it can't have been your intuition talking!"

This time his knife and fork clanked down on the plate. He was done, a small amount of kale remained, withered. "Well that's the guidance I received, okay? And I felt okay at the start of the week. I still believe the cough is just a hangover from the cold I've had. I want you to stop now. Please."

I could hear the vexation creeping into his voice. I understood. My being like this wasn't making things any easier for him and, Lord knew, he had to be as drained as I was after last night's humdinger. Message received loud and clear – keep my thoughts to myself. The truth was they wouldn't help right now. Even though they were rattling around in my head like snakes about to lurch, I knew that for the time being at any rate, they were better in than out.

"Should we pack you an overnight bag, just in case?"

"Honestly don't think I'll need one. It's just a routine procedure. We walk in, we do it, and we walk out." He checked his phone. "Shit, we need to get a move on. C'mon!" He stood up and gathered the plates, taking them to the sink to rinse before padding off surefooted across the sun-drenched floorboards and towards the bathroom, to brush his teeth and have a final pee. Rising, I went to close my laptop but not before instinct had me firing off a post on my social media page:

Gordon unwell. Going to hospital to be admitted. Am reliving nightmares and feeling vulnerable. We'll be okay but am sure your loving vibes to him would be warmly received. Thank you. Xx

Within the ten minutes that it took for us to leave the house, my update had received a surprising number of well-wishes from friends. There was no time to read any of the comments, only to follow Gordon down the metal stairs and step out onto the porch, my feet meeting with a scrabble of fallen leaves swirling across the mat in the wind. A last hasty check for my keys and then I closed the solidness of our huge blue door, our life behind it.

CHAPTER TWO

Day 1

10.30 a.m. – En route to the hospital

DRIVING UP THE HILL, we left the spangled waters of the bay behind us. Though the splashes of golden wattle caught my eye as we hugged the edge of the National Park, my mind was elsewhere, replaying the night before. There was no doubt about it, we'd both given as good as we'd got, dredging up all the hurts and stories of a past that was, in practical terms, still rippling unwanted consequences in our life. Despite fretting yesterday after hearing how unwell Gordon had said he'd felt in the afternoon, it hadn't been long before my unease had turned into something I could better handle: annoyance that he had not chosen to leave work for the day and see a doctor, and anger that he wasn't taking responsibility for his health when I was trying to get my body ready to conceive. I had yelled at him that I wasn't signing up to be a single mother, fumed at what I saw as his pattern of burrowing his head in the sand, and the ridiculousness of his addiction to trying to keep his world an "even-keeled" fairy-tale all the time. And oh how I had screamed like a banshee, shrieking that I wanted a man who was willing to dive into the depths of relationship, one who wouldn't be scared by an animated discussion if it screeched into play, someone committed to the full ride and not to just skimming and playing about on the froth and surface of things. That if it wasn't his desire to get "real" about where we were going, well we needed to part. I had flown out of the house at that juncture and charged up the steep driveway, panting from the exertion of the impulse and from the exhaustion of venting. Coming to a standstill at the top, I had stared up at the stars in hopelessness, not expecting the text message from him which came through on the phone two minutes later: *I do want you and I do want to dive deeper in our relationship. I do want that richness and that fullness of relationship with you. It's just that sometimes my subconscious gets scared and it needs to be held.*

The impromptu change in angle of the car, now pointing downhill as it navigated the descent towards the main road below, brought me back to the towering grace of the trees outside, a reminder that we were off to the hospital. Looking over at Gordon as he focused on the bends, I felt a surge of love, a touch of fear, and an ache to be with him so strong in its hunger that it stammered and blurted itself out with heartfelt intensity.

"I feel odd. I can't explain. I so want to make love to you, right now I mean, for a long, long time and, I don't know, but I want to *hold* you and not let go and jeez it's a crazy huge feeling in this moment. I love you so much, darling!"

"Oh Babes, I love you too. I wish all this wasn't happening today."

His eyes welled up as he continued to concentrate on the road, cupping my hand in my lap. A lump burgeoned in my throat, tears pricking at my eyes. I didn't understand why I'd just declared myself like that. I'd never spoken it in that way before now, with that degree of oddness, nor felt it with that brand of charge. It seemed to me as if my volume had been louder as I'd spoken but that I hadn't turned it up myself – as if all those words I'd uttered had come out in the wash and been pegged on the line, to flap in the wind between speech marks. I frowned, sensing a significance that I did not understand.

Twenty minutes later we arrived at the hospital. It lay in wait for us at the dead-end of an unassuming street in suburbia, a long, single-storey affair that bore its name in gold letters on brown bricks. It didn't look much like a hospital and for that I was grateful. We squeezed into the last space of the cramped car park and Gordon turned off the engine. Being here was enough to quicken my heart rate, its drumming becoming the calling song for the awakening of my phobia for all things medical. I steeled myself. *Alright Caroline, let's do this.*

The tint of the glass doors at the entrance bounced back our reflections as we approached – me with my long brown hair, and in my jumper and jeans, Gordon, in his red fleece and hoisting up the waistband on his trousers. It was disconcerting being unable to discern anything behind the doors, to not know what I was going to be walking into until I found myself right in it. Of course, I imagined that what lay on the other side was the means to what I wanted – Gordon's heart being flicked back into rhythm and us getting back to our home and our lives. Something nagged in the back of my mind. *It's not always about what you want. Sometimes it's about what you need.* I fobbed it off as silliness. Crossing over the invisible line, the glass panes responded, pulling apart in true *Open Sesame* style and allowing us to walk into reception.

A cursory glance around the foyer was enough to disarm me. We were the only ones here and the interior didn't look like I had expected it to. Chocolate and copper furnishings, small leather sofas, a trendy glass vase of orchids, and forgettable art on the walls all brought to mind a lobby for executive apartments. We veered over to the curve of the high reception counter and waited to the left of a sign that instructed us to keep a distance from the people being seen to. A set of panda eyes behind clunky glasses looked up from the keyboard. The brunette welcomed Gordon with such enthusiasm that for a second I thought everything else this morning might have been a dream and that we were now checking in to a hotel – somewhere else, someplace happy.

"Ah yes, the 11 a.m. bed. We've been expecting you. Did you have a smooth trip down here?" she trilled. Gordon said something about traffic. "Right, well, if you'd like to fill in these forms . . . this one here is about the BUPA insurance, yes? Um, why don't you take a seat over there, it's more comfortable for you to write. And a nurse will come for you soon."

We settled ourselves back into the sofa and Gordon busied himself with his paperwork. The receptionist pattered her fingers across the keyboard whilst discussing workers compensation with someone on the other end of the phone. There was nothing else for me to do except sit and wait – and grapple with my memories. It had been two years since we had last been to hospital for Gordon. The palpitations he had been experiencing then, both on our trip and the year before it, had worsened. Of course, I was still in the dark at that point, with no idea about how much stress he was dealing with and hiding from me. I was also yet to make my discovery about the devastation and carnage that had kicked in halfway around Australia when our property development went bad under his management and he'd used the funds from the sale of our home to prop it up. The bank statements might have alerted me but we were on the road, often in the middle of nowhere, using a service to forward our mail but that kept failing to send these statements and half our other post to the pick-up addresses we'd identified. There had seemed no reason for me to think to check the account, despite the fact that Gordon seemed to be the one going to the cashpoint to get our cash whenever we were in a town. Sitting here now, I raised my eyebrows, finding it a struggle to believe it had all been two years ago. Months had passed afterwards, until the day when the palpitations had increased, and just like now, his heart had gone out of rhythm and he'd been administered the routine drip he was waiting for today. The medications back then had been slow to take effect and the consultant had made the decision to help things along by giving Gordon the paddles to his chest. I remembered it as though it were yesterday. It had been a procedure for which I'd needed to sit in the waiting room, alone, having to calm myself after being told there was an outside chance that Gordon's heart could stop during the process but that he was in the best place for them be able to start it again if it did. After an hour spent frantic with worry, I'd gone back onto the ward to ask what was happening. The nurse, realising that nobody had been sent to update me, had apologised profusely of course and relayed with a smile that the procedure had been a success and I could go in and see Gordon, who had long been sitting up and was now eating a sandwich.

That was then – and a different hospital. It was a challenge for me to accept that we were back in one at all. Peering at Gordon, I could see the forms were still consuming him. I curled my toes inside my boots. The oversized clock up on the wall behind reception showed ten minutes to eleven. Was it my imagination, or was it the more I stared at it, the more my heart rate fell in line with the unrelenting march of the red ticker counting round the seconds? *Change focus, Caroline.* I picked up one of the magazines on the table. All about travelling to the remoteness of outback Australia, something Gordon and I had enjoyed doing for months on end during our trip – before our life had started caving in. We yearned to go again as soon as we were able. For a minute I became lost in the evocative photos and headlines, the spirit of ochre and cobalt, allowing myself to be whisked away to the magic and adventures we'd had. The day we'd spent connecting with indigenous elders of Kakadu and Arnhem Land – laughing with them in the space beyond words; me getting feathers up my nose in my dismal attempts under their tutelage to pluck geese like they could; watching Gordon make the fire with them; both of us mucking in as they cooked dinner in the ground; and later, passion and kisses with my man as the flamed sun dipped behind the horizon, the Whistling Kites calling out on the thermals, and thousands of Magpie Geese deafening us with their honking. Happiness. It all felt like lifetimes ago now.

"Whatchya looking at?" Gordon asked, pausing from his forms for a second and nodding over at the magazine in my hand.

I showed him the double-page spread. He did his wistful face. I knew he was itching to get back there.

"So . . . how are you feeling? How's your chest?"

"I'm surprisingly okay, actually."

"You know, I was thinking earlier about how lucky we were that we ended up at the surgery that we did this morning . . ."

"Indeed!"

"That you were able to be seen first thing, rather than the 2 p.m. slot you would have had at the other clinic you'd booked into. You know, something told me to get you into this one instead."

"Yeah, well Dr Grayson was saying it was handy too because she had the ECG machine right there in her room. According to her, if I'd ended up at the other place they would have ended up sending me to Hawksford Public to get it checked out there. I got a distinct sense of relief from her that I had been seen first thing, rather than later on in the day by someone else."

"Hmm. And then there was one bed left when she rang up. You have to admit, there has been a certain flow to all this. Maybe life is looking after us after all, eh?" It was a meek attempt at a joke. I flashed a "happy" smile over at Gordon.

"Maybe it is!"

The sliding doors activated and rattled along their runners as the squawking of lorikeets in the trees came rushing in for a few seconds while a portly woman entered. Grey trousers and corporate blue, she clopped with purpose across the floor and passed the desk. No stranger to this terrain, but rather someone who could saunter with confidence down a corridor known to her and disappear out of sight. In her coming and going, she had alerted me to the clacking of a busy stapler from somewhere beyond the lobby, along with the yakking of two women there as they worked.

"Mr Cumming? Gordon Cumming?"

We looked up. She stood to the left of the desk, a wiry nurse, at the start of the passageway down which we couldn't see.

"We're ready for you now," she smiled. "Would you like to come through? Yes, yes, that's right, both of you." She ushered us to her with her clipboard.

It was bang on eleven o'clock.

And yet not one of us had any idea that this moment, this summons, and this scene were to be the last things that Gordon would ever remember of his stay here.

CHAPTER THREE

Day 1

11.00 a.m. – Hospital

SWAPPING FLOOR TILES for a dark patterned carpet that hypnotised into the distance, we followed the nurse down her tramline, contained as it was by the blandness of its walls and the sickly taupe doors and handrails. The realisation that I had no idea how far down we were going, made me uncomfortable. I hated not being in control, not knowing – especially today. Guffawing broke out from somewhere ahead, colliding with the clamour and abruptness of an ear-piercing tone that suggested an emergency: "Ping! Ping! Ping! Ping!" I didn't know what the alarm was or if it did indeed herald trouble for somebody. What I did know was that I didn't like hearing it.

On and on we went. Gobbled up by the jaws of double doors, and trying to avoid glimpses into the private rooms where single doors cocked ajar at angles so as to obscure the patients. Passing wards too numerous to count and a repetition of hand-sanitizer dispensers along the walls that bordered on obsession.

Approaching the kerfuffle of Nursing Station Number Three where umpteen conversations were fighting for the same air, including the dialogue about Mr Peter's lung-function test and the female nurse jibing her colleague for pigging out on too much cake. We swivelled sharp left, another artery. More pings. Nursing Station Number Four. Finally, Coronary Care. The whole escapade brought to mind the voodoo tradition of burial I'd learned about once in New Orleans. The coffin-bearers would go on some crazy, round-the-houses route to the graveyard in the centre of town, all in a bid to ward off any evil spirits that might try to follow the deceased in their journey to the after-life. Right now, I felt I knew how those spirits might have experienced such discombobulation.

Stepping inside the ward, I caught the whiff of a sweet but distinct medical odour that knew its place and did not venture out into the corridor. The scent of it took me back to age thirteen, to something similar that had been in the room when Nan had been dying at home from cancer. A swell of queasiness rose into my throat but before it could amount to anything we were introduced to Robert, our charge nurse for the day. As compact and quiet as the five-bed ward he served, he dipped his thick head of short brown curls in welcome, inviting us in with a warmth of smile that suggested he was a family man in the life that ran outside of the one we were meeting him in today. We allowed him to smooth the way, steering us toward the cubicle tucked in the far corner. His energy made me feel safe and the more he talked, the more I relaxed.

"Well Gordon, if you'd like to get changed . . . pop the gown on . . . then we can have a chat about what's brought you here. I know it's the atrial fibrillation but let's jot down some notes and we can get you on the drip. You're fine to stay here of course, Mrs Cumming. Make yourselves comfortable and I'll be back in a tick."

"He seems nice, like he cares." I whispered to Gordon, although Robert was already at his nursing station. "Not like that dinosaur at the hospital last time, eh?"

"Yeah, he seems human at least. Let's hope we won't be in here too long though. I want my weekend and for . . ." Gordon's words turned to mumbles as he disappeared into the T-shirt he'd pulled up over his head in a bid to undress.

Having completed his consultation and set up the drip, Robert once again returned to his station, promising to check in on Gordon at intervals and leaving us with nothing else to do but twiddle our thumbs in boredom and idle our time with chit chat. Positioned in the corner as we were, there wasn't a great deal to see other than a section of the station Robert was not sitting at. The patient in the cubicle opposite Gordon's bed lay hidden, courtesy of a blue curtain pulled all the way around. Likewise, a wall of fabric blocked out the man next to us, while the opening to the corridor outside – though absent from our line of sight – sent in only the clatter of the tea trolley as it trundled by. We remained waiting within the cotton-wool hush. The only other sign of life belonged to a vague thrumming in the background: the whoosh of the air vent in the ceiling above us, breathing the outside in. I looked over at Gordon. His blink lasted a fraction longer than normal, as if getting here and into bed had triggered his brain into thinking it was time to sleep.

Two hours dragged by. Each time Robert checked on Gordon, I nipped out to the toilet in the corridor, glad to be able to step away and release my hospital nerves. By the third time, however, I struggled to fight back the tears after seeing Robert furrow his brow at how long the drip was taking, and hearing him say that they may have to consider using the paddles after all. I just wanted everything to be fixed without a repeat of the paddles, and to go home and resume normality.

I'd been gone five minutes. When I returned, Gordon's pallor unnerved me and his queasiness had worsened. Robert deftly hooked up another drip. I perched on the edge of my chair, eyeing the number on the heart monitor for a few minutes, as it chopped and changed yet refused to reduce. Unsettled and somewhat at a loss as to how I could help, I persuaded Gordon to let me nip into town and buy him some jellybeans, thinking that perhaps he was suffering from a drop in his blood sugar.

The errand took half an hour. Propped up on his pillows, he gave a wan smile to see me again. I offered the jellybeans but by now the force of his nausea made even contemplating opening them a no go. I honed in on the monitor. The number I'd been pegging all this time had decreased. I was relieved but the increase in Gordon's shortness of breath seemed to be an anomaly – an observation perhaps shared by Robert, whose own ruddiness now seemed to be deepening in direct proportion to the draining of colour in Gordon's cheeks. He strode off to fetch the registrar and returned with her minutes later. Slim and comely, in her thirties, and sporting a pink-popsicle smile, it was clear she kept every hair on her head in immaculate order. Each one was strained back into a sleek ebony mane that, I was sure, would flare like a proud ribbon behind her if she ever had cause to gallop into a headwind. She didn't get far with her questions before Gordon announced he needed to go to the toilet. There was a private one beside his cubicle, but the space around his bed was cramped with all of us there and so I offered to leave again for a few minutes. By the time I reappeared I was shocked to learn that he hadn't been able to walk without their help, that he had been overcome by faintness and weakness after some shuffles across the floor, and had panted and flopped down on the nearby chair. It had been an effort and drama just to get him back to the bed. I studied his face, biting my lip. He was not so much pale now as the slightest hint of grey. I latched onto Robert by the drip, pinning him down with my widening stare.

"What the hell is wrong?"

"We're not sure. We've had success in flicking his heart back into normal rhythm with the drip but . . . we can't understand why he is continuing to have these difficulties. It's a bit of a mystery."

"His breathing wasn't like this this morning. I don't understand."

"We think he may be having a reaction to the treatment we gave him for the nausea. It can happen. So we've given him something for that and, well, let's see."

The registrar promised to check back later, leaving Robert to ask me questions about Gordon which I answered as best I could, and thinking to mention again some of the signs I had observed over the past weeks and that Gordon had dismissed as "nothing" – including the oddity of that infernal snoring pattern he'd developed. I tracked Robert for any reactions to my comments, searching for clues as to what he thought. All he offered was a thank you, a taciturn smile, and a return to his monitoring of Gordon's drips and blood pressure.

The tracing arc of the afternoon sun finally closed up the patch of light on the floor beside Gordon's cubicle. No longer willing to leave my man's side, I clasped his hand in mine. He was chatting less now, his eyelids heavy, beads of perspiration gathering on his forehead. As ashen as the remnants of all the campfires he had ever enjoyed, this tinge was now spreading to his parted lips as he laboured to breathe. All of a sudden, the inhalations and exhalations switched to rattling within his throat and he winced. Same noises my Nan made on her deathbed. The hairs on my arms stiffened as I felt my heart being squeezed in my chest. The ward's sickly medicinal odour intensified as my eyes darted between the numbers on the machine and Gordon. Inside my head the danger sirens blared, exacerbated by the timely reappearance of the registrar and the attempts by both her and Robert to try Gordon with two different kinds of oxygen masks, neither of which seemed to be working for him. They wanted to try something else. I didn't understand what. Again I offered to make room in the cubicle by stepping outside, torn between not wanting to let go of Gordon's hand and allowing them all the space they needed to help him.

I let go.

Out in the corridor, a cleaner rammed his sodden mop into the guts of the wringer, screwing the mop handle around as he jammed and wedged the head down further till no air could get in or out, crushing the fibres, squishing the life out of it before yanking it apart from the bucket and slapping its wretchedness back onto the floor, humming a low tune as he continued. It wasn't long before the compulsion to be with Gordon drove my feet back into the ward. I lingered by the nursing station where I could see diagonally across to his bed. During my hiatus, two additional nurses had joined Robert and the registrar in the cubicle. I chewed down hard on my bottom lip. A frantic, high-speed train of thought screeched its carriages along the steel rails of the dark tunnel in my mind. *More nurses? That has to be bad. That's the most staff with Gordon since we arrived. What the hell is going on?*

Still able to scope out the scene, my eyes fixated on Gordon as if both our lives depended on it. He saw me too, locking his gaze with mine across the distance, but his face was now expressionless, as if the lights in him were still on but dimming – and fast. He just wasn't looking good. Fear hammered at my chest, hollering and demanding to be let in. Intuition told me something was horribly, horribly wrong. The right side of my neck pulsed in agitation, the blood inside the vein fighting to bust out. *Come on Robert. Sort this out for heaven's sake. Come ON.*

Robert flitted around the bed to the other side, obstructing my view of Gordon's face. *MOVE goddammit! I need to see his face! Please.* But Robert stayed put, oblivious to my needs while a juggernaut of anxiety now ripped through my system, knocking the wind out of me for a moment. My heart thundered blood down to the muscles in my legs. I needed to stay where I was but the energy demanded to be expended somehow and had me bolting back out into the now blurred corridor. Pacing up and down seemed to be the answer – a series of steps without wanting to go too far away. *Forwards and turn around. Forwards and turn around. Forwards and turn around.* A commotion soon brought my attention back up from my feet in time to see a young nurse pelting down the corridor towards me, clutching something that looked like a tube in a surgical bag. She scooted into the ward and, alarmed, I dived straight in after her, being sure to hang back again at the nursing station to allow them to do what they needed to do, yet managing to stand myself far enough in that I could also see what was going on.

There were four nurses in his cubicle now, plus Robert and the registrar. *Shit. Shit. Shit!* I had Gordon back in my line of sight. He had the larger oxygen mask on. His eyes met mine again for a minute or so and then, without warning, his head lolled onto his chest and landed slightly to the side – a World War II pilot going down with his plane after taking a hit. Before I could assimilate what had just happened, yet another nurse shot from behind me to join the throng of those around his bed. With her advent, the final gap of sight I'd had through this frontline of hunched bodies and darting heads and pushing elbows was sealed. I craned my neck but it was to no avail as the human curtain of medical intervention pulled tight around my beautiful husband. They might as well have pushed me out of a plane. Stomach lurching into my throat, the blood gushed in my ears as my mouth turned to dust. My mind became confused, clammy hands losing their grip. *This cannot be happening.* I charged out of there, clutching at chunks of hair on my head as I went, the little girl inside me mouthing a silent scream.

Away from the ward, the corridor railed in on my tremors. *Please, God. Please, God.* My eyes swept here, there and everywhere again, scanning for anything I could find that would make this nightmare go away. *How long has it been now? Why do I have no idea?* My head shook in denial. *No. No. No!* Having plunged from my freefall I was in an unforgiving sea, tossed around by waves so herculean in their size and energy that I didn't know if I had the capability to withstand them. I heard my breathing, jagged now, as it pushed itself out past realisations so confronting I dared not speak them. *Please-please-please-please-please-please-please! Don't let this be happening. Why isn't anyone coming out to tell me what's wrong? What's going on? I need news!* Jelly replaced muscle as my body slumped down the wall in the part of the corridor that expanded out to the open area of seating. *Please, God, help me. Don't make this happen. What are they doing? Somebody help me! Please God, help! Don't let him die!* There was no holding in the sobs anymore.

A giant dinner trolley crashed past me with plates of lasagne on its lower shelf. The reek of it pushed bitter, hot bile up into my throat. I pulled myself to standing, needing to escape from the stench, only to discover that it permeated and hung in the air, acrid smoke in the devastating bushfire that was my man's decline. In and out of teary focus, I glimpsed a grandma sitting up in bed in the ward opposite, tucking into the pile of congealed cheese and meat on her plate. *How can you just be calmly eating that? Can you see me? Why isn't anybody coming to HELP me? How can anyone be eating right now?* But the woman kept shovelling her food in and the day to day of people kept ghosting by me and moving on. My mind fogged up, just like the goggles I'd worn the day Gordon and I had gone snorkelling with whale sharks in that three metre swell. Like then, sounds were now muffled. The walls were lurching too, billowing. A man materialised in front of me. I hadn't seen him coming. *Robert.* His mouth was moving but there was a delay with the sound and I couldn't hear anything. When it did get through to me, I wished it hadn't.

"Caroline! Are you with me?"

Blink.

"I don't have long to talk to you, okay? We have to put Gordon into a coma."

"Co . . . coma?"

"Yes."

"What do you mean? Oh my God. Coma? No, please, no!"

He jumbled out more words and jargon, firing off explanations. I heard "acute respiratory-distress syndrome" and how Gordon had gone into fight mode to get breath. That this had put a strain on his heart, which then went back out of rhythm. The word "paddles" surfaced. He dropped a big phrase: "heart failure". Gordon had suffered the failure of his heart. Then, an even bigger phrase: "multiple organ failure". I was sinking but nothing was sinking in for me. It was as if Robert were describing someone else, not my husband. I gawped as he bent his arm at a ninety-degree angle and turning his palm upwards.

"See? This . . ." He was explaining again, pulling his forearm towards his chest in a fast and repetitive rhythm. "This is what a normal heart does when it pumps. And this . . ." He had paused, giving the arm just a flicker of movement. "This is where Gordon had landed: near death. He was about three minutes away from death."

Suspended in time, I didn't register anything else Robert said. I was still reeling at the word I had heard. The one before my ears had started ringing and drowning everything else out. *Death.* Finally, his voice flooded into my awareness again, something about having to intubate Gordon. He came back at me with the horror of that word again – coma. I must have spoken but I hadn't heard it, only his reply.

"No, Caroline, it's not that type of coma. This is a chemically-induced coma. It's not as dangerous in the same way an ordinary coma is, where a person knocks their head or something. That said, we have to put his body and mind into very deep sleep or he won't survive right now. Even then, in this case, there are no guarantees."

Survive?

"We *do* get to control when we wake him up from it – likely in the next 24 to 48 hours. But you need to understand the gravity of the situation, Caroline. He is seriously ill. I've got to get back now. I am so sorry for you. You will be able to see him later in ICU once we stabilise him. But I have to go now."

"ICU? No!"

But Robert had already sped back off to the ward, leaving me stunned and alone in the corridor, swallowed up by the waters of my worst nightmare. Babbling with hysteria, I began my descent into a dark and tortuous underworld, hyperventilating as I went.

CHAPTER FOUR

Day 1

6.00 p.m. – Hospital

"**L**OVE, YOU NEED TO DRINK THIS, there's sugar in it. C'mon, you need it lovey, you're in shock."

Looking up, I was met with the comfort and kindness of a pair of eyes that reached out to me from beyond their crepe crinkles. Her liver-spotted hand offered me a paper cup of steaming tea. I didn't want it but she motioned again, insisting.

"I'm Sally, Caroline. I was on the nursing station, outside this ward, when you first came in to the unit this morning with . . . Gordon . . . that's right, isn't it? Gordon's his name?"

"Where am I?"

"You're in the waiting room lovey, the one for the whole cardiac unit. It's by the nursing station outside the . . . well, yes, the, um, Coronary Care ward."

"Is he okay?"

"I'm so sorry this has happened to you – with Gordon, I mean. Can I call anyone for you? Who can I get in touch with so they can come and be with you?"

Blink.

"You got family nearby? You got a phone? Maybe in your bag?"

I peered down at my feet to where she pointed. There was indeed a bag there. Fumbling inside it, I retrieved my mobile only to discover the battery had died. The charger was not in the bag. Mind gone to slush, I let the implications sink in. *I have no contact numbers.* Without the address book, there was no chance I could remember anyone's number, not even my mother's and anyway, it was the middle of the night where she was in the UK, and I didn't want to rip her out of sleep to this news. It occurred to me to ask Sally if I could go and get Gordon's phone as he too had the numbers of our friends stored there – but she shook her head, saying that I wasn't allowed to go back into Coronary Care yet.

"Anybody live near the hospital, love? Perhaps someone can go fetch somebody for you?"

I thought of Jeff and Tammy. Sally could perhaps trace them on the internet through the website for their business. It seemed to take ages but when she returned with both a phone and the number in tow, I made the call and gave Tammy a summary of my situation. Bowled over by the shock, she was unable to grasp what I was saying at first and even I felt odd speaking about myself and Gordon the way I was. They were working on a job, driving to their gig ninety minutes away and unable to be with me until they wound back here at around 1 a.m. or so. I didn't know how long I had to wait for it to be 1 a.m. She filled in my blanks; it was only 6 p.m. In the end we agreed she would make a call to another friend and ask them to come and be with me until then. Happy that somebody was going to turn up, Sally whisked back to her nursing station, inviting me to come and get her if I needed anything at all. I was alone again.

The room was an iceberg, its chilling and penetrating rawness far worse than frostbite. A whooshing sound like the one I had remembered in Gordon's cubicle filled the otherwise near-muted space. Following its source, I realised it was the air vent in the ceiling. I looked around, trying to orientate myself within the context of the hospital but the three walls that flanked me also denied me a view, and the floor to ceiling divide of glass revealed only a section of the corridor in all its barrenness. A tapping made me turn around to see the registrar in the doorway. She began to offer her regrets that I was going through all this, assuring me that everybody had been taken aback by Gordon's rapid decline.

"We looked over Gordon's notes from the other hospital, when he'd had atrial fibrillation back in 2009."

"And?"

"The report says that the team hadn't known for sure what caused the weakening of the muscle around his heart at that time but that they believed it was triggered by a specific virus – one that is uncommon and only attacks that part of the body." She perched down next to me. "We can't guarantee it but we think this has happened to him again. He has just had a cold, and that was the case last time too."

"Okay."

"What we *can* say is that it's as if Gordon's heart has been stunned. It's been paralysed by something. And that is typical of what that virus can cause."

I nodded but couldn't feel my head moving. She asked questions again, trying to elicit anything they could have missed during the consultation. I repeated that he had been falling asleep in his chair during the early evenings; that for months, the skin on the soles of his feet had been flaking on what I knew – as a reflexologist – to be the part of the foot energetically connected to the heart and lungs;

and that for weeks he had been having a strange pattern during the night of noisy breathing that spiralled in volume and culminated in a holding of the breath itself. They had all been signs that I had urged him to get checked out, but he had insisted nothing was wrong.

"It was all so *quick*." She knitted the arches of her brows. "To go from being a walk-in patient I mean, to nearly dying just hours later. We do at least still have him with us. But he is hanging by a thread. I am so very sorry for you. All I can add is that it was fortuitous that he came to us at eleven o'clock. Any later and he would likely have died."

I blinked at her again. The word "died" still sounded foreign to me. I asked if I could go and see him but then felt her energy replaced with guardedness.

"Not yet, I'm afraid. They're still getting him sorted. But somebody will come to get you as soon as you are allowed."

She squeezed my knee as her lips made a joined-up line of sympathy across her face. Then, she left. I didn't know how long I sat there facing the rows of empty chairs. It felt like ages yet also no time at all. Now and again, there was colour and movement outside the glass but I didn't register anything much, didn't even know if I was thinking or not. I didn't know anything. Not until a colour and shape turned up at the doorway that morphed into the familiarity of a face from my outside world. Brian.

"Caroline! Hey, jeez, I came as soon as I could . . ."

He came into the room, a barrel bobbing on the surface of the ocean and onto which I could cling for dear life, a barrel with enough substance to not become submerged by my gripping. Though we were not close friends we often socialised together, sharing a love of music and dance and attending – with Gordon – the classes in African drumming through which we had all met two years before. From within his bear hug, I now let the honest scent of plain soap calm me for a moment, my murmurs of gratitude for his presence absorbed by us both.

We flopped down onto the seats. He asked questions, wanting to understand what had happened. As I relayed and relived things that didn't sound like they could be about me or Gordon, I broke down, sobbing, panic re-emerging at the sense I was teetering on the edge of something in my life from which there could be no return. It felt dangerous as hell.

At some point, a nurse took us to collect Gordon's things from the ward in which he had collapsed. I was not prepared for what I saw. The cubicle, littered with the remnants of chaos and confusion, was also rife with the energetic traces of a twister of turmoil and panic, anxiety and adrenalin. Even worse, the bed was unoccupied. Gordon wasn't *there*. Which meant it was true – they *had* taken him to ICU. The blood roared in my ears at the realisation, body flashing hot as spots passed before my eyes. My legs buckled beneath me but thankfully I stayed upright. Leaving the ward, I blindly clutched the bag of Gordon's belongings to my chest as if I would never let them go again. Scrunched up inside the plastic were his wallet, phone, keys, clothes – and the bag of unopened jelly beans.

I balked at the thought of having to make the calls to the family. At ninety-one years old, Gordon's mother Dorothy was frail and my worry about traumatising her clashed with the belief that she had a right to know. I already knew that to get in touch with her I had to phone Gordon's sister Brenda with whom she now lived. I wasn't sure how the call would unfold. Brenda had a strained relationship with Gordon and a dislike of me that bordered on hatred – circumstances that, in turn, had created challenges for both Gordon and me in being able to access Dorothy either on the phone or in person ever since she had moved in a year earlier. As for Gordon's boys, it broke my heart to have to tell them about the gravity of his situation. And my own Mum, I feared, would become overwrought and too fretful. I wasn't relishing the thought of speaking to any of them but it had to be done and at least now I had their numbers. I opted for the boys first.

Trying to sound like I had it together, I urged Jim and Steve to get on the first plane they could out of Melbourne and be with their dad. I relayed the basics of what had happened, impressing upon them the seriousness of things and telling them both that I was so sorry for them. Not ones to display their feelings much, they confirmed they would be on the first plane out in the morning. That was it. We said our goodbyes but I sensed from the new alertness in his usually soft voice that Steve was scared.

The call to Dorothy proved a lot more upsetting. Brenda's husband, Bob, answered the phone. With gruffness and hostility in his tone, he denied me access on principle. A rush of white-hot fury ripped its way up from my depths, a force that wanted to smash him to smithereens. I knew unleashing it wouldn't serve anything or anyone in that moment but it was all I could do to transmute it into the fiery ice and tight control of a voice that imparted in no uncertain terms that Dorothy's son was in a coma and Bob could bloody well go and get her. It shut him up and he fetched Dorothy but the energy I had needed to assert myself with him left me drained. As I told Dorothy the facts and discriminated where I needed to, I intuited her guardedness and her own feeling that she couldn't be normal with me because Brenda and Bob were listening. It had been a problem Gordon and I had been experiencing with her since her relocation. Shock also seemed to be shutting her down right now. She croaked "Okay!" after each piece of information I gave her, as if she were receiving a check list of grocery items that she had to write down. When I finished, she thanked me and told me I had to be strong. That was all. My shoulders sagged. I asked her to put me on to Brenda.

Monotone and terse, Brenda let the barest bones of a "hello" go down the line. I began to speak, the words in my throat like a battalion of infantry boots up against it in slurries of mud. After I'd finished filling her in, I pleaded with her that Gordon needed to know right now that he was loved by the family – of which she was a key member. That he had carried the grief around in his heart for so long, of feeling like he didn't belong to his family or indeed belong anywhere. Tears streamed down my face. I implored her to connect with the fact that he was a good man, worthy of all our love and that, at times like these, we needed to drop the stories that kept us separate. I held my breath, could hear her sniffling down the phone. In that second I had hope. Hope that she had opened her heart to me and to Gordon, and to love – and that we finally had a connection based in authenticity. I bit the bullet and asked her the question that meant so much to me.

"Will you come down tonight and be with Gordon? Or tomorrow even. We are still in Central Bay and still only an hour and a half away from you."

As soon as I had uttered the request I felt her energy pull back as she yanked up her drawbridge, clanked it shut and ratcheted the bolts across, creating so wide a gulf between us that I could not cross it.

"No. I won't be coming. And I'm not bringing Mum either."

There was a finality in her declaration, the brusqueness of the "no" a well-aimed slug to my stomach by a fist that I had hoped would open out as a hand of peace. Aside from feeling winded and bruised, I cringed at the rawness and vulnerability I had shown her, at my foolishness for imagining that she could bury a hatchet she had been holding onto for so long and wielding with all her might. Mouth gaping, my mind spewed. *For Christ's sake woman! How can you be so damned hard? So damned heartless?*

"Thanks for letting us know the situation."

There was nothing else to say. I told her I would be in touch later with any updates and hung up. By the time I dialled Mum in the UK, I was so depleted from being the messenger, that the chat was brief. In a way, that was fine for now. Much as I loved her and could register and have gratitude for her love and concern for me, the spontaneous outpouring of sobs and utter worry coming down the line felt like a heavy, suffocating drape over my head. It was more than I could handle in my own torn-up state.

I stood in the deserted street, not knowing what on earth to do. A leaf, pushed along by the coolness of evening, scratched deafeningly along the pavement at my feet. I didn't know what time it was, though the lorikeets had flown home to roost and the car park was almost bereft of cars. Looking up, the last fingers of burnished light clutched on to the remnants of the day, an eleventh-hour attempt at an S.O.S. flare across the swathe of sky. *This is it then. No one from the family is coming for me.* Mum had offered. But she was in the UK, without funds. In any case, I'd suggested to her that we wait and see what played out before making any decisions about booking a flight. Of course, Dad and my brother didn't know. Neither man was in my life. As for Jim and Steve, they would be here for their dad, not for me. I understood – I was not their mother and we didn't have any relationship to speak of. Dorothy, well, she was already sticking her head in the sand, an old woman who relied on her daughter and would not bite the hand that fed her to be there for me in any way. This just left Brenda. I tried to tell myself that people responded to shocks in different ways. That perhaps she too had gone into denial and would soon "come around". In truth, my hope was fading. Eyes stinging now, I swallowed past the lump of glass shards in my throat. A rock had found its way into my heart, sinking it into the black hole deepening inside me. There was nothing else for it but to turn around and head back to Brian in the waiting room. I was so grateful he was there.

Her energy preceded her into the room. I felt it before I'd even looked up to see that there was a "her" there at all. Plumping up the doorway, she was as much a match for its angular frame as she was a softening force upon it. I took her in with a single sweep of my glance. The gloss on her cropped honey-blond haircut; the voice that now asked me how I was. The shine on her small gold earrings; those nails with their red varnish; the sheen on her lacquered shoes. Dressed for business like that, all I knew was that she couldn't be a nurse. My alarm bells rang.

"Oh I'm sorry, Caroline, let me introduce myself." She fanned her fingers out onto her chest. "My name is Christine. I'm the General Manager of this hospital."

I nodded, wary. As Brian swapped seats to give us more room, she settled down beside me. Her hand was immaculate warmth on my arm and I listened to her extend her heartfelt sympathies for what I was going through. There were other things she mouthed, things that passed me by, verbal flotsam in my sea of anxiety. But all the while, her tone had a high degree of measure and calm, tactful without being patronising. I sensed she was treading a fragile line between telling the truth and holding back. She asked if I had any questions.

"How is he?"

"Well, we've been getting him *sorted*. It's taken us over an hour to progress him from critically unstable to critically stable. He's now on maximum life support in ICU. In fact, we actually had to reopen ICU tonight, just for him. I don't know if anybody told you about that . . . ?"

I shook my head, still reeling at the part about him having been critically *unstable*, not to mention thrown by the word "maximum".

"Ah okay, well yesterday our Board of Directors voted in favour of the closure of our ICU ward with immediate effect."

"Okay."

"Well, what I mean is that it has been a stroke of extraordinary luck that this was only decided then and that we were able to reopen for his emergency tonight, because otherwise . . ." Her eyes levelled with mine, "I think we could have lost him at the point of his crash."

"Okay." I couldn't think of anything else to say.

"Robert is with him now. He happens to be an ICU nurse too, so your husband is in the best of hands. But I have to warn you Caroline, Gordon is seriously, seriously ill. He is *hanging* by a thread tonight."

"I thought they said they were just putting him to sleep for 24 to 48 hours? That they were in control of when they brought him back? What do you mean, by a thread? Please, that can't be the case!"

Starting to sob, I shook my head over and over, my body rocking forwards and backwards in the chair and my hands over my ears, wanting to block out what she was telling me, the idea of his life hanging in the balance the way she was describing. There was an enormity behind her words that no-one else so far had conveyed in quite that way.

"Caroline, darling . . . *Caroline* . . . Caroline, *listen* to me. I came to say I can take you to him now. *If* you are ready and want to. But you are going to need to pull yourself together before I'll let you come. It won't help Gordon right now to hear you like this. We believe that patients in coma, even the induced ones, can still hear. So you are going to need to call on all your strength now, to talk to him, to help him, okay? Do you understand what I'm saying?"

I nodded, my nose trumpeting a snotty mess into the tissue. I did want to see him. Of course I did. Yet I squirmed with shame at the part of me that felt the reluctance and fear, and that wanted to run and hide. I understood what she was driving at though.

Satisfied, Christine levered herself up and made her way to the doorway. The stouteheartedness I needed to find within myself now preceded me in her form. With nothing more than blind faith and Brian, I stiffly followed her out of the room. A wave of adrenalin pumped ice through my body. ICU. A place I had never been to before in my entire life and about which I couldn't imagine a single good thing. I clenched my hands at the thought of what could be waiting for me there, with no idea at all whether I had the strength to face it or not.

Chapter Five

Day 1

9.00 p.m. – Hospital

Venturing out into the corridor and trailing Christine deeper into the hospital, I anchored my focus to the carpet at my feet, the alternating pattern of vertical and horizontal lines within the squares lending a certainty I believed I could count on. The abrupt shift to a shiny floor and the clip-clopping and squeaking of our shoes came as a rude awakening. I looked up. We had entered the claustrophobia of a white walkway that seemed more like a tunnel, its low ceiling surely designed to help push down – and leave no room for – the hysteria of all the loved ones who would ever have the misfortune of passing through here.

Level-headed, Christine was a few paces ahead of us on heels which suggested that balancing acts in this hospital were both her forte and a necessity for the role. I tried to keep up, squinting in the full shock of strip-lights that, in their glare, interrogated me as to why I was here. Soon the tunnel became shorter stretches of corridor that played their cards close to their chest, revealing left and right turns only once we were upon them. There were no other signs of life. An intimidating piece of medical equipment skulked against a wall, abandoned. Then, boom. And again, boom. Dull thuds reverberated from somewhere further down the corridor. I realised it was doors slamming and yet the sound had managed to conjure up all the finality of mortuary slabs being rolled back into their holdings. I was aware of whirring, something akin to the motors of a thousand fridges all operating at once but without any window to let out the noise. It felt like we were in a basement although I knew we hadn't descended any stairs to get here. I shivered. The whoosh of the air vents pronounced itself much more in this space, pulling the skin on my arms into goose bumps. To think that Gordon should be in a place like this! Fear parched my mouth, dusty like the dirt of the outback. *The Outback.* The thought of it brought the next lump up into my throat. Without warning, Christine stopped by an open door, curled her arm round inside, felt for a switch and flicked on a light.

"Here we are! This is the Relatives' Room." She invited us into the tiny space with its three chairs, small table, sink and cupboards. "That's it . . . just make yourselves at home. Now, ICU will come and get you when it's okay for you to go in, alright? It shouldn't be long at all. I'm sorry I have to leave you but I'll be back later. And Brian, it's so good that you are here with Caroline."

She turned to go, gently squeezing my arm as if to inject me with the courage I was going to need. No sooner had she walked off, than my nostrils curled at the smell I'd experienced in coronary care. Here it was more intense. I didn't like it. It was the smell of danger and panic and disaster, the smell of an alien world in which I did not want to be. We slumped down onto the chairs in silence. Yet another air vent was turning the place into the biggest ice-cube so far. I looked towards the door, unable to see further than the wall of the corridor two steps outside it.

Perched on the edge of time, I waited within the crumpled-up tissue that was this room, its walls meeting at peculiar and awkward angles. Guilt unleashed inside me. Seeping through me like an enormous river that had burst its banks and met with its first house, the quiet and slow licks of water to arrive under my doorframe were innocuous at first. I should have forced him to go the doctor sooner. I'd seen the signs, hadn't I? Should have acted on them, should have known better. Soon enough the volume of water behind those licks was enough to push the door right in and flood the rooms on a scale bordering destruction.

"Oh my God, Brian, I've caused this! I've done this to Gordon! It's my fault. We had an argument last night. I said things, dreadful things. I had so much anger for so much stuff that's gone on between us. But I should have shut up! He hadn't been well that day. I mean I *knew* that, he'd told me!"

I yowled, rocking back and forth again. Brian tried to reach out, the usually jovial cheeks no longer pushing his eyes into twinkling slits as he tried now to console me and talk reason and offer a cup of tea even – but I was past receiving any of it. Blubbering, I submerged in murky stormwaters, convinced of what I had done, shriven. I'd been a terrible wife, bad to my core, and now the Universe, and maybe even Gordon too, was teaching me a lesson. I was getting punished for my badness. For being a woman who could rage and who couldn't move past the wrongs she perceived had been done to her; who still hadn't sorted out her unlovable shadow after all these years; and who obviously refused to choose happiness in life. What the hell was the matter with me? Had I driven him to leave me? Was *that* what I had done? The river water kept coming, bringing with it abject terror at the prospect of losing him forever, and plunging me into remorse at the thought of maybe never being able to say sorry to him, or have him understand and forgive me for not having loved him or me the way I should have. I was lost to myself, eddying in my thoughts and the emotions they generated. Lost, that is, until the surging subsided and all that remained was the spent ache of nothing less than a drowned devastation.

It was Christine who in the end came to take me next door to ICU while Brian, understanding my request to first see Gordon on my own, stayed put. Ushered to the entrance, I paused. A pair of heavy PVC flaps overlapped and ran from floor to ceiling. *PVC.* My eyes rushed at the overload of instructions splattered in black and red across the opaqueness, while my mind raced to assimilate the way that I had to be here. Christine announced that I had to wash my hands. As I pressed down the nozzle on the soap dispenser, I discovered the source of the smell I disliked. The alcohol in the liquid was sharp, catching in the back of my throat as I smelt it and forcing me to suppress a dry heave. She asked if I was okay, a splash of concern in her voice. I nodded and with trepidation rang the bell, waiting until I heard the invitation to come in. Then, tender-footed, I stepped into another world.

As I crossed the threshold into the dimness, the pungency of the sickly-sweet smell suffocated me, flipping the insides of my stomach. It saturated the air, had seeped into the walls, the beds, the floor – and with no windows to release it. *No. Don't faint.* A myriad bright spots swam before my eyes and I breathed a sigh of relief when they passed as quickly. There was no time to faint, no time to take anything in other than that the ward was small but without patients. A nurse in scrubs said something and stood aside, motioning my gaze to the far corner that now revealed the one bed that did indeed have someone lying in it. Confusion reigned for a second and then I realised the "someone" was Gordon. I hadn't recognised him. Swallowing my shock, I stepped towards the bed but not even cautiousness could have prepared me for what I saw. A pneumatic drill intent on smashing up the paltry remains of my foundations took up its shuddering residence inside me.

My man.

Oh God. No. My man who once skippered a yacht through the Whitsundays, qualified as a recreational pilot and loved flying, built his own home with his bare hands, mountain-biked up the Picos Mountains in Spain, managed international and multi-million dollar I.T. projects with success, and who loved me and made love to me with passion and heart and soul . . . that man now lay here, motionless, yet not because of ordinary sleep. His body was connected in various places to a paraphernalia of wires and tubes that hooked him up to a mass of consoles, to machines that beeped and clunked and whirred, to monitors with numbers that moved and coloured zigzags and squiggles and lines that traced, to drips with stickers on the bags that used words for which my schooldays of biology and chemistry offered no help in understanding. I drew in a sharp breath. My distress wasn't so much because of the life support equipment all around him but more because of what I now saw in Gordon himself. It *was* my husband lying there – but it wasn't. The eyelids did belong to him but in their bulge they looked wrong and frightened me. The livid hue around the rim of his ears wasn't right either, nor the tinge of mauve to lips that had parted unnaturally to accommodate the thickness of tube that was now intruding into his mouth and down his throat. His body and arms were swelling too, already making him look like a puffed-up sumo wrestler. I scanned further down the bed to his toes, the only other part of his body not covered by the sheet and blanket. These too, seemed imposters. Turgid and purple, they hinted at feet that might look the same. It was all inconceivable. Gordon was there in front of me but he wasn't. And of all the sounds by his bed, one now came into my awareness. Hiss . . . poofft. Hiss . . . poofft. Hiss . . . poofft. I glanced across to see that it was coming from the unit beside him. He was being breathed.

"You can talk to him. We believe he can hear. It can help."

I leant over to tremble a kiss upon his forehead and to tell him that I loved him so very, very much. But as my lips brushed his brow, it was with horror to discover that his unique scent had gone. Not just the citrus of his aftershave that he would have used that morning, or even the spice of his deodorant, but his actual skin-smell, the one we'd laugh about me snorting whenever I brushed my nose through the soft hairs on his arms or chest. That smell was no longer there, replaced instead by antimicrobial fumes. Biting my lip, I tried not to cry.

"It's good to stroke him too." She was trying to encourage me, I knew. "And we'd also like you to massage his feet tonight, it can help things. Here . . . let me show you . . . like this . . . okay?"

I was afraid to touch him. When I did I was aghast to discover that the soles of his feet – those "bear pads" that I loved to warm my own feet on in bed in winter – were as ice-cold as my grandmother's face had been when, at thirteen, I had gone to see her in the morgue.

"It's all the drugs he's on right now for his heart and blood pressure." *Why is she whispering? Not as if she'll wake him up.* "He's on five different ones for the heart alone. That's what's causing the discoloration and the coldness of his skin." I watched as she returned to her station. It looked like an air-traffic-control console in communication with a plane in deep trouble.

Trying for normality, I told Gordon I would massage his feet for him. It unnerved me to speak to him and have him not respond, to feel that his energy was "further away" than just being asleep.

I set up a chair at the end of his bed and stroked his ankles and calves, caressing but with firmness in the way that the nurse had shown me, pushing his soles and toes towards his body, holding for a few seconds and flexing them away from him. Tears streamed down my face but they were quiet ones. I was beyond wretched. It occurred to me how much he loved having his feet stroked but I doubted if he was feeling my touch now. There was no pleasure on his face, only an expressionless mask lay upon the cold, starched pillow. Deep regret stirred in me for not having given him rubs in the past months or as often as I knew he would have enjoyed. It would have been such a simple act of loving touch and connection that I could have gifted him most nights. But I hadn't done it – and now I'd have given anything to have those nights back or, better still, more like them to come.

When I finished, I rose and joined him at his left side. His hand was heavy and cool as I held it in the clamminess of mine. My thumb stroked over his wedding band and his fingers. I talked to him, whispering in his ear now too, telling him I was so very, very sorry, that I was afraid, that I loved him, wanted him, and needed him. I don't know how long I sat there because my heart didn't have a watch. But it felt like forever. And all the while, the pump in the ventilator sighed up . . . and down . . . up . . . and down . . . up . . . and down. Breathing him alive although I could feel he was a long, long way out, floating somewhere indefinable, perhaps no longer a pilot of a plane in trouble, but an astronaut adrift in space.

Brian had been gone two hours now since emerging from his visit with Gordon. The short spikes of his hair had lent him all the air of a hedgehog that had been hit by a truck and had gone into a ball for self-preservation. He had blamed tiredness for his departure, conceding that he needed to get some rest and would be back tomorrow. I'd understood of course, feeling gratitude that he had come at all but also feeling my aloneness again as I saw him wander off.

When Jeff and Tammy finally turned up outside main reception at 1 a.m., it was a relief. They stomped out their cigarettes as soon as they saw me, and strode on over. I clocked the dreadlocks woven into Tammy's blonde hair, spied the T-shirt logo peeking out of Jeff's unzipped jacket, and then I remembered. *Ah yes, of course, the gig. They've come from their gig.* I tried to give them a smile but my lips and cheeks flattened out and wouldn't play ball. Jeff and Tammy. Our best friends since we were first marooned in the area after losing our money. They had taught us drumming and had been there for us at every pivotal turn of events that had followed as our lives had dismantled in chaos and then rebuilt. And now they were here again. For this. I shivered.

"Hey, Caroline, we came as fast as we could!"

Doing what Tammy did best she wrapped around me, the gentleness of her hand meeting with the back of my head, murmurs of "Oh honey!" wafting near to my ear. I nestled into her chest and breathed in the familiarity of her, that initial burst of radiance, and then the way her perfume enveloped and blanketed me in layers of comfort – deep and warm, delicate and sweet, all ashram and gingerbread and toasted marshmallows. For a moment, I wanted to stay in her hug, or to be at home in my bed socks with a book and cup of chai as if nothing had happened. But feeling the weight of Jeff's hand on my back, I pulled away from her to hug him too, burrowing my nose into his thickset neck. The tang from the goatskin of his drums, together with soggy nicotine and stale sweat, were all still belting out a lively rhythm there. It felt grounding and real and solid, medicine for my shakes. Minutes later we made the journey to ICU.

"Wow! Guys – did you *see* that?"

My outburst stopped Jeff in his tracks. We'd been chatting to Gordon for a while now, Tammy and Jeff from their respective places by his side, and me whilst massaging his feet. There had been plenty of quips from the two of them, the kind you say to a person in coma when you want to be all light-heartedness and convince them, or maybe yourself, that it's all going to be okay and there's nothing to worry about. Peppering the air had been comments like "what do you think you're playing at, dragging us from our gig at such an ungodly hour!" and, "you know this isn't the best way to ensure a mate buys you some beers, Gordon!" They had been telling him they loved him too. And they had shared with him about their day and their week. It was the four of us again, but not business as usual.

"Did you *see* that?" I'd had to bite the bullet and ask again because the thing had happened so fast that my brain had kicked in seconds after the direct experience, questioning whether it had happened at all.

"See what?"

"Gordon's *toes,* Jeff! His toes jerked just then, when you said about the mentoring! It happened, I know it! You were talking about how you met the Aboriginal elder and what he had to say about the mentoring programme for boys, right?" Jeff nodded, his eyebrows now raised. "Well, right at the point where you said the words 'Aboriginal mentoring programme for boys', that's when his toes jerked under my fingers. The toes on his left foot . . . they jerked across to the *right*! He's been interested in mentoring indigenous youth. And then you mentioned it, and his toes *jerked*."

"Yes, honey. I believe you," Tammy said with a smile. "His hand sort of squeezed mine for a split second right at the same time too."

"Oh my God, Tammy, Jeff, he can *hear* us. That must be so, no?

He is letting us know he can hear us . . . surely?"

I didn't dare breathe. We stared at Gordon and exchanged glances with each other. My mind wanted to dismiss it, to tell me that coma patients do twitch from time to time and that what he had done didn't mean anything. But the timing of it felt like the jerking was conveying a message, as if he was saying, "I'm still here. Just. I haven't gone yet," and that he had waited until others were there who had felt it too so that I would truly "get" the message and not think that it was a coincidence.

It gave me a meagre flicker of hope though I didn't dare clutch on to anything too tight.

I had no idea what time it was. Jeff had left earlier, at 3 a.m., to go home. Quivering in the darkness, I lay on the bed in the room beside Gordon's cubicle. Though the nurse had insisted upon it as the only way in which she would agree to let me stay the rest of the night, sleep seemed out of the question. From the armchair, Tammy stroked my hair and hushed me into the lightest of swirling places where it felt like I was falling out of the sky, only for my muscles to seize and yank me awake and back into my real nightmare.

"Shhh, we're going to get through this," Tammy whispered. "You're going to get through this . . . one breath at a time, one step at a time. You have to surrender, honey. Surrender my darling Caroline."

CHAPTER SIX

Day 2

7.45 a.m. – Home

I<small>T WAS A WHIRLWIND</small> once I arrived back at my place after dropping Tammy home. All I wanted was to be with Gordon in the hospital. I grabbed the phone chargers, had a snappy shower and, in anticipation of the boys staying here during their visit, did the briefest of tidy ups in the lounge, dealing with all its mess by shoving it into a cupboard as I went. In the kitchen, I spied that my laptop hadn't shut down properly from the day before. I was astonished to see so many replies and well-wishes to the short post I had written as Gordon and I had left for the hospital. It was surreal to consider how much my world had changed since then and that while it had been going on, so much support and love had been laid out for both of us on my social media page. I felt the need to thank people and so posted another update with a brief overview of the medical situation, and asked for everyone to send healing thoughts. In the time it took for me to brush my teeth and get dressed, friends had already replied. I allowed myself a minute to read their words before grabbing my keys from the table and leaving for the hospital again.

Update from me: The hospital is now only able to treat signs and symptoms and to try to keep Gordon stable. But the rest is up to Gordon and his body and Higher Self. I don't know what is going to happen to him. Please send healing as if he were healed and already well. In Gordon's vision for the future, he would love, amongst other things: to mentor Aboriginal children, to have a family, to claim himself as an artist, and to convert a truck and travel a bit more round Australia. If you would love to think of him doing that when he gets better, it would be so wonderful. Many thanks and for the love you have already sent here.

Sara: Keeping him in my vision today as the healthiest, most fulfilled, lively, and joyful parts of him. And keeping you in my vision with him.

Claire: Thinking of you both, sending much light and love your way, and visualising that all your dreams come true very soon. Don't forget to also take care of you, get as much rest as possible and eat well. (Maybe some friends close by might be able to cook you some nutritious meals so you can eat on the go still.) Xx

Helena: My mother in law is staying with us. She is a spiritual healer so together we'll send you love and healing.

Sabine: Sending Gordon & you lots of love and healing energy. If you need a hug, someone to come and keep you company or someone to talk to, I am here. Xxx

Gareth: So sad to hear that my old mate's in the midst of a struggle. Am thinking of him – and you – and hope that he gets through it soon and that he gets to do all the things he wants to do. Lots of love to you both, Caroline. X

Nadia: Sending you both much, much love. I can see art classes with the Aboriginal children where he teaches them and they teach him and you with a bubba talking to the women. It is a sunny day like today. Loving the image and sending it your way. Xxx

Francesca: Have been thinking of you all day. Love you both, will put my imagination to work. Am here if you want to talk. Xxx

CHAPTER SEVEN

Day 2

8.45 a.m. – Hospital

WALKING INTO THE RELATIVES' ROOM, I was taken aback to see Larry reclining in a chair, attired in designer jeans and casual black jacket, and immersed in the screen of a laptop balancing on his thighs. He looked up, his hair salt and peppered from seasoned experience and wisdom, his piercing blue eyes smiling a warmth and concern for me over the rim of the tortoiseshell glasses perched halfway down his nose.

"Hey, how you doing?" He set his things aside and rose to hug me.

"I don't know. My emotions are all over the place. Um, thanks for coming. They won't let me in to see him yet. You know anything about why?"

"No, honey, I don't. And I'm so sorry this is all happening for you. So sorry we weren't able to come last night. I got here as early as I could this morning. There's a creative brief I have to look over so I thought I'd set up my office here, you know, wait for you . . ."

"I don't like not knowing what's going on. Since we came here yesterday, it feels like every time I leave Gordon, he takes a turn for the worse."

"I get it. Really, I do. But my intuition says no news is also good news right now."

I nodded. I was glad to see him, even though we didn't go back that far as friends. It had been over eighteen months since Gordon and I had become part of the lively community of people from all over the country and from all walks of life, who called themselves magicians. That was where we had met Larry and his wife Ruth, attending with them and all the others, the trainings and gatherings where intuition and consciously creating your life and living from the heart were taught and practised. The connection between us had really only come to the fore more recently, as we prepared to embark on the same safari to Africa to deepen the work.

"You know, you have so many people that are sending love and wishes. They want to help." He reached for his coffee on the table, taking a slow sip with appreciation before speaking again. "That's why Ruth set up a special online page for Gordon this morning. She's called it Gordon's Journey Page. You should take a look, it's amazing."

"Gordon's *Journey Page*?" I arched my neck back, hearing the edge in my voice but unable to help it.

He smiled a nod, easing back into his chair and motioning me to sit with him. It transpired that Ruth, with her gift for leading groups and projects in the corporate world, had used social media to organise and invite those magicians I was not in connection with, plus all the followers of my personal page, to join a community page that she had just created. I bristled to hear about this intervention, especially when I hadn't requested it and she hadn't asked me if it would be okay to invite my friends. The name of it aggravated me and I told Larry so, maintaining my stance that my husband's situation was not something to ogle over and that people were already seeing my posts on my personal page and so there was no need for a group page. Though I didn't say it, I felt like Ruth was trying to muscle in and take charge of me and of Gordon's situation. Larry did one of those smiles where it wasn't an obvious smile and yet it was there nonetheless. Unhurried, he tried to assuage my fears, impressing upon me that I was underestimating how many people were expressing concern for us, people who were feeling the effects of our plight and wanting to know how they could help. Some of these were folk who didn't even know Gordon or me but had heard the news from those who did. With a group page, Larry advocated, there could be a singular place where these online friends could gather for the purpose of supporting Gordon, a hub where my updates could be shared and followed by those who may not have permission to access my personal page but who still may want to help us. I was assured the communal space could be administrated by me as well as Ruth and Larry, so that I could focus on the business of being with my man.

"It will only be of benefit, Caroline. You'll see when you go on there that it is already being used with power. In an hour, there is to be a session of group healing for Gordon. It's being organised through the page. You asked people last night to send prayers. This page and this organised healing today is a way to answer your request that people send their healing and thoughts. It's a means to channel and harness the desires people have to do something *practical*." He rested his hand on my arm as if to reassure me, as if it was his steady gaze that was the one seeing the heart of the matter here.

I listened as he revealed that as well as the healing at 10 a.m. there was to be another session at 10 p.m. The idea, he championed, was that at these times everyone – no matter where they were or what they were doing – would send healing to Gordon for fifteen minutes or as much of that time that they could. It could take the form of prayers, wishes, of imagining him in health, of people sitting in the heart and sending love or remembering times they had with him, or however else people felt drawn to do it. Fifteen minutes where everybody's energy could unite for the same man and with the same purpose.

I sighed. Maybe he had a point. Maybe I wasn't grasping how much people wanted to be of practical assistance. At least we were both in agreement that amassing people to send healing at these specific times was a great initiative, one for which I had gratitude. I was about to tell Larry I had once read somewhere about the power of organising group prayer or meditation when Robert popped his head round the door with news. They had carried out some tests, he confirmed, but there had been no change since I'd gone home and come back. He went on to list the signs they wanted to be able to see over the hours to come, told us we could go in shortly, and ducked back out again.

Borrowing Larry's computer, I typed an update onto my page, telling him that if he wanted to share it onto the group page, he could. Again, I noted that a handful of responses appeared underneath within seconds but the majority of them – as would become the pattern from now on – would land throughout the day, waiting for me to read them in the early hours of the following morning when I arrived home.

> Update from me: Today is the day where Gordon's organs need to rally and blood tests need to show that there is an improvement in white blood cell count, liver and kidneys. We will also get results of cultures which hopefully might show what is causing the chest infection. He is stable. I have not been able to stop

kissing him and he moved his toes and fingers last night if but for a moment. It didn't feel like that was just muscle relaxant stuff going on. I will be reading the messages to him today that everyone sent yesterday. I am also being asked to give foot and hand massages which is easy because he has always loved having his feet rubbed.

Jake: I will play some didge sounds today to send the healing spirit into Gordo. Let my vibe bless him.

Larry: To all the amazing hearts supporting both Gordon and Caroline Cumming: Many of you have expressed a desire to come to the hospital. Gordon is not allowed many visitors and Caroline wants to spend her time with him today. She feels all the love and support, thanks you, and trusts that you'll understand. Keep it coming!

Marissa: It's such an honour to be able to be of service and to belong to such a wonderful community who are choosing to be in their hearts, as one heart, supporting and holding the heart of another. Best medicine ever!

Eryn: Hi Caroline, I remember working with Gordon at the training weekend in Sydney . . . It was inspiring and powerful . . . I join everyone in calling him to stay and live out his heart's journey.

Chapter Eight

Day 2

9.30 a.m. – Hospital

NIPPING OUT FROM GORDON and on my way to the toilets, I turned a corner of the corridor to see Rebecca coming towards me, a little red hen immersed in her dream world and wearing all the layers and colours of a rainbow after a downpour. Lopped over her shoulders were two of her trademark cloth bags, contents bulging with love yet weighing her down.

"Rebecca! Oh, my gosh. It's so good to see you!"

"Well now, where else would I be?" She spoke with the sort of quiet love that could heal a grazed knee in an instant. "I only heard from Brian this morning. He said you were in here. That Gordon is in coma. My intuition just said to get here for exactly ten o'clock. So, I followed that groove. Here for you, whatever you want, okay?"

"You're unbelievable!" I smiled. "There's supposed to be a group healing happening at ten! Many people will be sending love and healing to Gordon for fifteen minutes, wherever they are."

Though I was amazed at her timing, I had no idea how much this sort of thing was to become a trend that would continue to unfold at intervals throughout the rest of the day: friends who would get the 'hit' to arrive one by one at just the right time, bringing with them embraces, a desire to understand what had happened, and questions about what it was I wanted or needed. But as with Rebecca's invitation now, I didn't know what I should want. Other than wanting my man out of coma and asking for people to agree to all send him healing at specific times of the day, I was oblivious to my own needs.

"Well now if you don't know, how about the fact that you haven't slept or eaten in over forty hours, hmm?"

"My stomach says there's no hunger, and I am way too wired to be tired."

"Well, I've brought you some things anyway, for later, okay?" She squatted down, started rummaging through her bags for containers and packages. "They're my gluten-free rhubarb muffins. I've packed a salad for you in that one – oh and it has celery and greens in it from the patch. Um, that's some raw chocolate I made with superfood supplements. Apples, of course. What else . . . Oh yeah, raw nuts. Anyway, heaps of other things in there to give you energy, okay? Oh and some chamomile teabags, in case they don't have any here."

Moved to tears, I hugged her and for the next ten minutes, we parked ourselves on the chairs and she listened while I brought her up to speed with events. By the time we had re-joined Larry and fanned out by Gordon's bedside, the first group healing was already unfolding.

Despite the distractions and noises from the nurses carrying out their checks, the session felt as if it had been of value and after it was over, I decided I wanted more of them during the day. My priority was my man out of coma and out of danger. If these sessions could play a role in that, I wanted to increase that potential. Back in the Relatives' Room, Larry and I agreed upon the new times and he posted the update on the page. From now on, group healing would happen at 10 a.m., 2 p.m., 6 p.m., and 10 p.m. each day. Pressing "send", the call of urgency went out to everyone who was ready to help. The clock was ticking.

Gordon's boys, Jim and Steve, turned up at around lunchtime as we were coming out of ICU. Raked into plum and beige trousers respectively, with pointed suede shoes and snug shirts and jumpers, they flanked one another in the corridor in a way only twins know how. Rebecca and Larry bid me farewell in an act of tact, promising to be back again tomorrow. My guts twisted to see them go. I was unsure how it was going to be for me with the boys. Despite being bleary-eyed from their flight, they did manage to greet me with a combined floppy smile and hello. For a moment, my heart lifted.

I watched them offload their rucksacks in the Relatives' Room. Jim seemed thinner. I was concerned but didn't mention it. Really, for someone who was such a lover of words and writing, he had always seemed perfectly built for his craft, perhaps now just even more so. His new haircut with the bushy quiff of black curls sitting higher to the left of his parting, lent him all the appearance of a pencil whose smudged eraser had been worn down on one side from overuse. I noted Steve had changed a bit too, with extra muscle on his arms and hands. Was it all the overtime loading his truck and operating the plant? Maybe the nights spent drumming at their gigs, or the hours building their recording studio. They would be 29 this year. Time really did fly.

I went to give each of them a hug only to feel again in their bodies how they weren't into big hugs or maybe just not ones from me. I slipped out of the embrace and resorted to a parting pat or two at their backs instead. We remained standing, as if none of us wanted to acknowledge that we were here, or get too comfortable together. Jim and Steve leaned shoulder to shoulder up against the kitchen sink, while I shifted about on my seat opposite them, feeling that blood was indeed thicker than water. But they both asked me how I was, and we glided over pleasantries about their journey from Melbourne and the five days off work they had been granted. As I updated them from the night before, I made sure to guard against leaking any distress, sensing they did not want it. Finally, they went into ICU. I stayed behind, figuring that was the right thing to do. Sons would want to have privacy with their dad – for that first visit anyway – and the dad's wife was better off leaving them to it. It stung me to pass up on time with Gordon but the boys were here now and, for as long as they were here, I knew I had to share him with them. Sinking back down in the seat, the shakes in my legs revealed the truth about the adrenalin I had just fired off to help me handle the situation.

I stared hard at Gordon. The changes to him now were giving us more cause for alarm, as the three of us sat there and wondered what was developing. It had been a couple of hours since I'd joined the boys, courtesy of a waiver of the "no more than two visitors at a time" rule again. The gesture from staff had of course been appreciated but now I was wondering if their motivation had been more to do with a concern that Gordon wasn't going to make it. The thought made me shudder, adding to my ongoing bristles at the changeover of staff that had taken place during my absence. The new nurse, Ed, was a stocky young Asian man whose cheeks were stuffed with words he did not speak, presenting yet another different set of clues to have to read and interpret. Since meeting him, my hyperawareness had already latched itself onto his manner of pinning Gordon through his silver glasses. He displayed all the sharpness and point of focus one would use to slip the thinnest of threads through the tiniest eye of the smallest of needles. Managing to avoid meeting our gaze, he had woven in and out amongst us as if surgically stitching together our collective wound. I was in awe at the complexity of care he appeared to be administering on what felt like a minute by minute basis – evaluating Gordon's reactions to the medications, adjusting the flow based on what he saw, noticing outputs, and so on. It had helped to reassure me but I still hadn't liked that he avoided saying too much whenever I asked how Gordon was doing.

For a while I massaged Gordon's feet and the boys sat either side of him and held his hands. All of us had attempted our pretence at normality. Jim, stroking the three-day growth scribbled across his chin like 3 a.m. creative downloads after black coffee, had told his dad with soft earnestness about his music writing. Steve had joined in too, as snippets of news about his achievements with work and the band drum-rolled their way out from between the fur of his starter beard and moustache. There had been silliness here and there as well, the same jibes to their dad they would have given if he had been awake and able to grab them by surprise and tickle them with vigour. Yet all the while, Gordon lay there unmoved, unmoving, and unmoveable. It was taking time to get used to this version of him.

As one IV bag after another had dripped dry and been replaced, my unease circled, a shark beneath the surface of what lay at stake. Neither the boys nor I had been able to ignore Gordon's escalating temperature. Shiny beads of sweat had formed on his brow and a flush had swept over his otherwise lifeless face. At first we hadn't wanted to name the elephant in the room. But it was a tension trumpeting to be resolved. So I pointed out the obvious to Ed. He had already taken Gordon's temperature twice without saying anything but he duly re-tested and noted it, only to pad away with the same steadiness and deliberation with which he seemed to do everything else. My edginess ramped up. I needed to know what the number was and what Ed thought about it. I hated not being kept in the loop. All the nurses seemed mute and, as if to exacerbate this, the alarms on the machines had been sounding more frequently, their warnings grating upon my fragile nervous system. I wanted to understand what messages their tones were imparting, but neither Ed nor the other nurse had offered explanations nor displayed any sense of urgency. Instead I had been left to try to figure it out myself, based on what I could see – a new IV bag that needed fitting, a twiddle of this monitor, a reading that needed to be taken on another. After a couple of hours like this, the sweat on Gordon's forehead multiplied like something undesirable in a petri dish, the boys fell into silence, and I could suddenly bear it no more.

"Ed!" I made no apologies for my conviction bolstered by irritation. "Gordon's temperature is worsening. That can't be good. He must have an infection or something. I mean . . . if you're on life support and you have a temperature, well, what does that *mean* exactly? Can his body withstand that?"

"Yes he has a temperature at the moment."

I watched him amble away again.

This is their policy, isn't it? Their BLOODY "keep quiet, don't tell the relatives much" policy. Shit. That doesn't bode well, surely? They only see him as a body and a set of numbers and lines, a reason to monitor bloody input and output! For Christ sake, people – he isn't just a damn body! He's my husband, their father, his mother's son! What is going ON? I clenched my sweaty hands together on the bed-sheet and prayed.

At around 5.30 p.m., I could bear it no longer and went to seek out Christine, the General Manager. Standing at her door I drew myself taller, cheeks burning, feeling myself to be both the pyre and the sacrificial lamb. Anger masked my fear, a lividness that had as its driving force the fact that nobody senior had come to tell me anything about Gordon's condition since Christine herself had taken me to ICU the night before. She welcomed me with understanding and promised to arrange an immediate meeting with the Senior Anaesthetist and Intensivist, Dr Brentwood. I sighed with relief that I didn't have to do battle with her, though I squirmed at having to ask what an Intensivist was. If she noticed my own sense of inadequacy or ignorance, she had the compassion and sensitivity not to show it. Her voice chinked like a teaspoon against the rim of a porcelain teacup as she proceeded to brief me on the sorts of things I should ask to maximise my slot with him. I was invited to consider what else I might want to get answers to and whether I had any questions for her about what had happened in Coronary Care the day before. My mind swam as the focus that had delivered me to Christine and to this conversation now threatened to dissipate and dissolve into an unhelpful blur. *Come back, Caroline. This is important. You can do this. You are good at detail.*

Twenty minutes later I was fidgeting in the Relatives' Room with Jim and Steve, every cell in my body on alert as I waited for Dr Brentwood to grace us with his presence and his report on Gordon. No matter how many questions I'd been briefed to ask him, I felt woefully unprepared.

Dr Brentwood brought a desolate coldness with him as he entered the room, a chill that seemed at odds with the warmth and earthiness of his corduroys, suede loafers and red and white-checked flannelette shirt. He kept his head bowed, making it a challenge for me to discern whether the rosiness of his cheeks was a result of an inherent bashfulness or the chronic symptom of a refrigerated and bleak demeanour. A lone wolf, he stood his ground and leaned against the kitchen unit with his arms bent behind him, the blood draining from his knuckles as his fingers gripped the edge of the sink-basin. In a crazy second of anxiety that needed release, I noted the humour in such an intense man having a job as an Intensivist. We all looked at him, holding our breath. When he lifted his head, it was to draw the steel of his gaze level with mine.

"Right, well hello everyone. Sorry I haven't been in to brief you until now. It's been pandemonium. And I don't have long. It's the weekend and I want to have what's left of it, so let's get started shall we? Okay, so, what would you like to know?"

Oh my God. You cold fish! I gulped, feeling a sense of my own ridiculousness and insignificance in the face of his authority and power. But my desire for clarity trumped the sense of intimidation I felt, and I cleared my voice.

"I would like an update on Gordon, where we are at, what the infection is . . ."

Without blinking he launched into his answer. I thought I saw a grimace yet, in truth, there seemed no pain for him at all in the sentence he was handing down to Gordon and to all of us.

"Well, as you know, Gordon suffered multiple organ failure yesterday. Heart, kidney, and liver. He also went into acute respiratory distress. Right now, he is hanging by the thinnest of threads. It is absolutely touch and go. I have slung all the life support at him that there is to sling. There's nothing else for him, he's on the lot."

Jim looked to the ground, scuffing the toe of his shoe into the carpet. Steve and I stared at Dr Brentwood.

"Okay, so now to the details. His ejection fraction is at 5%. As you will be aware, normal is around 50%. He has extensive sepsis – that's blood poisoning – and the severity of a chest infection which, it seems, has turned out to be pneumonia. We don't know yet whether the pneumonia has been caused by virus or bacteria, though we need to find out." He blew his nose. "Myself and Dr Karl, the Senior Cardiologist, very much want to transfer him out to St Mary's but to do that, St Mary's have, as their stipulations for receiving the patient, insisted that his sepsis is cleared and the pneumonia too because they will not admit him with that either. If – and I do mean if – we could do both those things in time, he still wouldn't be able to be transferred to St Mary's right now. Mainly because to get him out of here, we need to chopper him out. But there's no space in the chopper for the ventilator. So we would need to get him to a point first where he could breathe for himself again. And we are just not there yet. We also can't transfer him right now because any move of his body, any slightest of slight moves, *will* likely kill him."

He paused, as if aware of us again. Maybe he remembered he was not in a lecture theatre in front of his students. Or had he heard the scream exploding inside me at decibels only audible to wild animals when he'd said the words "*will* likely kill him"? Our eyes locked for a second – his glacial, mine wide open and instructed by a brain grappling with the enormity of the picture he was painting. He resumed looking at the floor, about to speak again, only to be interrupted by the boys.

"So . . . we need to move him but . . . we can't move him?" Jim pushed his glasses back up a notch.

"Bottom line: how many hours before we would be able to move him?" Typical Steve. Cut to the chase.

"*If* he can survive the gravity of the situation he's in *right now* – and I stress again, the odds *are* overwhelmingly stacked against him – then he is going to need a heart transplant to have any chance at some semblance of a normal life again. That's why, in theory, we are so keen to get him to St Mary's. Once they take him in he can go on their waiting list for a new heart and in the meantime, they could put a pump into the organ so that he could be released as an outpatient and he could be at home. But listen, we are a long way from *that* outcome. Right now, the new deadly things are that he has a temperature and a chest infection but we don't as yet know what from."

I watched as he folded his arms, crossed one foot over the other and looked up at us once again.

"You need to prepare yourselves. It isn't looking good. But . . . it is always important to try to keep hope."

For a man who numbed people senseless for a living, he had more than displayed his talent. My mouth wouldn't work. I couldn't feel my body. The world as I knew it was slipping away and I was stalled at number six in the part where you get asked to count down from ten to one when being wheeled into surgery, and the strip-lights on the ceiling start colliding with one another. In fact, the calamity, the shock, and the silence from me and the boys punctuated the air like the "dot, dot, dot" on a line in a book where The Mustard Seed of Hope, The Devastatingly Unspeakable and The Sheer Despair all get to uncomfortably hang out together. *He said I need to prepare myself. PREPARE. That it's not looking good. Please, God. Please, no!*

Dr Brentwood quizzed me. When did Gordon's cold start? Was there anything about his getting it that had stood out to me? Anguished, I recalled the night when we had argued and Gordon had left without a coat, to go out walking for hours on end. It had been drizzling. I told Dr Brentwood the basics. He came back at me with more questions. Was Gordon still taking his drugs from the episode last time with his heart? I told him no, he wasn't, that he had weaned off them and had talked to the GP about that. When did he get the next check-up? I didn't know. I felt stupid and that it was something I should know about. He sighed, folded his arms.

"Well, you see, the thing is this: everyone else is saying that in all likelihood this has been caused by a repeat performance of three years ago, a specific virus that has stunned and paralysed his heart again. I am of the opinion however, that whilst he may have suffered this viral attack, this alone would not and could not have been enough to create the catastrophe that we have now ended up with. If you ask me, I believe his heart muscle had been weakening over time since coming off his medication. There would have been signs for you to see in the past months . . . him falling asleep earlier in the evening, not doing as much exercise . . . ?"

The memories of the signs I had indeed noticed came flooding back and I offered up what I knew. It was like trying to piece together a jigsaw of a thousand pieces without having the picture on the box to use as a guide. The more that clicked into place, the worse I felt. Dr Brentwood announced he had to leave, repeating that it was the weekend and that he had delayed it to be with us, and reiterating that we needed to see Gordon's numbers rally and fast. It was obvious that he planned to depart with the same cheerlessness with which he had entered. It occurred to me that whilst his job was to keep death at bay, he looked more like the Grim Reaper, his non-existent smile equivalent to the dash between the "born" and "died" on a tombstone.

Jim and Steve shuffled out for some air. I understood their need. But it left me alone, stranded on the edge of my seat and tuned in to the tap that was dripping at the sink. I felt lightheaded, my stomach churning. Though he had said we should always try to have hope, I didn't believe Dr Brentwood held out any hope for my man. And I had the impression he sure as hell didn't want to give me any.

Gordon's mobile flashed. It was a text from Ruth, asking what news there was. I rang her from the room, managing to keep a handle on the aftershocks ripping through me. As I was to discover later, she went straight off the call and posted her update on the Journey Page:

> GORDON UPDATE: Things are not great. Caroline is with him. Charles is on the way and Larry and I are going to take shifts so that she has someone with her.

With the boys still gone, I could think of nowhere to be but back inside ICU with Gordon. Pressing the bell again, I had no idea of what I was about to walk into, the conversation I was about to have, or its extraordinary repercussions. The nurse on the other side called out for me to come in. Pushing open the veil between worlds, I entered.

Chapter Nine

Day 2

9.00 p.m. – Hospital

THE DIMNESS OF THE WARD reminded me somehow of a morgue. As I sat down beside Gordon, the nurse from yesterday with the brown bob and the mole under her eye came over and whispered her greeting, asking me how I was.

"I've been in the waiting room, talking about everything with Dr Brentwood."

"Ah . . ." She drew the word out as if it guarded a boundary, her tone dropping off at the end. "What do you know?"

I relayed what he had said, finishing by gabbling my fear to her that Gordon would, in all likelihood, go but that he would first hang on for a few days more because there were things that I had to learn or go through. That when his coma had enabled this, he would depart from this world.

"No, no, Caroline. When patients are like this, we don't let them carry on for a few days, we usually only give them 24 to 48 hours . . ."

"What? You mean then you . . . switch life support off?"

"Yes. We would bring him back to consciousness so that you could . . . speak to him and . . ."

"Speak to him? But, how would he breathe?" I was frowning now, trying to comprehend the consequences of removing the very machinery that was supposed to be inflating and deflating his lungs and keeping him alive. Then, it dawned on me. *Oh my God. Surely not . . .*

"Well, it would be difficult for him but . . . we would make him as comfortable as we could. You would at least be able to speak to him. You know, to say . . . to speak . . ."

"*No!* Definitely *not!* Bring him back to consciousness just so that I could say *goodbye?* Oh my God, no way could I do that to him! I *won't* do that to him. Imagine the trauma that would bring to him!" My whisper was a cross between a sob and a hiss. A new layer of my heart ripped open, bleeding into the emptiness of the spaces between my words as I struggled to let in the enormity of what she was driving at.

She didn't say anything, only looked at me and placed her hand on mine for a second. Hanging in the air was a threat that could not be denied. As our conversation died, she stood up to go, saying I knew where she was if I needed her. My body was shaking, terror on ice. I felt powerless to do anything about the situation we were facing. *But you can make calls. You need to make calls, to the family . . . more difficult than the ones when he had crashed.* It was 9.30 p.m. The group healing was imminent. Not much time to get the word out and ask everyone to please take part. And yet, much as I wanted my man back and knew that the next 48 hours were of paramount importance, I also somehow knew from within the calmness of my core that we were to all now pray for – and choose – the highest good, whatever that may look like. I knew it was the only way.

Leaving the ward, I felt as if I were walking on cotton wool. Almost as surreal was the sight of Charles, one of our magician friends, standing tall inside the doorway of the Relatives' Room, with all the solidity and stateliness of the elephants from his homeland Africa. I hadn't expected him to come. Seeing me, he broke off mid-sentence from the boys to ask me how I was and how Gordon was faring. Not one for even blending into his orchestra's chorus group, the crispness and clarity of his reedy voice penetrated the space between us, projecting a sense of order and leadership onto me that I didn't feel. Ringing and rushing sounded in my ears as I relayed what the nurse had said. I wanted to scream but instead a strange sound came out only to be caught and muffled inside Charles's hug as he wrapped his arms around me. It was a moment of vulnerability. I had to pull myself together, make those calls, and ask people to please send love for the outcome that would be for the highest good – whatever that was going to be.

I had been remarkably present during the healing session. No thoughts, just being the sending of Love. It came as something of a shock therefore to see the nurse storming towards me as I was about to leave, her eyes flashing with fury.

"I've just had Gordon's sister in distress on the phone, saying that you told her we were going to switch off the life-support in 24 hours if there was no change!"

"Well, yes, I had to tell her what situation we are in. She is his sister even if they don't get along much."

"I *never* said we would be switching off Gordon's life support in the next 24 hours if there is no change, what I . . ."

"Yes you *did!* We sat there and had an entire conversation about it!"

"I most definitely did *not* say that, thank you very much. I said that a *review* would take place in the next 24 hours."

"But that isn't true! I know what I heard! I may not have slept in nearly two days but I'm not deaf. You never once said the word *review*. I don't understand you."

"How *dare* you say that it . . ."

"Stop!" My head reeled in disbelief as my palm faced her. "*Stop.* I've heard enough!"

I pushed past her and barged through the PVC flaps, pausing at the Relatives' Room only long enough to tell Charles and the boys what had just happened and how she lied through the back of her teeth. Then I fled. Down the corridor in all its twists and turns, running with hot tears streaming down my face, running until I was out on the pavement, running until I was in the car-park that was empty save for my four wheel drive, running until my lungs needed me to stop. Exhausted, I flopped onto the curb, sitting in the shadows of the bush behind me. I wanted to rail at the night, my fear and anger the eye of a tornado bearing down on a ravaged terrain within.

"The world's gone mad!"

Declaring it seemed to provide an unexpected comfort, as if at least there was one thing I could be certain of right now. I puffed out my exasperation, shoulders slumping. Over to my left, a movement caught my eye. I turned, froze on the spot as a white rabbit, all lit up by the streetlamp, came into view from out of the bushes. Twitching its nose, it sat there for a moment and proceeded to hop across the tarmac until it paused in front of me. Staring at it, I saw the word "magic" in my mind's eye, intuitively heard the words "*believe* in magic." No sooner had it happened than the rabbit bounded away until the shadows claimed him and he disappeared from sight.

I didn't move, still holding my breath in surprise, wondering if I could trust my intuition about the encounter, if I could rely on the strangest yet strongest sense that this was a sign from none other than Gordon himself. In the weeks prior to his coma, we had seen white rabbits jumping out in front of us in unlikely places. Had he sent me one now? Was he telling me to trust? That despite my misgivings about his situation I was to believe in a higher vibration that could move mountains? Was this visitation a replacement for the exaggerated "thumbs up" Gordon liked to do whenever I needed reassurance? But how could he be alright when he was hanging by a thread?

The air was crisping up and I shivered. From across the tarmac, Charles strode towards me. He didn't say anything as he sat down beside me, allowing instead a cushion of silence. Finally, I spoke. I shared about the rabbit and the message to believe in the possibility of magic. That I felt stupid and that the nurse *had* said what she had later denied uttering. I sensed that Charles thought I was mistaken about her. Too tired to argue, I let it be.

Magic. Believe in magic. That had been the message.

Hadn't it?

CHAPTER TEN

Day 3

1.30 a.m. – Home

ALMOST 48 HOURS HAD PASSED since The Unthinkable had erupted, blasting the lid off my world and spewing out ash and rocks with such ferocity that it had left me stranded, disoriented and choking within a cloud of dust. The irony was, that in the explosion of events and the way that the "fixed" had become volatile and unstable, obscurity was beginning to actually serve visibility. Now that the eruption had happened, I could do nothing but start to see how much I had held onto limitations – limitations born of fears and perceptions and assumptions and beliefs about what was real and true. Forming a plug of confusion, they had served only to create my experience of separation from Love and truth. The blast had sent them sky high, from where they were already starting to fall to the ground. There was no doubt about it, the horror of Gordon's crash into coma was burning down everything in its way, rendering all of my plans of how life should be and should have been and should never have been – and all my other stories about that – as just "things" burning in the aftermath.

I glanced over at the laptop. It was 2 a.m. and I was still fighting off sleep on the sofa, a combination of my unwillingness to be in our bed and fear that if I didn't stay awake I would miss a call from the hospital. I could not get the rabbit out of my mind. Furthermore, for an hour now, I'd had a jingle playing between my ears on stubborn repeat and driving me to distraction. I realised it was the jangling of the jack-in-the-box from my childhood. *Humpty Dumpty sat on the wall . . . Humpty Dumpty had a great fall . . .* Why on earth tonight? I used to play it a lot as a child, sitting on the rug and cranking the metal arm round and round. Sometimes I had even kept my hand on the lid so that I wouldn't get any nasty surprises from it. If only life was indeed that simple.

The tune had me thinking. Maybe sometimes things do have to happen on an earth-shattering scale if the patterns of limitation that imprison us are to break apart. Gordon and I had been through a lot in four years, a heady concoction triggered by his financial betrayal, my unwitting enabling of it, and all the stress, conflict and hardship that it had led to. I had thought the pain and learning back then had been sufficient to bring to consciousness both his and my conditioned stories and patterns of behaviour, and end them once and for all. Tonight however, I was the only one taking up space on our sofa and I had to acknowledge that on the contrary, both of us had continued to "play out" this thing of sitting on our respective walls of fear and indecision. For Gordon, it had been about whether he would dare to claim himself as an artist and as someone who wanted to work with the land, whether he would go out into the world and contribute to the workplace and community in ways that had meaning for him, and whether he would choose to be all he had come here to be. As for me, doubts had given rise to questions: could I trust to start a family or not? Was I right to have still chosen Gordon and the marriage after The Things That Had Gone On? Was he even still a match for me? Could I or would I ever be able to trust him again?

Infinite Possibility – sitting on the wall. That's what we had been doing. Could it have been the case that by giving in to our fears and stopping our growth as humans and spiritual beings, we had led ourselves to a fall from grace of sorts? Right now, a part of me did believe we were both being punished. Just opening the door to that assumption caused a hit of heaviness to descend over me. I breathed into the familiarity of the sensation, exhaling deeply, my chest crushed and pushed down by the exacting weight of the scales of justice.

Punishment.

I closed my eyes.

Six years old. Heart pounding as the policeman stands there in the lounge. This is Dad's doing. He needs to teach me a lesson, he says. There are no words from Mum but the ones from Dad cut to my core. I am a wicked, wicked, wicked girl, he decrees. My cheeks blaze as I hang my head. After all, who can love a wicked girl? It's a crime to steal money from your Mum's purse just so that you can buy biscuits for everyone in the playground. I am sent to my room, eyes stinging as I repeat the words "wicked girl" over and over, so that I never forget who I am.

Six years old. Mum in hospital getting ready to give birth to my brother. Me standing on a dining chair I'd dragged to the cooker so I can properly reach the stovetop and frypan. Wanting to make my first fried breakfast for dad, surprise him, show him I can be a grown up. I crack the egg on the rim of the pan, just like I'd seen her do so many times before. But it doesn't work right. I misjudge things and the yolk and white splat all over the floor. In comes Dad, yells at me, tells me I am useless and to get down and come away from there. My cheeks are on fire. Later that night I am sent to stay with my best friend for the duration of Mum's stay in hospital.

Tonight I can still see traces of the story. Karma punishes. God punishes. The masculine punishes. The best way to reprimand and teach a lesson is to withdraw the love, no? Was this what was happening? Was the Divine chastising me? Was Gordon avenging me because I had not been good enough or loving enough or open-hearted enough as a wife? Was my badness and wickedness so inherent that I could not be loved? There it was, my pain, my story that had entrenched itself since childhood and that I was now projecting onto my husband in coma! Here was the filter that had never done anything but separate me from my essence and from the Love that I was! This was the pain – the fear that I could be so unworthy of love that this love could be withdrawn by another, and withdrawn to such an extent that I might never survive in this world without it. I had insisted on holding this tattered script for years, and was allowing my attention on it now to fuel the fire that said Gordon and I had failed in how we had lived our lives, had flunked at being the mighty Creators that the world of personal development had told us that we were and should be. That we had powered our agendas of sabotage and therefore only had ourselves to blame for the set of results we were now facing.

Yet somewhere in all of this was also a greater realisation that there was no getting it "wrong" in life and therefore no "punishment" either. Part of me innately knew that on some level we needed to do this thing we humans called "fall". That it was our destiny to freefall into the depths of our humanity, to explore and experience the darkness inside us that we fear so that we may grow and awaken to the lies and illusions, and return to Love. That along the way, we are *meant* to have our shell of defence and its storied armour smashed to smithereens so that we can receive once again the soft heart of our true nature. Right now with my man in ICU, I had indeed been brought to my knees, forced into humility because I did not know what was going to happen to him and now had to even consider his dying, not to mention what that might mean for me. In the face of all this, I felt my smallness and helplessness. I yawned and rolled onto my side on the couch. Sleep was out of the question.

Throughout my life, my unconscious reaction to believing some of these fears, and my conditioning and path of least resistance regarding them, had always been the same: I had avoided sitting in my vulnerability. I had focused instead on being who I thought I needed to be and doing what I thought I needed to do to assure my safety. Strategies for control that I believed would secure my survival, a survival that had been in question for as long as I could remember because of my wickedness and unworthiness of love. I exhaled at the magnitude and yet smallness of the game I had played – and its flaws. How could I have ever controlled the ultimate Big Picture? To compound matters, I had operated from the assumption there *was* anything to have to control in my life, and that I *had* to have control to experience my wholeness and completeness and make it out of here alive. I had done nothing but wrap myself up in compensating agendas and strategies. When would I finally learn? Or was it that I should have unlearned? Whatever the answer, these core wounds were now peeled, exposing an original pain that had so overwhelmed me at the time, that as the years had passed I'd needed to enact my strategies with repetition and finesse to ensure that this wound would never see the light of day again so that my life could go on. Now that the light of day had arrived, however, it was not the light I had imagined. In the exposing of the wound, a portal had opened, shafting a slither of light from another reality. It was as if this light were the Divine itself, reaching through to hold my hand, inviting me to meet with and embark on a journey I now sensed I was being called to: a journey into Love, into higher forces, and into surrender.

Surrender.

I had never bloody liked the word. In the hospital I had been resisting "what is so" as if Gordon's life depended on it. But maybe I was resisting it as if *my* life depended on it. Only now I saw that all these hours hadn't just been about *Gordon's* survival. On an unconscious level they had been about mine too. We humans and our conditioning to fight and defend or run away from the sabre-toothed tigers of life! Believing there *is* something to fear and something to "lose" and that our resistance *will* save us. And yet, in that landmark moment before making those calls tonight for the group healing, I had experienced my first glimpse of the power that could come from true surrender. When the window of opportunity had opened up, I accepted and allowed the reality that Gordon might pass, acknowledging it without any further stories attached. It occurred to me now that we talk about surrender in life and stopping the fight but that in truth, there is no surrender and no actual 'stopping' of the fight. There is simply the acceptance that comes from being present to what is so. It was peculiar but somehow I had realised that surrender was not something I had to *do* but something that was happening because it was all that could happen. In truth, I was in hospital, with my husband in coma and with the odds of him dying. It was obvious to me now that the surrender of then was the degree to which, during that small window of time, I had been present with that truth.

Pondering it now, it had been my presence that had enabled me to respond with consciousness rather than react on autopilot, and to take actions with a clarity of focus that had put me in my power. I had made the calls I needed to make and had also asked something new of everyone, that they prayed not for Gordon to live but for the outcome that would best serve the highest good of his soul. Through this alone, my decision had been an act of releasing into the unknown, a release that had come to me as natural as breathing. Presence and acceptance became the bridge, allowing me to acknowledge my desire for Gordon to come back to me, and to access the knowing that there might be a higher outcome than "what Caroline wanted". Allowing all that was happening and allowing that which could yet happen, whatever it was. It was not a giving up. It was an offering up. It was not passivity or doing nothing. It was a deliberate change in a state of being. During that window there were no tears and no hysteria. There was only now. When I had returned to sit with Gordon for the 10 p.m. healing, there was a softening in me, a coming home, and of being how Love is. I had realised I'd never loved Gordon or indeed anyone in this way before. It was different to romantic or emotional love. If only during that moment, I'd glimpsed the realisation that I could maybe love so freely, that I would let go of asking Gordon to stay around in the physical here on earth for me.

Downstairs, one of the boys flushed the toilet. Bare feet slapped against the floorboards and the bedroom door tapped shut again. Sighing, I picked up my laptop from the table beside me. Though reluctant, I felt I should take a look at the Journey Page that Ruth had set up. As I scrolled down the newsfeed, scanning the succession of updates from the hospital that I had given to Larry and others, and reading the flood of comments from all those who were supporting Gordon and me, a ball of crackles formed in my throat. Licking the hot saltiness from tears of appreciation, grief and fear, I honed in on some of the chop and change that had been the day.

Larry: This is the 1 p.m. update from Caroline. "The liver has rallied and is good. Kidneys have worsened a little. Gordon has responded to the latest blood pressure intervention. I feel the group energy is benefiting him. I feel he does not want to go. He is fighting! This is so much to do with the healing and love being sent. Please keep it up. Your support is such a gift, thank you."

Charles: Next global tune in is 2 p.m. Let's all be there for him!

Marty: Dear Gordon, I humbly offer "The Medicine Buddha Mantra": Om namo bhagavate bhaiṣajyaguru vaidūrya prabha rājāya tathāgatāya arhate samyaksam buddhāya tadyathā . . .

Rebecca: This is the 9.45 p.m. update from Caroline. "Gordon has been given 24–48 hours on life support if no change. Please pray for the outcome that will serve the highest good of Gordon's soul."

Ruth: The call has gone out. Our hearts are with you both. Healing energy is pouring in. Come on Gordy, we're pulling for you.

Ella: Oh my God, I don't know what to say, am sending prayers.

Wilson: Hey darling, I'm holding a massive vision for you and Gordy. You are not alone! Call me if there is anything I can do. Xx

Kathy: I'm praying my heart out. Don't know what else to say. Xx

Ruth: Between 10 and 10.15 p.m. tonight over 80 people (and counting) across the world are uniting together in prayers and healing for Gordon. I invite you to join us.

CHAPTER ELEVEN

Day 3

2.40 a.m. – Home

I CRAWLED OFF THE COUCH to get a drink, pattered across the floorboards so as not to disturb the boys. For an hour, wildfires had been lighting up my mind, igniting wakefulness in the face of drowsiness. I let the water from the jug glug into my glass. I was still thinking about the notion that it had only been after my point of surrender at the hospital tonight and the group healing that followed, that both the retraction from the nurse and the appearance of the white rabbit with its message to "believe in magic" had played out. My skin pulled itself into goosebumps once more at this sense of the extraordinary at play. I felt humbled. It begged a repeat of the question: what was Life showing me? And what was it asking of me?

I couldn't get the nurse and her recanted statement out of my thoughts. That she should deny our conversation having taken place defied reason. It opened me to wondering about "parallel realities". Was there indeed a reality where the nurse had mentioned switching off life-support and another reality where she had never said it all? And had I somehow been privy to both? If everything was vibration, both would co-exist and the only thing that could have made the difference to what I had perceived and experienced, would have been what I was choosing to focus upon. Making my way back to the couch, it struck me that the nurse's behaviour might have taken place to show me this nature of focus, pointing me back to my studies in alchemy and vibration and the premise of using the higher against the lower to change lead into gold.

The timings of the original conversation and then her pullback intrigued me. The first dialogue with her had happened after the meeting with Dr Brentwood. Was it the case I had so believed him and his Grim Reaper diagnosis that I had taken it on as The Truth? This would have been easy to do considering his air. The coolness and declarations from him had supported and validated all my underlying beliefs that the people you love let go or leave, and that life doesn't work out. Were these beliefs so ingrained in me that this was all I could hear or see, all I could expect, and all I could then have as my experience of reality with the nurse? What if her words had been just a projection of my addictive belief system, a result of my terror about what could happen? Had she indeed said something else?

I shook my head, digging my heels into the arm of the sofa in a moment of irritation. *No.* She *had* said it. I frowned. So what about the timing of her retraction? Not half an hour before, I had already surrendered and asked people to pray for the highest good of Gordon's soul. Could those moments of presence and acceptance have opened me, with such swiftness, to receiving an experience of possibilities that lay outside of my belief system? The rabbit had indeed messaged me to believe in magic. Had a change in focus and the power of unconditional love really been able to veer

Gordon's train off the "certain" track it had been on? And what was Gordon doing in all this, what part was *he* playing?

Right now at 2.50 a.m. it wasn't so much a case of me needing to know, as it was a deep-seated sensation of being in the not-knowing, in the mystery. I was in awe at all the twists and turns of the past days and of the kaleidoscope of potentialities and realities that seemed to be shifting, tumbling, collapsing into one another, and being created anew. I had to admit, I didn't know how everything was going to land. Yet within the extraordinary was the strongest feeling of connection that I'd ever remembered having – of feeling tapped into something higher than reason or what logic could point to, where *not* knowing offered itself as a faint pulse amidst the crash and burn. Like Gordon in a way, my heart had failed, had been stunned and paralysed since the devastation of his crash. Yet with all the peculiarities that had followed and the surprise of so much support from friends, it seemed that my heart was now being offered life support too, albeit of a different kind. I felt a stirring. Somewhere inside I knew that what I was going through had significance, that I had to pay attention, perhaps even be vulnerable enough to share it with others and communicate my insights with as much honesty as I could muster. Whatever happened now, I already felt like there could be no going back to who I was before Gordon went into hospital.

The notification of a private message beeped and flashed on the screen of my laptop. I clicked on it and read.

> At 10 p.m. tonight, I sat in the stillness thinking of Gordon when this mouse came out and scurried in my kitchen. For some reason, I felt it had something to do with him because we never see it in the open. Then I happened to look over to the fridge. Someone had put magnets there that I've never seen before, and they

> said "still here, waiting for you." Well actually, I only
> saw the "still here" part at first but I think the whole
> message was for you. Love, Linda.

My heart skipped a beat as the words and their implication seemed
to leap off the screen. Was Gordon messaging me again, through a
mouse this time, and through a friend? I paused and read the words
again, feeling the hairs prick on the back of my neck. I turned my
attention back to the posts and comments on the Journey Page and
witnessed once again all the friends who had been sending their
love, people who were with us in spirit and energy and a part of
this crisis as much as I was. The tips of my fingers tingled. Before
I knew it, I was typing a status update, the keys responding to my
flurry of thoughts, agreeing to organise themselves in heartfelt
marks on the screen that would serve not only me but also whoever
else they would find out in the world that could be served by them.

> Update from me: Thank you so much everybody for
> your energy and love. I am shaking and crying at it all
> right now, in overwhelm and humbled.
>
> During the last group healing tonight I felt such
> expansion of love and heart that I felt I would explode.
> The "downloads" have been happening thick and fast
> for me today as I surrender to the transformation that
> is happening in me, in my gorgeous man, and within our
> relationship. Too much to write here but I have been
> having profound experiences of the truth of multiple
> possibilities existing all at once – experiencing this in
> deep and magical ways. I have had glimpses today from
> the level of soul. This is a rich and amazing ride we are
> all on, where Gordon is the conductor bringing together
> at just the right times and in the perfect combinations,
> the people who are meant to be on this journey . . .

gifting us not only with his evolution but also with ours.

I've been in a lot of fear again at the hospital. The thought that I hold, and keep buying into, is that his life before coma had so much upset in it that it had caused him to see the world and most things as unloving, unsafe, and rejecting of his heart – and that he might not therefore want to come back.

I've been kissing Gordon even more. I have spoken to him about the support that can be available for him to take his heart out into the world and that he no longer needs to have heart failure and machines as a way to have his heart supported. I also experienced a celebration of and a commitment to the deepening of our relationship, and fully opening to what that might look like if he chooses to come back. It was liberating!

Yesterday afternoon something struck me with such clarity that I had to smile at the irony of it. I have suggested that Gordon's soul is up to amazing work here – both with Gordon the man, and with all of us. And not without a sense of humour either, because here we all are, "seeing" Gordon in his "truth", his "Greatness", his pain, his story – and we are saying "I see you." Yet where is this journey unfolding? From inside the Intensive Care Unit! ICU! Wow.

I want to say again, I am overwhelmed by your messages to me and to Gordy. I don't get to read them during the day as my focus is with him. So to sit down and read them when I get home buoys me, and gives me a new point of focus at night in the house. You see, I feel too wired to relax and rest, even though I know I haven't rested properly in nearly two days.

It's getting late now. I feel like I can let myself sleep for the couple of hours that are left before it's time to

get up and go back to the hospital.
But then I just felt such fear again.
Thank you again for your love.

I placed the laptop back on the table and pulled the blanket up over me, nudging down into the couch. Oblivion was instant. While I slept, others posted their love, keeping the fires of the heart burning and sending light into the dark.

Nadia: So much learning for me from your messages and from the power of community when support is needed – reminds me that I do not have to feel alone. I am grown and am growing from all your beauty and sorrow and feminine strength. I shine a light on you beautiful woman. And I see Gordy with a cheeky smile and thongs!

Joyce: Caroline it is exciting to be a part of both your soul journeys at this time. It is teaching me a great deal. As I face major surgery in the morning I am fully aware of the power of love. Most importantly . . . love of oneself. Standing with you and Gordon has made that hit home. Many tears have fallen for Gordon and yourself, mixed with joy and a connection that is difficult to articulate. I find that my fears for my situation have far less hold as I focus on love for Gordon, love for all. I thank you, I bow down to you, and I love you. Xx

Lauren: This is where life has real meaning, where lessons learned can be put to practice, where fear can be confronted and unexpected strength surfaces . . . Xx

Marissa: Dear Caroline, the angels are supporting you . . . remember to breathe into the earth and reconnect with your beloved plants in that white environment. Imagine the scent of flowers and know the universe supports and is eternally patient with each of us.

Evelyn: Blessings, Caroline. What a journey you are both on and we are all on the ride with you in spirit. Makes me realise the past is over and that any story I'm telling myself is just a lie from the past. I see Gordon's Greatness and yours and it's helping me see my own. Let's hope this whole group gets to express our hearts in the world. I believe we will.

CHAPTER TWELVE

Day 3

6.30 a.m. – Home

RUBBING THE CRUSTS OF SLEEP out of my eyes, I asked Mum to repeat it, thinking I had misheard her over the crackling of the connection to the UK. But no, there it was again. Leaning forwards on the couch, I pressed the mobile to my ear a little harder, suddenly wide awake. Up until this point in the call, her voice had been full of concern and emotion. I had held myself back, giving only brief details of yesterday, not wanting to spend long on the phone, not wanting what I sensed was churning inside of her and bubbling to the surface to spill out and onto me. I didn't feel I could handle that if it happened. But now I wanted to hear more from her. She said the words again. Gordon had come to visit her tonight, an hour ago in fact. I listened as she described her experience. A distinct and tall shadow had passed across her bedroom wall. Instinct had told her it was him and so she had spoken aloud: "Hello Gordon." It was a peaceful meeting, she'd added. I blinked, not knowing what to say. There was no doubt in my mind she had experienced it. I was glad that she had too. I just wondered why he had not done that with me.

After the call, I sat still for a few minutes, gathered my thoughts, typed a status update, pressed send and went and had my shower. There was only the briefest of opportunities to read a couple of replies on the page, before the boys came up the stairs for their coffee.

Update from me: Glad the night has gone and without a call from the hospital. At the same time I am in trepidation about what today will bring. But I know I have to remember this thing I am experiencing about multiple possibilities existing in the same "moment", and that there is a possibility or actuality existing in this moment called Gordon Cumming pulling through and recovering and living an amazing life. I still choose whatever is going to serve the outcome for the highest good of his soul – whatever it is. And I know in my humanness that I just want my man back and for him to be well. I guess this is the dance of being spirit and having a human experience.

Last night I had the conversation with the nurse about switching off life support in the next 24–48 hours if Gordon's numbers didn't rally. I saw her again after the group healing and she was furious and retracted her statement, saying that she had only said a review would take place instead. I stormed out and went and sat in the car park thinking I had gone mad – only for a white rabbit to then appear! Its message to me was to believe in magic. I have had a couple of new thoughts about this since last night. I believe the retraction happened because Gordon's soul chose to remain in the Gordon experience. That there was a paradigm shift, one of multiple-possibilities-all-at-once, where we moved to a different reality in a different vibrational time and space. And so yes, in *that* reality the nurse had *not* said any such thing, that's quite right. I think the rabbit in the car-park was trying to get me to see that. So today I have to believe in the power of magic. I am buoyed by the fact Gordon is clearly hanging in there against all odds. And this morning, Mum even said that Gordon had come to visit her as a tall shadow across her bedroom wall. I believe his soul is still doing a "review".

It's time to go back to the hospital for the day. We will continue to have group healings from 10 a.m. every four hours. Please continue to send your prayers and love to Gordon. I believe it is helping him to make whatever decision he has to make.

Thank you. Xx

Amber: Caroline you are an inspiration. This is such a powerful insight that shows us the truth of this magical existence. You are teaching me all about the power of love, trust, faith and so many things I can't even put a name to but do know as the truth because right now I have those tears in my eyes that aren't sad or happy but the ones when you feel you have glimpsed the slightest comprehension of reality. Gordon's heart problems are making us all aware of our own hearts. Amazing teachers you both are! Sending you so much love. Hang in there. Xx

Nadia: What a powerful coming together of community this is as everyone focuses on something so much bigger than their everyday woes. This is what true creating is. I am moved by the experience that is being shared.

CHAPTER THIRTEEN

Day 3

7.45 a.m. – En route to hospital

I FELT AS IF I HELD MY BREATH during the drive from the house to the hospital. Jim was in the back of the car, Steve next to me, but nobody said much. The tiny hairs on the top of my forearms had become radars, on guard and poised to receive the energy flying around. I knew something was brewing in both of the boys, had felt it back in the kitchen when I had invited Jim to read the online posts everyone was writing for his dad. Gazing out of the windows, he hadn't even turned round to look at me. Instead, I had watched his body stiffen like a board and felt myself wince at the clipped "no thanks" that had cut back. Steve hadn't wanted to read them either and so I had dropped it. Even now, in the car, I felt like I was treading on eggshells around them both. One moment my eyes were on the traffic and the road ahead, the next focusing in the rear-view mirror to scan Jim's face for clues, and sneak glances across at Steve. *What should I say? Should I ask them what's happening for them? Ask if they want to talk about it? Shit, I don't bloody know.* A muscle twinged in the side of my neck, shooting a pain down into my shoulder. I decided to not ask them anything, to give them their space, and refocus on the road. My grip on the wheel and the impatience of my foot on the accelerator now seemed my only allies in a bid to rescue us from the claustrophobia of the car and expedite us to Gordon's bedside.

Dropping to a terrain beneath the tension, my mind wandered off again to all the online messages that had been piling in over the past 72 hours. It heartened and inspired me that such a volume and quality of support should exist for Gordon but I was blown away that it was being offered to me too. In a flash I realised the reason for my surprise. It wasn't just a reaction to the challenge to a lifetime spent harbouring the belief that neither others nor life supported me. It was more that I, Caroline, could be *that* loveable, that *worthy* of love and so much so that people across four continents would gift their care for *me* around the clock too, even though Gordon was the one in danger. It was that some of these people were strangers to us both and yet were willing to send unconditional love . . . and that I was worthy of that. I felt the tears prick.

As the lights changed and I eased the car back into motion, I checked for Jim in the mirror again, only to be met by my own eyes before refocusing on the car ahead and returning to my thoughts. I couldn't stop circling around this concept of worthiness. To experience the power of such a challenge to my mythology was one thing. It was quite another to be able to see the insidiousness with which it still weaved itself through my life despite recent years of bringing awareness to it and efforts to stop acting from it so much. This clarity brought with it confrontation but also liberation. Those decisions I had made about myself so long ago, did nothing but create an experience of the illusion of being separate from Love as the source of everything. And yet here I had been since Saturday, on my knees and cracked open in the only position, it would seem, that could have enabled this light to stream in and illuminate my path of "seeing" the truth behind the fable. *We are always loveable - because we are Love itself.*

Reflecting upon it all, I was starting to come to terms with the idea that Gordon's crash had opened up a gateway so that we might all receive the experience of consciously connecting as Love. Not only as emotional love, seeded in the humanness of need and desire and affection, but as Love that is pure vibration and Source energy. The same animating force that moves through our bodies; the current that had sent ripples pulsing through Gordon's abdomen and stomach in the session yesterday; the power that had caused my body to feel like it had been plugged into a socket whenever people jumped on-board to send healing. Whether we name it Source or Love, it is the force that keeps atoms together, holds a person's body together, and joins a body of people together. The vibration that moves through and between all things and no things and that ultimately, *is* who we really are. Without precedence, emerging for me now was a visceral understanding that although what separates is our "wounds" and the imagining of them to be the truth, what *connects* is being conscious of the Love that we are and choosing to experience that. Perhaps this explained what the community forming around us was feeling. Maybe some of these people – like me – were experiencing this consciousness for the first time.

For a moment it seemed unimaginable that the failure of Gordon's heart should be in such service to so many of us and to him too. And yet, wasn't it so often the case that through the shutdown of a heart – whether emotional, energetic or physical – and the situation or reaction this creates or invites, we finally have the ability to see and feel what it is we have repressed, what we have been blind to seeing and numb to feeling in ourselves, and what we need to acknowledge, honour and reclaim? After all, what is heart failure if not the failure, first of all, of our emotional and spiritual heart to function as it is meant to? And the heart functions in a state of openness. From there it can receive Love, transmit Love, and vibrate Love in its myriad forms of creative expression.

I flicked the indicator on, turning at the roundabout. How many people were already so shut down in some way, already at the stage of "emotional" heart failure or "spiritual" heart failure and therefore well on their way to the physical trauma? Was not Gordon acting as a wake-up call for us all? Why did we even need such an alarm? I sighed. Maybe for some of us it does have to take the physical shutdown of the heart of a loved one to wrench and reopen and resuscitate our own heart, the hearts of others, and the heart of the collective. While I suffered in my humanness, I began to comprehend that "my" wounds weren't just "mine" but were on some level an experience shared and felt in everyone else's life too, with each individual in their own way having the same or similar wounds. They were "our" wounds, the wounds of the collective, and we were all feeling them. While we went through this, we all endured the opening of our hearts to Love . . . for ourselves . . . for one another. And then, seeing that there was no "other".

I steeled myself with a breath and switched off the engine. We had arrived. As far as I knew, Gordon was still with us, still in life. Just.

CHAPTER FOURTEEN

Day 3

10.00 a.m. – Hospital

ABOUT HALFWAY THROUGH SITTING at Gordon's feet in the 10 a.m. healing, I had the oddest sense that I was *being moved* to pick up and hold the rose quartz from between his calves. It was a smaller piece than the flatter one that rested on his chest and I now nestled it in my palm. Surprised by my action, I looked over at the only other person in the room who was perched to his left, but Rebecca's eyes were closed, as mine had been. For the last few minutes we had been sitting in innocence, a being-ness that served as the gateway to connecting with everything that ever was or is or will be. It was a state of openness, of "not knowing" and "not needing to know" how things might turn out. So far, the group healings were the only times I could sit with Gordon like this without the worry or the grief or the dread. The intention – as for so many of the others who jumped onto the healings from afar – was to allow Love or source energy to come through us for Gordon and for the benefits of healing. All the while, the ventilator hissed and the machines beeped and a whole other world outside went about its day in streets and houses, offices and shops, planes, trains and cars.

That the quartz should even be here at all was perhaps no coincidence, since intuition had nudged both Rebecca and me to grab our pieces before leaving our houses today, and to bring them in and place them on or around Gordon in whichever ways we felt necessary. Used with an intention of healing, the crystal was reputed to help stimulate the functioning of the heart and circulation, to assist in stabilising irregularities with the rhythm of the heart, to ease stress and tension, and even to be useful in helping to clear fluids and support healing in the kidneys and adrenals and lungs. All of this was in line with what the specialists, within their conventions of treatment, had said Gordon needed. It also spoke to their urgency and focus today on clearing the sepsis from his veins. Yet there had been something else about the crystals' presence on this day. Something else about the third piece too – a smooth and large sphere nested in the tip of a long metal holder – which had been brought in at 8 a.m. by an acquaintance who had said only that her intuition had told her to do so. We had placed that piece on the ledge above his head behind the bed. So much rose quartz! It felt as if the energy of the feminine was being called in for Gordon. Rose quartz, carrying within itself the energy of the soft and sacred feminine, activating and opening on all levels that centre in the body's energy system associated with unconditional love: the heart chakra, located in the chest.

I had only been holding the crystal for a minute, my other palm hovering just above Gordon's left foot, yet already I was feeling distinct waves of energy emanating from it. It had aliveness, a heartbeat, as if it were flowing and emanating life force. For the first time, I realised I was experiencing its vibration. The feeling was of being held by Mother in the safety and security of her hug. *You are love-d.* Or of the lullaby as the cradle is rocked. *You are love-d.* And even the gentleness of the kiss upon the sweet-smelling head of a newborn. *You are love-d.* Just like the heart of the cosmos, it pulsed through me, from me, and into me all at once. The more I opened to the sensations, the more the beeps and hisses of the machines faded from my awareness and I received the magic of what was happening. Without explanation, I could literally feel the healing energy everyone else was sending. Both the vibrations of the quartz and the vibrations of all our intentions, were the one energy, flowing. Divine Love, healing light, and peace were circulating throughout not only Gordon's heart and body and aura but through all of ours too. It was penetrating the energetic chambers of *all* our heart chakras, finding that place where our emotional experiences had been recorded and stored since the day we were born. This energy was helping to dissolve and release and heal, not only in Gordon but also within this healing group. It was helping to transmute all sorrows and fears, bitterness and resentments, traumas and wounds, and the limitations of behaviour that had contributed to suppressing the heart's ability to gift and receive Love.

Though Love had been the point of all our group healings, today and in the presence of the rose quartz there was an amplification of the experience. A suffusion of warmth in my chest fanned itself with the boundlessness of stardust in the cosmos. At the same time, it penetrated and took root into the earthy depths of every cell within me. It was as if a gentle nourishing was taking place, a re-patterning and re-energising of my heart as part of the "new", a foundation for peace instead of fear, joy instead of despair, and longevity instead of death. As I stood there I had the impression that a similar effect was happening in Gordon's chest and in Rebecca's chest and in each individual who had joined us on this healing at this time. It was also taking place within the collective heart of our community, and even contributing to the heart of humanity itself. I didn't know how I knew that. I only knew that I did.

I snapped back, feeling a rolling sensation in the space just above Gordon's toes, as if he were flexing them back and forth. He wasn't though because I had been watching him and had seen that they had been stock still. I stood there for a second, not daring to breathe before intuition sent in the truth of what was happening, letting it arrive into my heart like a lilting feather coming to its place of rest: I was touching the Divine. And the Divine was touching me back. And then I realised that *all* of it was the Divine, that there was no "me" and "it", there was only Divinity being conscious of itself.

I looked at Gordon, who appeared at peace and then I glanced over at Rebecca. She radiated, her eyes still closed, as a slight smile played about her lips.

With Jim and Steve out for a walk, Sarah, the American nurse, approached me. I liked her. She was the aunt who, with hands squarely on her hips, could be trusted to tell you the truth whether you liked it or not. I smiled and said hello but she tucked the coarseness of her copper hair behind her ears and returned my gesture with lips that had flatlined.

"Caroline honey, we need you to take off Gordon's wedding ring. He's still swelling. We're concerned that if the ring doesn't come off now, then by this evening we won't be able to remove it without cutting it off."

I blinked at her, stunned, a fish just hauled out of water and gasping for air. *Take his ring off?* I tried to swallow but my throat wouldn't work. I didn't know what to say. Years ago I'd been the happiest woman in the world when the celebrant had motioned me to slip the ring onto his finger. Now an ICU nurse was telling me I had to try to wriggle it off before a time would come for it to be sheared off. I took his hand in mine, stroking the band with my thumb as I stared down at it for a moment.

Mostly, our rings had stayed on during our marriage. In the main, they had been cherished and worn as sacred. But like us, they too had been on a journey. At one time or another and in the heat of an argument, they had been yanked from fingers pumped with fury, with righteousness, and with a blood that boiled and coursed thick and ugly through veins that had struggled to bear such an overload of rage and destructiveness. I winced at the memories. That time of defiance, slamming a ring down on the bench as an attempt to hit the other below-the-belt, to hurt them just as much as we were hurting, to show our anger in a way that said, "I am not connected to you, in no way ever want to *be* connected to you, nor be so in any way, ever again."

On another occasion, the rush of striding ahead like a madman whilst blindly hurling a ring onto the footpath behind, an expression of powerlessness in the moment, and the projection of an inner disconnect that had escaped recognition and was instead being perceived as a disconnect from "the other". And lastly, there had been the pain of finding the abandoned ring waiting next to "the note" on the table in the emptiness of dusk, statements of hopelessness that had provided a distraction from that which had needed to be felt in the body: the depth and the ache of a cavernous grief. All of it – the yanking, the slamming, the hurling, and the abandoning – had been nothing but a plea expressed with desperation and dysfunction, an S.O.S. that would go out from one or the other. It was the plea for love and to come back to a place of love, the plea for the things we didn't want happening between us to finally stop.

As I looked across at Gordon and the marbles of sweat on his brow, a familiar and insidious shadow slithered over me, through me, around me. It was shame. Shame and regret for all the times of unconsciousness in our marriage. I shuddered. For Gordon to release his ring *this* way, for me to take it back in this way, well it was unthinkable.

"Caroline, honey . . ."

I nodded, history washing itself clean as un-cried moments filed their way in silent procession out towards their exit to see the light of day. The ring proved stubborn in the face of my tentativeness and then pulling. Sarah watched me and I felt my cheeks prickle as a tear splat onto the sheet. Heavy, full and wet. Then, another one. The first fat drops of rain on quivering leaves before the torrential downpour. *Oh my love!* A dry sob.

Once it was off, I studied it. Sarah, content the job was done, strode off to her nursing station. It was an unusual ring of substance and beauty, with both a width and size, and a strength and heaviness that was in contrast and complement to my own. Etched into and running around the middle of it, a squiggly line separated and yet joined the half that was gold with the half that was titanium. It had never struck me before but now I could see that the line looked like a snake, reminding me of the Rainbow Serpent in the Australian Aboriginal dreamtime. I stroked the grooves with my thumb, recalling the day I'd slid this ring onto his finger. How my own fingers had trembled and my face had flushed under the smoulder of his gaze! Somewhere along the way, the reading by Dorothy from Dr Seuss: *Congratulations! Today is your day. You're off to Great Places! You're off and away!* I smiled at the memory. There had been so much love in the air it had flowed out of the pavilion we were standing under and into the rest of the botanical gardens that overlooked the sensation of a Perth city skyline in summer. You may now kiss the bride, the celebrant had trilled. We had held hands as we did it, my thumb somehow resting on his ring, grounded there. There was much clapping and cheering and even the lemon-scented gum-trees lining the avenue had released their confetti of scent in jubilation. After the ceremony there had been the photo-shoot. And then our private tram, cherry-red and decked out in white bows, had wheeled us all away to the winery and vineyard. Gosh, that night had gone by so fast! Toasts, hilarity, wafts of lamb amongst the canapés flying around on the waiter's trays, and Gordon and I canoodling during our wedding dance to "Moon River." His handsomeness had taken my breath away, my body tingling to feel his hand run down the back of my slinky gown of sequins, satin and lace. He was the man of my dreams, my rock, strong and dependable. A man who would never betray me. A man who would keep me safe. That had been my belief. It had been the best day of my life.

A series of beeps brought me back to the noxiousness of medicinal smells around me and the scurrying footsteps of a nurse who had come to push a button on the screen, which made the sound stop. She looked at Gordon, frowned, bit the end of her pen, wrote something down on a chart and left. My head spun. *Are you going to leave me, Gordon? Are we getting to the 'till death do us part' bit of our marriage? Is that where we are up to?* Immersed in the vibration that I sensed from it, I stared down again at the ring, an unbroken circle with no beginning and no end, a symbol of infinite Love. *There is no separation. A love experienced in freedom, in truth, has no giver or receiver because we are One.* I stroked the serpent, reminded of powerful snake energy – the source of all Life, infinite Love in physical form. Powerful snake energy, reptilian nature, our unconscious drives and base humanness. Powerful snake energy, gifting transmutation, bringing healing and change in vital transitions.

It was only now, in the release of Gordon's ring, that I received and appreciated all the energy it held and the truths that it whispered. Both it and the snake pointed me to what I needed to understand: to the deepest essence and function of marriage. Marriage as sacred sexual union, as spiritual vehicle designed to facilitate healing, as the mirror in which to "see" ourselves. It was a birthing canal for the born-anew we had come here to be, a conduit for our remembering of the Love we are. With a rush, I got it, more than ever before. All the arguments we had experienced, the way we had brandished our rings like swords with which we were prepared to fight to the death, the times of doubting whether the other was the "right" or "best" partner for us – I could now see it was all perfection. Our conflict had been the vehicle we had used to get around in so that we could receive and expand into wisdom, the wisdom that knows that marriage isn't about getting our needs met by the other but rather, the place to see that we have those needs in the first place, that they came from childhood and were unmet there. We processed those needs into a bunch of stuff we made it mean about us back then, including how loveable we were. Marriage had helped us expand into the wisdom that knows that for the majority of us, when we said "I do", we were in a state of unconsciousness, handing over to our life-partner the job of having to fill up our well day and night with water so that we might not thirst again, yet never comprehending that we were the source of our own replenishment. Our journey together had been helping us arrive at all this wisdom, to see that marriage as a sacred and sexual union awakens all this, provides the snake bites that have us sit up and take notice of the repression and unconsciousness in us, whilst also providing the opportunities to heal and transmute. Handing us back to ourselves so that *we* may be our own medicine and nourishment, and so that we may receive ourselves more deeply than perhaps we have ever received ourselves before – as the light and shadow of our humanity, and as the divinity we really are: Love. The wisdom that knows we already are the Love we seek outside ourselves, we are that already, wholeness and completeness. Just like the ring itself promised by its very design.

A profusion of peace warmed my heart as I exhaled, feeling gratitude and appreciation for my man lying there. How he had served me in our marriage and how I had served him! In this moment I had nothing but compassion for our times of unconsciousness, nothing but admiration for his path and for mine, and nothing but total awe and wonder at the realisation that, ultimately, there was no he and I. I knew we were that energy out of which all creations spring – snake energy, Infinite Love. Without thinking, I found myself removing my white-gold engagement ring. I slipped on Gordon's ring next to my own wedding band and replaced my other one back into position.

"Ah no, I wouldn't keep it there, Caroline!" I hadn't been aware Sarah had returned to the bedside and her voice now rang out like an alarm. "I wouldn't recommend you do that. I'm just concerned that you'll lose it . . ."

I surveyed her for a second. Was she thinking that this was all I was going to have left of Gordon, was that it? And that to lose the last thing I had, when I would have lost so much, well, that it would be too much to bear?

"Why don't you let us get a necklace that you can tie it onto? That'll be much better, to have it around your neck. It won't be in any danger of coming off that way, or of you losing it. What do you say? Will you let us do that for you?"

Instinctively my hand reached up to my throat, feeling the gemstone already hanging from there. It was purple chaorite, a stone for courage, the necklace I had been wearing by chance on the day we had come in here. But I didn't want the ring hanging from there. Testing, I pulled at Gordon's band sandwiched between my own rings, and looked to see if its size meant it could slide over them and fall off my finger. But it wasn't going anywhere. The design of my engagement ring, with its raised and diagonal diamond, meant that it blocked Gordon's from slipping off at all, even though the width of his band exceeded that of my finger. My heart skipped a beat. Although I knew that who we really were could never ultimately be parted, intuition whispered that this could be a sign that Gordon was going to come back to me in this lifetime still. But I didn't dare speak it out. Not aloud, not to the nurses, not to anyone. Not yet.

I tested the ring again. It couldn't fall off nor be yanked off. I sat there, twizzling it around absent-mindedly. Somehow, it was a comfort to have it there.

Back in the Relatives' Room, while the nurses did something with Gordon's machines, I noted the new arrival of magazines on the table. My eyes widened to spy the monthly lying on top. It was for lovers of the outback. The front cover portrayed a scene of a Ute on red dirt under a cobalt sky and bore the tagline: "Going Outback Again!" I took a sharp intake of breath, recalling the times during healings when I had been sitting in a state of innocence and had "travelled to" or was "shown" the two of us driving in the outback in the truck Gordon had wanted to convert. These moments had been experienced with an aliveness that surpassed simple imagination, as if we actually were right there with my feet up on the dashboard and both of us laughing as he drove. To brush with this publication now, right after receiving his wedding band, felt like such a message from Gordon, such a message from the Divine, a nudge to say that he *was* returning to this lifetime, to continue adventures to be had here.

The journal underneath was a golfing magazine. This time I felt a quickening of my heartbeat, a rush of excitement. Its title reminded me of the opening chapter of a book that Gordon and I had read and which had formed the basis of the workshops and training community we were a part of. The book had been all about a magical golf lesson. The lesson was a metaphor for living life from the guidance of intuition and with connection to the heart, in a way that had you transcending your limitations and beliefs and assumptions about how life is and should be or could be. Throughout the chapter, the hero was shown how to stop focusing on his swing circle – the "how" of taking the shot – and instead to focus on his true outcome – the "what" – and to play from that place of focus. To see this magazine here on the table felt like a clear message. *Caroline, stop fretting, stop obsessing and focusing on how this will all work out. Make yourself available to the state of innocence, of not-knowing. Then you can stay present to infinite Love and to the action steps that infinite Love shows you to take. Keep choosing the outcome that will serve the highest good for Gordon. Whatever that is will, by definition, also be the highest good for you and for everyone else who is involved here.*

In a flash, my conditioning kicked in, the conditioning that had me living in the disconnect of my mind with all its limiting beliefs, the conditioning that wanted me to ground myself only in the physical world and trust only what science and evidence had to say about my man's chances of survival. The conditioning that had me questioning what I saw here on this table, and doubting my interpretation of it. I didn't trust my intuition – or couldn't – and I had slipped right back into the unconscious investment in my story that said loved ones let go of me and abandon me, and that I wouldn't be able to survive without them when they went. I had returned to the belief that I wasn't even worthy of receiving Divine Love and its gifts of grace. Scepticism angled to shut down my heart to the potential messages of the magazines, to close off communication with the Divine. Like the addiction it was, I had turned back to the pain of assuming myself to be anything other than Love, had retreated to that over the truth. I had chosen to power the notion once more that I was separate from Divinity, and separate from the wisdom that I as Divinity was trying to send through to me as Caroline. To let in the messages would mean opening my heart again. It would require me to be vulnerable to the fact that the human me wanted my man back and that yes, he could die. It meant sitting once again in full acceptance of that possibility, and all possibilities.

I sighed, my own voice ringing out from somewhere inside me. *It isn't enough to just make the decision once to accept and allow! You know you have to make it every time you notice that you have gone back to closing the heart. You have to acknowledge you've closed it and refocus back to opening it again. No avoiding of pain! Simply make that conscious shift toward accepting Love and letting Love in.* The voice was right. I sat there waiting to be called back in to ICU, aware of the ever-present airflow whooshing through the ceiling vent.

By late afternoon, the storm front I had felt brewing with the boys in the house and that I had been eyeing all day finally blew in full throttle, whipping its words of anger to gale force, rumbling its menace throughout the atmosphere of the room in which we stood, and forking and flashing its barbs from hostile eyes. I knew it was inevitable. After all, it was their dad in there all hooked up in a jungle of wires and these boys were in pain, navigating it their own way. Shock, grief, fear, and the feeling of not being in control are potent catalysts for releasing from the depths whatever needs to emerge, so that it can be healed and met with Love – especially if we prefer avoiding our feelings and our vulnerability, or if we haven't had much practice with being with either. In a way, it couldn't have happened on a better day. My participation in all the group healings over the previous 72 hours had done much to help keep my heart open, not to mention my having been in the presence of all that powerfully charged rose quartz.

Ironically, it was the rose quartz in the 6 p.m. healing that provided the outward trigger to trip things off. Steve and I had been the only ones in the room, Steve at Gordon's feet and me over to Gordon's left side, both of us in silence. The energy I felt coursing through my body and through the crystal sandwiched between mine and Gordon's hand was extreme. So too was the feeling that I had been "switched off" the minute the designated time was up and people had stopped sending their loving thoughts en masse. In amazement at the intensity of the experience, and in the spontaneity of the moment, I blurted out my astonishment with a grin on my face, declaring the healing to have had power indeed.

"*Shut up!*" Steve snarled without looking at me. "You're getting in the way of me being able to connect with my Dad!"

His nostrils flared, eyes a dark alley I didn't want to go down. He continued to stare at his dad, blanking me in the process. Stabbed by what I was sure was his loathing of me, I felt winded, the heat of the blade giving rise to a cold flame that burned nerve endings more sensitive than I had dared to realise. After the extraordinary experience of the vibrations that had radiated through me in the group healing, the magnitude of the shock caused by his tone and words hit home. With a lump in my throat two sizes too big to swallow, and feeling like a stunned child about to crumple its face and start crying, I murmured my apologies and slunk outside so that he could have his privacy. I understood, felt bad even. The mother within me had concern for him, and for Jim. But the little girl in me just wanted to be picked up and held so that she could hear the comforting beat of a heart that loved her.

Jim and Steve filed in to the Relatives' Room later on, accompanied by their slim, brunette girlfriends who had now arrived from Melbourne. With only a strip of carpet separating their feet from mine, the four of them formed a frontline, leaning against the sink and the wall while I sat facing them in a chair that felt as if it had shrunk. An earthy whiff heavied the air, warmed by the outbreaths of surging emotions. Jim pushed his horn-rimmed glasses back up his nose, the thickness of their plastic as black as ink and just as expressive. I wondered how long he'd had these ones. They announced creative spark and cool intellectualism – two heady worlds colliding, intensity and playfulness the bridge. With the oversized frames that did as much to hide the narrowness of his face as to draw it out from the crowd, it was clear they were the lens through which he formed his views, the circles in which he moved.

As the front man for their band, I wasn't surprised when it was Jim who spoke first. The eye of the storm had arrived. The consensus from both of them was that I was indeed getting in the way of them connecting with their dad. There was an accusation that all my visitors to the hospital were crowding them in. And in particular, there seemed to be an objection to those friends of mine and Gordon's who called themselves magicians. Jim's tone was terse and, with cheeks flushing, he finally vented.

"You and Dad and them – you're all just part of a scene, man! You're part of a scene!"

His words struck with all the force of a hammer for the puck, instantly sending the blood in me high enough to ring my bell and boil with fury. I wanted to lash out and smack his face, cause him to smart with all the viciousness of the sting with which he had sent out his words. After having had the mindfulness to allow them both plenty of privacy with their father, it felt unjust to hear this accusation and declaration. I wanted to spew forth my indignation and righteousness, with a "How dare you!", but I bit my tongue and kept my mouth shut, and made sure I restrained the rage and the roar and the feistiness of my provoked lion. It hurt like hell to feel both of them were dismissing me and my ways and who I was, not to mention their insistence that because of my presence, their connection to their dad was compromised or in some way diminished.

I knew what they had touched in me. The pain that I felt was an old and unhealed wound ripping open within. It was my father's story about me and which I had carried, believed, and feared all these years. I wasn't even seeing Jim in front of me anymore. I was seeing my father, hearing my father in my head: "You just get in the way! You get in the way of me and your mother getting along. From being a proper husband and wife! It's because of you our marriage isn't happy." It was my father's story. I could hear Mum's story too, about his resentment at the hours I'd demanded from her as a newborn, about his jealousy of the closeness she'd had with me when I was a baby, and his anger at her disinterest in sex during the months of her depression after the birth. My father and mother had been Sentinels of the Story all these years, yet on some level I had also agreed with this story and become a Guardian for it. Somehow and at some point, I too had decided that it must have been the truth. That I *was* bad news, that my birth *had* created problems, and that my very existence in the world had caused them pain and disconnect and anguish and upset. In short, that just being me brought about the ruin of relationships for others and stopped them from experiencing closeness. Whenever my father had suggested this of me all those times in the past, I had stood there with defiance, locked my jaw and smiled right back at him. It was the only way I knew to mask the unbearable pain searing into the desolation of my heart. Afterwards, I would end up a snotty mess in my bedroom, sobbing in secret into my patchwork bedspread, my throat ribboned and ragged from the serrations of grief's edges, as my dog Ben whimpered and pawed at my back, only to flop himself down with resignation into the curve of my heaving belly.

Everyone in my family had been torn asunder by our conviction about The Story. We had been torn from ourselves, torn from each other, torn from the real truth and from our hearts, torn from peace and joy and love. Just as was threatening to happen now for me with Jim. *Breathe Caroline! Jim is not your father. This time is not then.* I eyeballed the floor, to stop the tears forming, fearing Jim would loathe them. Suddenly this mountain we were on felt too big to climb, the air in the room too thin to support any further exertion. Every cell and fibre and bone in my body ached for Gordon to put his arms around me and be here to support me in this. Right now I needed his solidity, his groundedness, his largeness of heart. These weren't my children and I wasn't anyone to them other than their father's wife. And yet I felt a responsibility towards them in Gordon's physical absence. How was I supposed to play this?

Breathe Caroline. But my mind snatched at thoughts flying in and out faster than the speed of light, trying to understand Jim and Steve's anger at me. I wondered if they were feeling the pain of not having their mother there, though it seemed unlikely they would want her at the hospital, given all the years of Gordon's separation from her. I dismissed the idea. Besides, Gordon had often noted that each twin had always been the most important family member for the other, that each was the other's main "go to" when it came to a sense of family and family support. And they did have their girlfriends here now.

So what was this judgement they had made in meeting mine and Gordon's world, in seeing the people who were in it, and with hearing how we lived our life? Was the version of their dad so many people were referencing somewhat alien to them? Perhaps, I couldn't tell.

What I did know was that Gordon had never borne them ill will for the irregularity of their contact with him. He would have loved it if they had visited him or called more often but he had never held any expectations. His loving them was about accepting whatever they had wanted for themselves and the fact was, they were living the vibrancy of an inner-city life on a shoestring, immersed in the band and their girlfriends. In his bones Gordon had felt it was all as it should be, as it *was*. I had never worked out if he feared losing them if he asked for more connection or whether he simply loved freely. He always maintained he never wanted them to feel duty-bound to call, and I had always been in awe of that position, but I knew Gordon missed them and had at times felt the distance all too keenly. I had wondered if the distance between the three of them, in part, stretched further into the past, to when the boys were fifteen and Gordon and Susan had separated. Gordon left to work in Hong Kong and, a year or so later, got together with me. I had no idea if they still had grief or anger or loss lurking in their hearts about that. All I knew from my own experience was that it could be hard to deeply connect with a lover or a parent if you hadn't fully connected with yourself. Perhaps this was some of what was happening for them, underneath their sense that it was others getting in the way of their connection. It was a possibility. But not something I dared to ask. I still felt a colossal separation between the four people in front of me. Again, how should I play this? *Breathe Caroline. Be here, right now. No need for tactics, no need for game-playing. You want connection? Connect. Sit into your heart. Choose Love.*

I made an effort to exhale and send the breath down into my heart and belly, feeling the softening of my body. It was time to let go of what I thought I knew, time to allow myself, in the softening, to open up to anything I might not yet know. No longer lost in my head, I embodied the here and now and something shifted in me. From this space, I could *feel*. With empathy I could see how it might be for them to watch our friends coming and going, even though these people did engage with them and were friendly, even though most of them did stay in the Relatives' Room rather than go into ICU, and even though their visits with me were brief.

"Guys, I understand if you're feeling the lack of your family here. I would be too, if I were you. I'm sorry it's this way for you. I'm sorry you don't even have your mum here. I did ask everyone to come. Whatever they feel their reasons are, they have said they're not coming. I am devastated by that as much as you are."

I paused, my voice cracking. I could feel Jim open a millimetre or so.

"I'm feeling the lack of family members here for me too," I ventured on. "My mum is in the UK as you probably remember, and it's not easy for her to come. She has offered, but I have said let's wait and see. I hurt that your aunt won't come. And I feel alone with regards to her choice. She isn't ringing me to give her support that way either. Neither is Dorothy. There's nothing from them. This was how your dad had been experiencing their behaviour before he fell sick, and how he's experienced the relationship with his sister for years. It broke his heart over time. He has never felt he belonged to the family. Always felt the outsider, the black sheep. It ripped him up. It can cause pain when there is a lack of a blood family here for you, I know."

Still, the millimetre. *Keep sharing, Caroline. Be gentle – and firm.*

"But look, there is a family of friends rallying to support all of us through this. They love us. They are here for him. They are here for me. They can be here for you too. It's true they are not our blood. But they are helping your dad. They bring parcels of food. Rebecca has even come twice on her pushbike, with a slow cooker of dinner in the front basket so that you and I can eat something nourishing! And you see this blanket? Rebecca brought it in today so that I don't freeze in this room at night! That's what I am talking about here. This is the family that is here for me. And I choose to receive this family! No, they are not blood and they are not your blood. But they are good people."

I watched as the boys shifted their posture, like mirror-images. Nobody said anything. *Carry on.*

"Yes, there are a few people that come during the course of the day. It is always in flow though and it's never all at the same time. So I am not going to stop them coming here or being here. And if there is a way we can arrange it so that you can still have your space and what you need, and so that they can still come, well, let's arrange it that way. What do you say?"

It felt like there was another slight opening from the boys, though they gave no reply. Everybody seemed to be avoiding eye contact with me, even their girlfriends who stood staring at the floor and twizzling the ends of their hair. My body tensed as I drew parallels with eighteen months before. How could I ever forget that night? They were all on a visit and camping in Dorothy's front yard while

Gordon and I, broke, were living in our camper in her backyard. The rock of that memory plunged to the bottom of my heart. Did they still have anger towards me for the vileness and toxicity that they had overheard that night? The night I had spewed and hissed at Gordon inside of our camper trailer, while our marriage was in freefall over his betrayal with the money and my inability to forgive it. Was that it? I felt the heat now rising in my blood and realised I still carried resentment towards the boys and their girlfriends, for their behaviour back then with me. Not once had any of them asked during that abomination or indeed the next day, if I was okay. Not once had any of them acknowledged Gordon's part in it either. Instead, the sympathy and the concern from them had been for him, the note in the morning was for Gordon, the offer of help . . . for Gordon. Feeling the humiliation and shame of wanting the earth to swallow me, I had simply concluded at the time that it was further proof I was so bad that people had to reject me, oust me, and exile me from the family. Jim brought me back to the here and now.

"Your experience isn't how it is for us, man! We don't *like* the word 'healing' and to be honest, we'd rather it wasn't used. Same with all those vocalisations man! The way you and your people keep on about 'intuition' and all the 'signs' you think are happening." His voice had an edge as hard as metal and I watched his fingers imitate the quotation marks that referenced the concepts he wanted to dismiss. "That's not our lexicon. It's just noise, utter psychic noise. It's totally invasive to my meta-cognitive processes, man! What with that and all your people who come . . . it encroaches . . . on my liminal – hell man, it just gets in the way of us connecting with our dad, man!"

Again I could have swung for him, felt the rush of hot anger as it whooshed in my throat, a panther ready to go in for the jugular.

Who the hell does he think he is, speaking to me like that, dismissing me and my experiences! I was aware of my hand covering my own throat, as if I knew I would regret it if I spoke from this place, even though the compulsion to do so was extreme. I felt the magnitude of my need to defend and stand up for myself. But instead, I curled my fingers under the arms of the chair and clamped my mouth shout, not trusting what it could unleash if I opened it right now. Other words arose and spoke themselves inside me. *You are not the image that you project, Caroline. You are not the image that others project onto you. You are not even this body!* The words were familiar somehow, causing me to pause and to remember to breathe down into my heart and belly again, to re-open to innocence and receive information from *there* and *not* from my mind - to choose Love.

For a second I struggled with the fact they could imagine that something outside of themselves, such as a word from someone else and its expression in the world, could prevent them from being in their heart and connecting with their dad. Wasn't experiencing connection a choice? After all, what created an experience of connection if not the simple decision to *have* that experience of connection right there and right then, regardless of others? I frowned. Then again, hadn't *I* just cringed at some of *his* word choices? My cheeks burned. It was true. I had reacted to his utterances of "lexicon" and "scene" and "meta-cognitive"; I had judged him for being cold and for always trying to sound so erudite and cool. Wasn't my reaction and judgement the same as his? To me, his expression had been nothing but a barrage, just descriptions of ways of being that I didn't relate to, a wall of words between us different from the ones I might have used. And yet if only for a second, had I not also imagined that it was because of him, and because of the way that he was and the words he was choosing, that I could not connect?

I softened, breathing into a shift I could feel happening within. I immediately saw that even the whole "magician" thing had been more of the same challenge for the boys. Now, from a place of presence, I felt compassion for them both again, for how they felt about these people being here, how they felt about the label, and even about the "scene" they thought we were in. Compassion showed me the futility of choosing to relate with another predominantly through the mind rather than the heart. When we over-identify with our words and thoughts and definitions, and when we fear what we do not understand or what we have shut down with the heart, then we create compelling experiences of this illusion called separation! We can imagine unhelpful scenarios of "them" and "us" in our reality, and we can either feel like we belong or we can sit in the conviction that we and others are outsiders.

If my time in the hospital and this exchange with the boys was teaching me anything, then with ruthlessness it continued to steer me on this path. Words can help us to connect and they can light our way into deeply enriching events, but oh how they can also so often become a block, a barrier to us being able to experience the very thing that the word or the label is trying to point to: the direct experience itself. In a way he was right about the label "magician". Maybe there was only one word, one label, one definition ever worth using that could transcend all barriers and blocks to understanding: Love.

"Guys, listen," I started up again, my voice as soft as my belly. "I want to level with you about these group healings. I get that it's not something you're into. And that's okay, I respect that. The healings are just about a lot of people living in different places who have agreed to sit down at appointed times to think about Gordon and what he loves. To think about his nature, his essence, and who he is as a man. And to send him love and wishes as they do so. Sometimes, when we have sent love and well-wishes to him from our heart like that, something particular about your dad has popped up in our imagination, or we have felt a feeling or physical sensation. But that's it, nothing more sinister than that. I understand and respect if it's not your thing."

Steve perked up, eyes shining as if a light had been switched on.

"Do you mean it's . . . like, earlier, right? . . . when I was with Dad . . . and I had my eyes closed and was thinking about him and how much I loved him . . . and right away I saw him in your kitchen, sitting on the stool that I was on this morning."

"Wow. Yes, that's exactly the sort of thing I mean! And you know what? That breakfast bar stool you refer to is exactly where he likes to sit! And that's intriguing because you wouldn't have known that, and yet you discovered it anyway."

"Yeah . . . when I had my eyes closed, I was walking up the stairs and I looked over and he waved at me and smiled!"

"But see, that's what I'm talking about, that's what innocence and intuition can be like. It can let you connect with people in this way, it lets you see things or know things your mind couldn't possibly have known!" I felt a rush of excitement and tried to keep it in check, respectful of their needs. "I'm curious though. When you saw it, what did you *feel* in your heart about it?"

Steve stared down at the table for a few seconds before venturing to reply.

"That he was with me . . . and . . . he wanted me to know that. That he is okay for the moment . . . where he is he is okay . . . for the moment."

Like the reassurance of the lantern from a traveller bound for home, something deep inside me felt a resonance in Steve's words and his sense about it.

"That's beautiful . . . to hear your sense about it." I took a deep breath in and bit the bullet. "Look, guys, can I say something?" Four pairs of eyes focused on me, their raised eyebrows and shoulder shrugs suggesting I could. "Well, I guess what I want to offer is that maybe there's no need for you to go and make this word 'healing' or 'intuition' mean anything other than this that Steve just shared. See, I will only speak for me now but I've found the more energy you put into powering your thoughts in being against something in life, or into powering meanings that have you disliking particular words, then the less energy and focus you have to connect with what really matters. And I guess for you that could mean the less energy and focus you have to connect with your dad and with what is right here for you."

I paused, as a shuffle seemed to Mexican-wave its way around the room, releasing pent up energy like an invisible out-breath, and breaking up the rigid barrier that had stood between us. Were we at a juncture for a parley?

"I love you guys." I meant it. "Jim, what do you need for *you* now? Before you fly back home in a couple of days, what do you need? What does it look like or sound like for you? How can I help you to have it?"

"Ummm . . . I'm not sure yet."

"Okay. How about if anything occurs to you tonight, we can talk about it tomorrow? And in the meantime I'm going to just say that for those of us who are still involved, we will continue to take part in these group healings. It matters to us. But you know, there are only four of these fifteen-minute sessions in a day and they won't get in the way, I promise. They won't get in *your* way. And, if you like, from now on I'll describe them as simply 'sending love' and I will be mindful to not share my experiences with you if that's what you would prefer right now."

There was another shift in the room. A hint of brightness like the sun emerging through fog, a lightening of spirit after the rain from a storm, a space again in which the clearing and ever present "whoosh" of the ceiling vent could now blow through. Though our conversation didn't feel fully complete, we had all helped ourselves into a better place – for now.

CHAPTER FIFTEEN

Day 3

11.45 p.m. – Home

"I KNEW HE'D BE ALRIGHT!" was what the receptionist had trilled that afternoon after the episode with the boys. As I lay on the couch back at home, I mulled over her words and the bizarreness of the episode that had played out. First, there had been the appearance of a local friend, Paula, in the doorway. Her hair was still in rattails from showering as she described how, in the midst of washing the dishes, she'd found herself stopping and going into the hallway to put her boots on, realising only then that it was because she was going to come to the hospital. For me, the timing had been impeccable. The boys and I had just finished our discussion and I was drained from my conflict with them, feeling like vital energy had been sucked out of a tank already running on empty. Seeing Paula had been a relief and I had more than welcomed the opportunity to leave the scene and head down the corridor so that we could catch up in the other room.

There had been so much to tell her. But then that woman had

barged in, full of joy to have spied Paula after years of not crossing paths with her. Ignoring me and my tear-stained cheeks, she'd unleashed a babble of questions and updates for her friend while I stared in disbelief at the rudeness she was displaying. It was only when she had asked why Paula was at the hospital and listened to the reply, that she remembered me and introduced herself again as Sally, the receptionist who had been on duty at the nursing station the night that Gordon had crashed. Upon hearing that, I recognised her as the lady who had brought me the cup of tea and who had found me the number for Jeff and Tammy. And that's when she had blurted it out to Paula and I, with a voice bordering on the fullness of cheer and the volume turned up: "Oh I just *knew* he'd be alright!" I'd gaped to hear such insensitivity and her words had danced before my face like a chain of letters that only I could see. She reiterated that she had always felt it would be a positive outcome for Gordon and had backed up her statement by referring to the availability of that last bed on the day of his arrival, Robert's agreement to stay on for an extra shift earlier that morning, and even to how that in itself had been an omen because . . . "Robert is an *angel!*" Again, the words had danced in front of me. *Angel. Robert is an angel.* Yet had she even understood the direness of Gordon's situation? If she had, how could she have proclaimed that he was alright?

No matter how I looked at it, I could not escape the peculiarity of how she had barged in, broken up our conversation and thrown it on another track entirely. There had been something odd about her conviction that I couldn't put my finger on. Now, in the stillness of my lounge, I wondered if it could be the truth that Gordon *was* already "alright" again, waiting in some other time/ space dimension for the body that needed to play catch up. What if, in the second the receptionist had spoken, we had switched timelines again? I wasn't even sure of the mechanics of how that could happen but, in support of it as a theory, I could not deny that the receptionist had spoken with a level of assurance that flew in the face of all the facts. It bore a resemblance to the scene from yesterday with the nurse. Did we have people – time travellers – walking amongst us who simply delivered messages from our "future"? Or were we "spoken through" in the "now", the receivers of messages that were delivered that way – and if so, by whom or what?

Opening up to the plasticity of time brought the white rabbit to mind again. I closed my eyes, re-picturing that event. There was something about the timing of that rabbit, something even about "time". I frowned, trying to understand the thoughts that were arising. The rabbit had appeared after an argument with the nurse over "time", over the concept we call "24–48 hours", over time that could only be measured in ticks and tocks and by hours and clocks. Saying it to myself like that made me recall Alice in Wonderland. It felt ridiculous to draw parallels and yet hadn't her rabbit been so focused on his watch that he had been blinded to the strangeness and unexpectedness of happenings around him? Was there a chance that this had been the message for me on the night with the nurse, and one that was now being repeated by the receptionist? That in being so focused on the time of fixed reality, I was forgetting the time of Spirit, the time of the present, of Now? Certainly, the talk with the nurse had been all about giving Gordon 24 hours to show improvement. This was the only kind of time the medics had on their radar. For them it was a question of getting their outcomes within their stipulated timeframes. I had joined them in that, fearing their deadline and racing myself against the clock with the phone calls I'd made. In that flurry, I hadn't considered the time of Spirit – a time that cannot be planned or mapped out, manipulated or controlled, measured or saved, or even watched or seen. From within the urgency, I had made no space to experience the time that unfurls in the heart, invites a letting go, stops the stopwatch . . . and allows magic to happen. And yet, what about *that* "time", where life is right now and not tomorrow, where "past" and "future" happen all at once, where "now" is always anew, and where "already healed" already exists?

It seemed such an insanity to even contemplate it but the rabbit, the nurse and the receptionist all seemed to be linking up. Because of the ways each of them had presented to me, my attention had continued to been drawn to making this same, deeper change in focus that Life seemed to be asking of me. All three of them had served to shock me into breaking the pattern I had been in at the time. My head now buzzed with a sense of the extraordinary once again.

Moving over to the door, I dimmed the main lights. The boys were not at the house tonight. They now had a rental they were sharing with their girlfriends for the rest of their stay. I had felt a knife in my heart but wasn't sure if they had meant to thrust it in or not. I was on my own again. Settling back down under the covers, I turned to my laptop and began to read through the Journey Page, updates from a day that had seemed like a lifetime ago, and posts from strangers and friends.

> Nicole: Message from Caroline, for the 10 a.m. healing today: "The main focus for the healing is for clearing the sepsis in Gordon's veins. Gordon is currently fighting an infection related to pneumonia."
>
> Larry: A powerful prayer group in L.A. has joined in, as well as a healing service there. And Caroline told me there are folks jumping on in England and Hong Kong. That's four continents. So powerful!

Ingrid: I will be surfing for you Gordon. The ocean represents love energy to me and I will combine mine with the whole, for you. Xx

Alexis: Loving you Gordon. (Posts music video, "The Lion Sleeps Tonight".)

Ruth: Hey Gordy, when I first met you I didn't realise how deep your soul runs. And over time as we have had time to be vulnerable and open, I have got to know your heart, your fears, your foibles and your joys. You are a most gentle and magnificent man. I love your connection to expression, your art, your love of the didge which reflects your connection to the souls of Australia. As you lay there on the razor's edge, no matter the path you choose, know you are well loved. It's funny you know, we often love from afar, and yet it is so simple to write the truth to you here. Xx

Melissa: Dear Gordon, I don't know you that well but I know you have a passionate wife and that tells me something of your passion for life . . . I pray that you recognise how the simplicity of being you has reached peoples' hearts beyond your imaginings. Much love x

Holly posts Aboriginal music video for Gordon; "Timeless Land" by Yothu Yindi.

Francesca: Caroline and Gordon I am sending you love through the stars that light up the night sky, through the network of roots that connect the great forests of this land, through the sounds of our voices carried on the breeze, through our connection to all that is. Love you both. Xx

Susan: I want you to know that I am thinking of you both in everything I do. I cried as I remember the love I have for my partner compared to the anger I show him.

Thank you for sharing your journey, you are not alone.

Charlotte: "Flash Gordon", who sprang to my celebration of my 50th in a red suit of expression! You helped me to celebrate an amazing weekend of connection, love, joy and huge FUN! Without your gentle yet effortless energy at my party and at Sunday breakfast it wouldn't have been the same vibe at all. Your soul is gentle and there is a journey for you to "fashion" into . . . allow it to unfold and, with our healing and prayers, let's see where and which party you go to next. Much love xx

Jenny: Sleep well Gordon and hopefully you too, Caroline. Let us all do the work while you have a pause and rest the weariness of fear. Hope, faith and love . . . we can do this for a long while yet.

CHAPTER SIXTEEN

Day 4

2.35 a.m. – Home

I COULDN'T SLEEP. Or was it that I wouldn't? The music video clip of Frank Sinatra's song, "Moon River", had just reduced me to sobbing all over again. Opening up my laptop, I posted online and attached the video clip to some words of my own.

> This was our wedding dance back in 2004. I love you Gordon Cumming. I would give anything to dance our wedding dance again on our anniversary in a few months. If it is to be so, I would be the happiest woman alive on that December 9th. My heart aches and at the same time feels like it could burst and fill the entire Universe. Right now, I am looking at your ring on my finger. I'm here darling, like the lyrics say . . .

It had felt second nature for me to write and post my promise to him. Afterwards though, I questioned whether I should be posting things like this and the other shares since Gordon had become ill. Was it too much? But then I had always been a person who needed to express! In recent months I had developed more authenticity via my online shares. Feeling and then expressing in writing seemed to be how I must navigate the situation I was in. But there was no space for this communication during the days at the hospital. Whilst I was there, my attention was with, and for, Gordon. By allowing my fingers to flurry across the keyboard like this tonight and on the other nights, I could process the day, my stream of consciousness unravelling with greater ease than a pen and paper could have ever afforded. Here, in the darkness of night, I preferred the brilliance of the white on the screen, as if it were a trusty friend. Outshining the capacities of any bound journal, the white could absorb the outpourings of my head and heart, with the bonus of illuminating them too. There was something about sending these words out into the online realm that gave weight to their expression, imbuing them with a longevity that wishing them in my head could never do.

Then again, maybe it was also because there was always somebody awake somewhere in the online world. For me to know I was not alone.

Chapter Seventeen

Day 4

8.00 a.m. – Hospital

T HE FIRST TO ARRIVE in the Relatives' Room for the day and anxious to receive news, I plonked my bags down and was about to take off my coat when Sarah, the nurse, popped her head round the door.

"Morning, Caroline. You can come in soon, just not yet."

"Is everything okay? Is Gordon alright?"

"There are things we have to sort out with him but . . . okay, look, let me give you a quick update in the meantime. We've not been able to take him off temporary dialysis yet. His heart rate reduced slightly during the night. And his BP's up a notch which we need to see continue. So I guess we could say there was a tiny change in his condition, which, overall was good. He did need more oxygen but that's a sign of the infection and to be expected. And his white blood cell count has continued to fall, another good thing."

"It *was* at 30. Where is it now?"

"It fell to 20 between yesterday and today. But we do need to see it come down to around 10. In other news, we've reduced his blood pressure medication slightly from the maximum dosage. That's a first; it's positive. Liver and kidneys *have* been damaged, but look, *if* he recovers they will rejuvenate so that's still not an immediate concern of ours. The heart is *not* good though. It's going to require work and medication if he pulls through. And we can't start that until the infection has cleared up. So, I guess what I'm saying is that what we need to have happen next is the following . . ."

She started to count off the steps on her fingers.

"Clear the pneumonia, keep the white blood-cell count falling, see the natural blood pressure rise (which will lead to less need for that ventilation) . . . and maybe *then* we can start addressing the heart itself."

She tapped the doorframe with her palm as if to punctuate the end of her list or to emphasise what was coming next.

"Caroline, it is categorically still touch and go, okay? He's critical. But he did remain stable overnight. I'll come back out and let you know when you can come in."

With lips pressed together as if drawing a line under her report, she let the side of her mouth and cheek suck in the harshness of reality, making a sound that suggested she felt for me and for Gordon. Once she'd left, I flopped down on the chair, feeling the exhaustion of the hours I had spent overnight and since dawn just waiting to hear news, only to receive this download. I was still acclimatising to starting my mornings in this way. I switched on my phone and texted an update to Charles for the Journey Page.

When I entered the ward, I was shocked that Gordon and his equipment were not in the cubicle. Rationality deserted me at the door for a second as I quivered out the question whether he had died.

"Good grief, no not at all!" Sarah rushed to put a hand on my shoulder. "We've moved him into the small room you slept in on the first night. It's more private in there."

"Private? But he's the only patient in ICU. So why move him? Is it because you don't believe he'll make it through the day? Is the privacy for that reason?" I could feel my tone rising as my throat constricted and anxiety needled at me.

"We thought being in the room would assist your group healings when you do them and that it would be nicer for the family, and for you. I pushed them to do it. Come on in!"

I followed her over and panned the room. On the whole I had to admit the space did convey a sense of protection somehow. It was also a relief to see light streaming in through a large window that ran the length of Gordon's bed and, that outside, three old trees were keeping watch on their strip of grass.

"They painted the ceiling a while back too." Sarah motioned me to look up. I smiled as I saw the aqua sky there, clouds painted like balls of cotton wool.

"See, it is better in here, isn't it?"

"Yeah, it's better." I smiled. We were being wrapped up in the safety and warmth of a cocoon and I was grateful. I moved across to the side of the bed, leaning over to say good morning to my man. Kissing him was an utter relief.

CHAPTER EIGHTEEN

Day 5

2.00 a.m. – Home

I CAME IN FROM THE VERANDA, too cold to stay standing out there under the moonless sky. The aloneness I felt now was in contrast from how it had been before midnight, when me and the boys and Charles and Rebecca had been sitting around together in the Relatives' Room. Somebody had said something and we had all burst out laughing, tears streaming down our faces. The moment had felt a bit surreal afterwards, but then again the laughing, the crying, the numbness, the screaming . . . it was all part of this journey and experience, part of all potentials existing at once. Perhaps it had been of benefit for Gordon to hear our laughter too. It had at least helped me to feel that there might have been a shift between the boys and myself, to think that perhaps a degree of healing had taken place between us the other day, even if they were choosing not to stay at the house with me.

The laughter had also served as a release, a letting go of tension, of fear, stress and strain. Maybe there had even been a tinge of relief in there. After all, as we had bid Gordon goodnight, the nurse had begun the process of cutting back on one of the drips and had suggested to us that Gordon's stability would likely continue overnight. This news had followed the briefing from Dr Brentwood hours before, which had revolved around the continued plan for moving forwards with Gordon. We had all taken heart as he hadn't followed up his comments with his trademark caution of "but it looks bad."

It wasn't to say that Gordon was out of danger, of course. But the fact that he had at least continued to hang on and had been responding to some of their interventions did inspire hope. Everybody was in no doubt about the gargantuan journey ahead. Dr Brentwood had again impressed upon us the urgency of clearing the sepsis and the pneumonia and of weaning Gordon off life support, both for Gordon's chances of survival and for the transfer he still favoured to St Mary's in the city. He had talked again of the insertion of the heart pump they were so keen to do there, the list for the heart transplant, and all the new drugs they could administer once his infections had gone and they didn't need to focus so much on maintaining the rise of his blood pressure.

I wriggled on the sofa, trying to get comfortable under the blanket, only to sigh out in a puffing of lips. It had been a long day with staff and visitors coming and going and yet all of it the breath in and the breath out, the ebb and the flow. Throughout the day Gordon had been still, except for a moment during the 2 p.m. healing when Sarah had checked a number on the monitor and had said "nice". Both of us had then watched as two jolts moved through Gordon's chest for no apparent reason. Sarah said nothing. But I had felt a quickening in my heart and I had held my breath. All day the staff had repeated the need for his lungs to repair, and Sarah herself had been asking that our healings focus on this for the day.

My opinion had been that the energy everyone was sending was intelligent and would go wherever it was needed anyway, but I had still put out her request to everyone on the Journey Page.

Had our efforts indeed created this happening in his body during that group healing? Was it proof that we *were* impacting something here? As I now read the comments in the forum, it appeared there were many people who had reacted with the same excitement I had felt. I continued to catch up on all the other posts, some of which jumped out at times, yet all of them triggering awe and humility as I beheld this community and how they had rallied together for yet another day.

Kevin: Can anyone post some of Gordon's drawings? Remember that elephant drawing he did a while back? Let's share his heart with the world. Get on board and share them, c'mon guys, let's post!

Francesca: you can find Gordon's artwork, including his extraordinary mandalas here. (posts link)

Nicole: (posts Gordon's drawing of an eagle totem) I love this drawing Gordon did. For me it represents a connection to all creations – Mother Earth and the spirit world. What an amazing open heart, a free spirit with Wisdom, Power and Strength. I see this Eagle as Gordy. Sending you, Gordon, and Caroline and the boys love and healing energy. Xx

Francesca: (posts music video clip of "Don't Give Up" by Peter Gabrielle and Kate Bush) I kept hearing this song in the 10 a.m. meditation. Xx

Matthew: I was lucky enough to be at the hospital with Caroline for today's 10 a.m. I'm not usually overly sensitive to energy but my hand was on his leg and I could feel and was aware of the honour of transmitting something powerful and healing and humbling. Xx

Martina: (posts music video clip of "Somewhere Over the Rainbow" by The Piano Guys) A beautiful song full of love, joy, hope, light, oneness and love. Let those vibes and energy pour into your veins, Gordon and Caroline!

Sharon: Hi Caroline and Gordon, this morning during prayer time at school I mentioned to the kids I particularly would like to offer healing prayers as a dear friend was very ill and his wife and family needed some help too. The kids were especially quiet this morning and some respectfully also asked for prayers for their sick family and friends, one child also wanted to offer a prayer as his uncle had recently died. I feel these were very powerful prayers of pure intention and it is wonderful to hear Gordon is "responding" so positively.

Lorraine: I joined in the healing at 10 a.m. I don't know how it's supposed to be done as I don't have much experience with this, but I pictured the "good guys" in Gordon's blood running around in their little superhero costumes, beating up the "bad guys" who disappeared in a puff of smoke, then I pictured that cleansed blood travelling to Gordon's heart, and helping it to beat strongly again. I also sent comforting thoughts to Caroline and Gordon's sons to help them through this ordeal. I hope it all helps in some way.

Ruth: Hi Angels, our next healings are 6 p.m. and 10 p.m. Click LIKE if you are joining us for 15 minutes of holding hands and pouring healing energy and love into Gordon and Caroline. We are a growing community, a growing group heart, full of unconditional love for self, others and our dear friend Gordon. Good on ya mate for hanging on there, thanks for showing us what love is all about. HEALING focus: the lungs need support so let's focus on deep breaths as we clear the infection with him, deep breaths as we hold hands at 6 p.m.

Owen: One heart, many lungs, breathing effortlessly. Xx

Ant: I don't know Gordon personally, but am his colleague and just heard the news. I do not intend to offend with what I share here, but I believe that the God of creation can miraculously heal, and will be praying for Gordon's speedy and complete recovery, in the name of Jesus Christ.

Nicole: At the 6 p.m. healing, Jess, our 9-year-old, saw her heart pour love-hearts into Gordon's body and him respond by getting up and dancing. I saw him whirling and dancing in Africa. Kevin saw him in a row boat in a sea of the universe.

Ingrid: Tonight at Community Choir we sang "River, River" to Gordon and family. "River, river come and take me flowing down to your ocean, my sorrow I will give it up to you, let this water come and heal me If I let you reveal me, like a shiny little pebble river, river I am yours."

For a moment all words swam in and out of focus as I felt the trembling that receiving this love and care from everyone precipitated. I experienced a swell of gratitude for the leadership of Ruth and Charles, both of whom were doing so much on the forum to help hold the space in which space could be held. The music clips touched me but it was perhaps the championing of Gordon's art that brought the sob out into the silence of the lounge, for I realised that in reposting these pieces of his, they were all seeing his Greatness and his essence as an artist. In bearing witness to him, they were doing what he had been unable to do for himself before his coma: to acknowledge his talent, his heart and what it loves, and to share that with the world. I knew that his greatest fear had been that of rejection if he were to go out into the world from his heart and with the gifts of his heart, that his belief was that he had nothing of worth to share in the first place. And I also knew that if he came back to us all, it would be his responsibility to continue to hold the space of self-acceptance and to claim his gifts.

In the meantime though, I wondered if on some level he could see that his heart had been far from rejected by the world.

CHAPTER NINETEEN

Day 5

2.47 a.m. – Home

ALTHOUGH DR BRENTWOOD had omitted the phrase tonight in his briefing, all the medics had shown constancy in their description of Gordon as "touch and go". I had the feeling that with their prognosis of "dire straits", they had a focus skewed more in the direction of "go". Yet I kept finding myself drawn to how the phrase "touch and go" suggested that he was both holding on and letting go at the same time, a state of flux where neither outcome appeared to be obvious. Like when light vibrates so fast that neither the colour nor the speed appear to exist and all that remains is transparency and stillness. My sense was that in this seeming non-movement and no-change, much movement and change was indeed happening, that Gordon's soul was undertaking a review. Perhaps this is what it looked like when a tipping point was reached, when it was not about stagnation but about the point from which the greatest leap of change could occur. It was a tension that sought to resolve itself – and resolve it would. Tonight, it brought to mind the sweet jasmine I'd planted at our home in Perth three years before. I had dug up the plants in disappointment over their lack of growth in the time the tag had promised. Gordon had laughed at the shock on my face as I stared at the bulk of their root system. The jasmine had been growing all along, albeit underground, getting ready for its shift, where the flowers could spring forth and expansion above ground could take place. It seemed like a lifetime ago now.

So many of the comments I'd seen on the Journey Page tonight were urging Gordon to "hold on" and encouraging me to "hold onto hope" and to "stay positive". I clung to their phrases on the screen like a woman from a shipwreck clings to a lifebuoy in the intrepidness of high seas. After all, telling me to hold on was better than telling me I was screwed, that was for sure. But there seemed to be a paradox with positivity, with holding onto hope. People's words were a reminder to continue to open to the possibility that Gordon could make a full recovery. In this way, holding onto hope was like holding on for a miracle and for magic to happen. And in my humanness, I hoped and prayed with fervour that higher forces might assist in bringing about that outcome. However, hope was only "clean" as long as I could allow myself to include in that hope the realisation that all potentials – even the one of him transitioning – were a possibility. To hope within the context of acceptance of all potentialities, was to hope cleanly. From this space, holding onto hope buoyed my spirit because all possibilities co-existed until such time as they didn't.

But hope was turning out to be a bit of a Jekyll-and-Hyde character that kept veering into the shadows of its expression. It was one thing to hope for Gordon's return to life for the joy of seeing it happen in and of itself, and because of what I believed it would mean for us both. It was another, when the hope came from my *need* for his return to happen, and when it was driven by my fear and resistance to his dying because of the pain of what that would mean and feel like. Yes, of course I wanted him back in my arms! But there was a part of me that desired it with such plunging and radiating heartache, such hammering and pounding in my chest, that I believed that the power of that desire not being met would be a force colossal enough to reduce me to a pile of dust and rubble.

Needing Gordon to come back exposed me to the terror of having him not return. So much so, that when I wasn't looking, hope turned into a rope that I held in desperation so that I might never have to endure the separation from what I loved. When I was like this, holding onto hope was more like "holding on" to the "not-letting-go". A hope like that may have seemed to some as powerful in its intention but I knew that it had as its underlying agenda the idea of not wanting to lose something. It may have looked to me like all my hope equated to positivity but the underlying reality revealed that what was in truth driving it – my need to secure safety and avoid the pain of loss – was what dominated my creative consciousness. It was as if Gordon had abseiled down a mountain-face and I was at the top holding on to his ropes, terrified to let go of them in case I facilitated him falling to his death and therefore exiting my life. Each fibre of the rope was a strand of the story of why I could not let the rope go. It was the kind of holding on where blistered hands would bleed from the intensity and ferocity of grabbing and gripping those fibres with all your might, and where your arms deadened and ached from the tension of it all. The kind of holding on with all your might because if the rope were to fray and unravel, if it were to rip from your grip or irrevocably slip and snatch away through your fingers at breakneck speed, then you, like the one on the other end, would not survive. It seemed better to hold onto that rope as long as I could – then Gordon could at least stay dangling as long as it took for him to have the strength to haul himself back up. In a way, there was nothing wrong with a hope that sometimes expressed in the shadow like this. After all, to hope – whether expressed from our shadow or the light – is what makes us human. It is part of the dance between humanity and divinity that we came here for, part of those simple steps and the fancy footwork, the flamboyant rhythms of pulling apart, and the subtle grooves and moves of coming together.

Whilst at times it was the darker side of hope that endured, it was only through what the lighter side of it sustained, that the power of faith managed to deepen. It intrigued me that faith, whenever I'd visited it so far, wasn't something I needed to hold onto like I held onto hope. Hope seemed to feel more of an action, something I did to feel my positivity or to try to en*courage* myself perhaps. Faith, however, was something that at times I'd just *had*. It didn't need holding onto, since all the uncertainty that Hope could see and that Hope wanted to resolve, wasn't visible to Faith. Faith lived by the blind resolution that no matter how the circumstances and facts stacked up, the "highest truth" would prevail in the end. I noticed that whenever I chose to align with Faith, I felt a sense of naturalness and a grace and surrender such as I hadn't experienced even with the light side of hope. Intention was everything though. I did have to *choose* to align with the highest.

With faith, I still found myself taking the obvious action as it arose but not with the grasping of wanting what I, Caroline, wanted. Instead, it was with the energy of knowing that things veering in favour of the Highest is how life works and how life moves, that life is always evolutionary even if it is a challenge to see it that way because we don't always live with awareness about the Big Picture, or always reside in "Spirit time." When I was able to hang out with faith, it was not a faith in the happy ending the way I, Caroline, envisaged it, even though that ending could have been a potentiality too. Rather, it was a faith in life being the highest good for *everyone*.

Faith required me to accept that this gift might not come wrapped the way I wanted it but that I would come to love the present, even if not at the time of the gifting. There was a peace, an acceptance, an outbreath, and an is-ness about everything with faith. And I had been there at times, including today. And when I was there, I hadn't arrived by *holding onto* faith. I had found myself there by *knowing* faith, by just *having* it, by just *being* it. Maybe in truth I didn't even *arrive* at all. Perhaps in those moments of stopping or letting go of "holding on" to hope, I discovered instead that Faith had always been holding *me* – that I was held by the infinite Love that had always been there, just like the ever-present air blowing through the vents in the ceilings of the hospital regardless of my whereabouts.

It was thought-provoking – the sense that when we let go we are still held but by something more powerful than what our holding-on can generate for us. I could see too, that there existed the holding of something or someone in a way that was the purest expression of "holding", and that there was the receiving of *being held*. Each of us were giving the gift of holding something or someone and receiving the gift of being held in some way, even though we were not doing one to get the other.

Gordon was the obvious example of being held. He was being held by a thread, by life support – with its tubes, drips, pumps and drugs – and by the diligence and care of the specialists. Held by the space that was the little room, and that in itself was held by the ICU ward, which in turn was held by the hospital as a whole. He was held by the hearts and intentions of me, of his sons, of all who came to visit him, and of all the friends and complete strangers taking part in the group healings. He was even being held, perhaps, by other realms and dimensions.

I thought about every friend and stranger who had joined the online group and those who hadn't but nonetheless were still sending energy. Each was holding the other, holding me, holding the space, holding the intention. Even I was holding the intention and, in a way, through my updates and my requests for where I felt the healing was most needed, playing my part in holding the community as it grew. And as much as Gordon was being held, he was also holding all of us as well. His body was the reason for, and held the physical space for, us gathering around him. His spirit held an energetic space that was enabling all of us to experience and go through what was needed for our evolution. All of us were life support. All of us were being held by a sacred holding, in which there was no scared.

A big breath rolled out of me, breaking onto the soft shore of silence that was the dimmed room, and releasing my hunched shoulders as it did so. How much I must have been holding my breath since his coma! Had I fantasised this could buy me the gift of time – a way to press pause on the action around me so that I could escape from all the tension? I'd been aware of doing it again today when Gordon's machines had beeped without warning. In fact, there were times when the fragility of the situation I was in had felt such that any exhalation – or too many of them close together – could be enough energy to tip the precariously crash-landed plane that we now both found ourselves in over the edge of the cliff. I had to acknowledge the irony: breath was the very thing giving us life in the physical, moving Spirit through us as us, and connecting our head with our heart and our body with our soul! To think that

Gordon now found himself having to *be breathed* by a machine, and by all of us whenever we held that intention during healings as we envisaged our lungs breathing to help clear his. And yet there was I, often *holding* my breath, unconsciously trying to refuse or to stem the flow of life within my own body. Wanting to staunch the haemorrhaging that I perceived from the natural flow of life in the world around me, in case that flow should transition Gordon from one form to another and take me to places that I didn't want to be taken to.

Sleep still eluding me, I closed my eyes, trying to breathe into the depth of my belly.

Chapter Twenty

Day 5

3:22 a.m. – Home

M Y FINGERTIPS WERE TINGLING. I was wide awake and tired all in one go, the night seeming to last for eternity. Something wanted to be written through me and *now*. I began to type, not necessarily knowing what I wanted to say.

> Update from me: Yesterday was day 4 in hospital which blows me away. It all feels like a bubble of never-ending "now", everything being felt with intensity and experienced on barely any sleep.
>
> The last two group healings yesterday had power. For one of them I was at Gordon's left foot and again I had this feeling of him wriggling his toes and flexing his foot except he was not doing that. Yet I could feel the energy of him doing that. It's like there is an "activation" happening in me because when healings happen, I experience huge outputs of energy flowing through me and all of my body buzzes like crazy when our sessions start.

As I left the hospital last night, I felt daunted and humbled. Gordon has severe heart failure, liver failure, kidney failure, pneumonia, sepsis, and oedema. The number of drips, tubes, medications and machines that are needed just to make these parts of his body function without his body having to do it, is staggering. What a work of sophistication the body is when it is all functioning and yet how clumsy and clunky it is when humans try to mimic that creation, using technology! But of course, thank goodness that we HAVE been able to mimic that technology.

I want to speak for a moment to the intricacy of the work that the staff do. I watch them in awe. They are meticulous, their job to notice every detail in every minute and half-hour and hour and log it all on paper as they go. They carry out this process of create and adjust, so we can "inch forward". That's why when I said bye to Gordon for the night I knew he was in the most brilliant of hands. The ICU team are all angels – two in particular are actually angels. I have received "messages" about this from people who have spoken to me, and I know this sounds weird but on one person, I can "see" their wings. Yes, I told you, it does sound like madness, doesn't it, but what can I say? For me, it is another piece of evidence that points to the fact that regardless of where this is all going to end up, Gordon and I are being led by the Divine and looked after right now. That all of this is and has been part of the Divine Plan which so far has unfolded in all its chaos and fear and trauma, yet nevertheless with an uncanny grace and flow.

Staff said yesterday that they want to see a few more days of "critical but stable", which will provide the foundation for small increments in function to occur, and which can then correspond to a weaning off drips and volumes and support. Gordon's job is to hang in there moment to moment, hour to hour, day to day, night to night.

Today we are going to be playing music in the room. I have been getting strong intuition for two days now for Gurrumul, which is one of Gordon's favourite CDs. We are playing it for the indigenous sound, but also for the gentleness and purity of spirit that is Gurrumul too, an honouring and reflection of these qualities in Gordon. We will be playing some didge CDs to him too – again, been getting the hit for this now for the past two days.

I am doing okay. But I am aware that alongside the grief and the shaking and trembling happening within and without, there are huge feelings of guilt. I know they are there, I know what they are about, but I also know I am trying to push them down for now as I need to be here for Gordon. The guilt would be making things be about me when, right now yes, there is me with needs but there is also Gordon on life support. I know his soul has already forgiven, it is me who has not forgiven myself and in truth, at the Higher Level there is nothing I need forgive myself for, for there is only Love. But I'm enmeshed in the human–divine dance of all this.

I have known for some time that I am learning about unconditional love. We all are. But I have been calling in this experience on purpose for the past three years. I wish I didn't have to learn what I needed to in the way that it has unfolded but, in being brought to my knees in such a painful way, my heart has cracked open in those places where it needed to. It seems like the hospital, this community, and Life itself has been the bowl that has received me as I have done this.

I have much awareness now about the small

percentage of time I chose to see and relate to Gordon through the filter of his Greatness as these past four years went by. Instead, I experienced him more through his flaws and his limiting story about himself. I had not even accepted those parts – and with love – as being part of the whole man. Needing him to be "more this" and "less of that" when in fact that is what I needed me to be and yet there I was, projecting that on to him. I have said before about the irony or the perfection of this situation of *ICU/"I see you"* that we find ourselves in now.

While we are in this holding station called ICU, I am being given ample opportunity to "see" Gordon. Not least because all of you are also showing me Gordon's Greatness in your comments, a Greatness that I am aware of and have always been aware of and yet the mass reflection back to me from all of you is part of the healing – for you, for Gordon and for me. How intricate is the connection between us all! For I also see that as Gordon keeps us all here, and we reflect this Greatness back, we are also reflecting our own Greatness back to ourselves. Likewise, with all the things that you have said over the past few days that are my Greatness, you have helped me to "see" and receive these aspects of the experience called "Caroline" that I am in. WOW.

Maybe this is why, for the moment, Gordon is keeping himself, me, family, and all of you, in this place called ICU. We need it. We need this love and this healing that comes from seeing the Divinity of who we are and who others really are . . . and then realising that at the highest level, there IS no other, when it boils down to it. There is only *One*.

I am grateful to all of you who continue to send your love and healing. I know we are not sure how many more days of this it could be, but I would like to ask that those who can to please carry on with the group healings. I know they are playing a huge part in all this. Goodnight everyone. X

I pressed send, allowing the words to fly off into cyberspace. My eyes burned in their demand for sleep and were no longer willing to stay open to negotiation. When I awoke, it was three hours later and to a watery sun streaming out through cracks in the cloud. I looked over to the phone. There was no red number flashing on the screen. That meant no missed calls, nobody from the hospital who had tried to ring. It meant my man was still alive. Instantly, I sobbed with relief – just a few seconds, and it was out.

Plodding over to the kitchen, I made a cup of tea and took it back with me to my blankets and the couch. The nerves were already kicking in. Though it was a gift that Gordon was still with us, I knew it also left the door wide open to all the potentials of another ride and another day where everything could change in a heartbeat. I flicked on the laptop. Whirring into life, it showed there were replies to my post. In what was fast becoming a ritual now, I sat and read, the comments fortifying me and helping to massage the knot in my stomach.

Vicky: I appreciate deeply your sharing of this process Caroline. We've not met in the flesh yet but when reading your posts I feel so close to you, with tears in my eyes and much love in my heart.

Harvey: I am overwhelmed by your strength and perspective, Caroline. We are ALL in this together, and we are here for you both. X

Francesca: Thanks for sharing, beautiful strong woman that you are. It cracks my heart open to read your words, and I'm so touched by your honesty and vulnerability. I'm still here, sending you love and courage. Xx

Nat: Hey Caroline, during the 10 a.m. healing on Tuesday I sang to Gordon and the words that came were: "you are the one, we are the ones." I felt much moved by this and afterwards when I was walking, I looked up at the sky and there was a cloud pointing behind me like an arrow. I turned around and behind me was a sign, where the visible letters that weren't covered by a tree read: "cure". Though I'm not sure what this means exactly I felt to share it and to thank you both because sending love to Gordon's heart is reminding me of mine, and the immense power of all of ours together. Xx

Holly: There was a time when I thought unconditional love was about being loving all the time and rising above all "lower" thoughts and feelings. Now I see it as the ability to love through anything and everything. To love ourselves and to love others no matter what is going on or what story we have about what is going on. To move and flow in accordance with our own hearts and to put the power in that and in the flow of the hearts of others . . . to honour all of our soul journeys. What I mean by love here is drawing our energy from a higher source and giving energy to each other from that infinite source rather than taking energy from each other. Seems to me this is what you are doing, what we are all doing here. I feel so privileged to be a part of it and am learning that I can live like that in simpler times, when there is no crisis or ICU, and where I can still see you. Xx

Helen: (posts picture of a white rabbit bearing the words "You are never alone") These are such tough lessons and you are brave. To be so honest, true and authentic is scary but also liberating. As it all comes into the light of consciousness it becomes strength and its power to hurt diminishes. You are generous to share as you do, when even as it is cathartic it is also clearly so painful. Xx

Patricia: I have no words Caroline that express how profoundly these words open my heart. Thank you and bless you for all that you are.

Ruth: Good morning angels. I was speaking last night about how much Gordon and Caroline are bringing to the world. We are all gifted with a new perspective on life. We are shown the power of friendship, community, truth, honouring the highest and love. Not one of us is untouched by this.

Holly: Today is Winter Solstice, one of the most significant landmarks of the year – the turning of the seasons at the darkest night and an opportunity to leave behind old worries and fears and step into a fresh new world. Steiner children in the southern hemisphere will be lighting lanterns and celebrating this day. Many other cultures too. Let this mark a turning point in Gordon's recovery. I have been feeling to call him back to his body the last few healings, as if his will is needed there now. It's a difficult thing – to return to a body that is suffering. May all the solstice lanterns light your way, Gordon. There is so much love waiting for you here.

CHAPTER TWENTY-ONE

Day 5

8.30 a.m. – Hospital

I ARRIVED AT THE HOSPITAL to discover there were breakthroughs with Gordon overnight; it made my heart flutter even though it didn't dare soar. Jim and Steve had been with me when Sarah came out to bring us up to speed with things, and I wondered if they were experiencing her news the way I was. We had to acknowledge the victories! The count for his white blood cells had normalised, meaning that it had reduced 8 points in 24 hours. They now had a hold on his pneumonia though would need to continue with the antibiotics to prevent it returning with a vengeance. His blood pressure had improved slightly. He had been taking the occasional breath for himself since the morning and, he was responding to dialysis in a way that now helped him. Yet Sarah's eyebrows still knitted together.

"He has been vomiting and that is something new. It means there is a problem with his stomach not working to digest the liquid food we are giving him. So we have to take a look at that and see what can be done."

"But the positive developments are . . . positive, right?"

"For sure Steve, and look, I would be the first to admit that your father has defied all odds to still be here. But without wanting to dampen your spirits, we still have a long haul ahead of us and every minute is touch and go. There's something else too, and it's why you can't come in for a while. He's been having trouble with oxygen this morning. It is an issue I'm afraid and we are trying our best to handle it."

"You said he was taking in the odd breath himself though?"

"True Jim, but this problem with oxygen is part of the forward march of the pneumonia. We need to put another drain into him. Please remember, he is critical but stable and though there have been improvements, there are also things of concern to deal with." She paused, directing her next comment to me. "I want to ask you and your group of friends to focus your healing today on his heart beating and contracting with efficiency and a good distribution of oxygen. It is imperative for him right now. I can't stress it to you enough." Her eyes seemed to bore through mine for an eternity, sending my heart racing.

After Sarah left, I went outside to text Ruth with an update so that she could add it to the Journey Page.

That Gordon had tried to take some breaths himself had me skirting around the edges of wondering whether he might well be coming back into the physical and making his passage back into his body. I took care not to speak my thoughts to the boys, mindful of giving them space and time alone with their dad as much as possible. But like the Whistling Kites in the sky over the bay at home, the thoughts circled nonetheless. As the day panned out with all the magic of who was turning up and when and with what, my wondering only increased.

It started with the 10 a.m. healing. Gordon's muscles were twitching, something the staff were attributing to his "lighter" state now that they were weaning him off aspects of life support. I had felt he was trying to connect with me, his head moving to the side as I arrived in the room. Then Rebecca turned up with an expanse of red cloth and a pair of wooden taiko drumsticks in tow, items her intuition had nudged her to bring. It was enough to prick the skin on the back of my neck again. Red, the colour of vitality and strength and the physicality of man! Red, the colour for the root chakra, the energy centre in the body concerned with linking us to the physical world and to solidity and support and to the body. We laid the cloth over his sheet and the nurses allowed us keep it there. As for the drumsticks, belonging to a style of warrior percussion that Gordon and I liked to practice, these were placed under the bed as per the guidance of Rebecca's intuition again. By lunchtime, an additional gift had found its way into his room – a piece of art by his friend Craig, expressed in an Aboriginal style. The nurses gave us permission to hang it on the wall by Gordon's bed.

Buoyed by the events of the morning and the way they seemed to have significance, I stood on the pavement outside the hospital and sent a text to update Charles. No sooner had I finished than I was surprised and overcome to see Mike, the friend who had taught Gordon how to play the didgeridoo. Wearing baggy hemp trousers and a loose fitting shirt he bore the energy of the sun, the clouds, the soil and the red desert sand, as he ambled towards me.

"Mike! It's so good to see you! I can't believe you've turned up today of all days!" I said, as we hugged. I nuzzled my cheek into the softness and curls of long, yogi hair.

"Why, what's happened?"

"No, what I mean is that today we have been playing the music of Gurrumul to him, and now here *you* are! Thank you so much for coming!"

"Well, you can play him some didge music now too. Here, I thought I would bring these with me." He smiled, handing me a pile of CDs as I shivered at the synchronicity of the one at the top called *Earth Rhythms*.

We headed back into the hospital and out into a courtyard, taking a seat under a palm tree. With all his trademark huskiness, quietness and gentleness, Mike offered his sympathies and expressed his shock. I had always found it ironic that the tone and volume of both his heart and Gordon's heart when expressed in words, sounded so muted and in stark contrast to the range and amplification and depth of their expression when they sang the land and their heart through the didge. As Mike talked now, touching the long and pointed clear-quartz crystal hanging by its leather strap around his neck, I could feel the love. And that was all that mattered. I let him have time alone with Gordon. It tied in with the boys taking a break, and I sensed that he wanted to tune into him and have a conversation, man to man, soul to soul.

By the time I met with Pam down at main reception, I was a mixture of elation and anxiety. The 2 p.m. healing had brought with it both promise and a reality check. During the session, with eyes closed and from the space of my heart, I had seen nothing other than a warrior returning home in a rite of passage. I had wondered if I could dare trust what my intuition was showing me but when I reopened my eyes and looked at Gordon, what was obvious was that his appearance was the most like his normal self that I had seen since he had been admitted. Was he coming back to the physical? I had mentioned it to Nurse Ed. But all he did was remind me of the seriousness of the issue with oxygen right now and my heart had sunk.

"Caroline!" Pam was a woman who boomed. Her voice was all nasal and drone but with concern now too. "So good to see you honey, and the timing has worked out just perfectly!"

I beamed to see her there in her block colours and flashes of gold and silver jewellery, as she jumped up out of her seat in the reception area. I'd missed seeing her at the last couple of meetings with the magicians. We hugged as if it were a reunion. Sitting back down, she asked about everything since the day Gordon had crashed. It was funny in a way, having her here in front of me. Her animation and larger-than-life persona made me realise just how deadpan so many of the faces in ICU could actually be, not to mention how little any of them really said anything. With her gift for storytelling, Pam's physicality could tell umpteen tales of its own. Her cheeks and skin florid from a lust for life and living – good times spent feasting on fine wine and food, luxuriating in the warmth of spa-tubs, indulging in the pleasure of massages, pampering with facials and manicures, and celebrating in joyous gatherings with her tribes. As I answered her questions, however, her face coloured only with love.

"What you are saying, Caroline . . . I *so* resonate." She murmured, placing a warm hand over mine as her eyes misted beneath rimless glasses. "I went through similar when my Jack was diagnosed with leukaemia. The veil between worlds was so thin for me also, and as for the insights, well!" She gave a low whistle as she exhaled. "I didn't know if he was going to live or die. And like you, I became a wide open channel. Gordon has been allowing me to remember all I learnt back then with Jack. I mean, illnesses of this magnitude Caroline, they are such a gateway to the learning of giving and receiving unconditional love!"

We talked some more. Sometimes I cried, sometimes she did. Now and then she leant over and hugged me in the chair, her bosom heaving a generosity of spirit and heart clearly not only reserved for her grown family. Once or twice we even joked and reminisced, Pam throwing her head back as the laughter shrieked out and jiggled her body.

"Now then, missy . . . you must get a massage, work out some of the stress in your body. Let's get that booked for you, yes? What about an energy treatment, a reiki session perhaps?"

"I can't think about that right now, couldn't relax enough I don't think, but thanks."

"You have to take care of yourself, Caroline. The trauma you have been through! A massage would do you the world of good. You could have one now, while I stay with Gordon."

"I can't. I know, I know, and I hear what you are saying, but please, not now." I heard my voice rise, knowing I didn't want to be controlled by anyone right now. Then I brightened again, softened. "How about a visit with Gordon, would you like to?"

"Well I'd *love* to, if that's okay with you. I thought I'd give him some reiki, if I get it from intuition that it's okay to do?"

"Well, okay, why not? You'll be able to have some time alone with him. The boys just stepped out for some lunch, so it's perfect, we can work in with that. They fly home tomorrow night, aren't allowed any more days off work. I'm trying to help both of them have as much time as possible with their dad, before they leave. So I'd say you've got an hour or so, if you want it."

I walked her through the corridors and up to the Relatives' Room, pointing her to the ICU entrance. As she strode off, it occurred to me that she had indeed picked a great vehicle for embodiment in this lifetime. Solid and strong, her hips and legs could not only accommodate the exuberance of her dancing, and the full force of her stomping whenever she cursed and vented, but also her power to take action in the world and to drive things forwards and to manifest. On a day that seemed to be all about Gordon perhaps making his way back to the body and this physical realm, I couldn't think of a better person to be sitting with him.

CHAPTER TWENTY-TWO

Day 5

11.50 p.m. – Home

LEAVING THE HOSPITAL ON MY OWN, I felt the familiar queasiness in my gut. The staff, out of the kindness of their hearts, had been allowing me to stay with Gordon beyond the curfew. Tonight however, they had requested I leave a bit earlier. Those issues with Gordon's oxygen were still proving to be a concern and although no alert was in place, the night nurse had preferred me to go home and get rest. He had given no acknowledgement to the wins I thought we had seen during the day, and so the churning in my belly made its return.

I slipped out of the after-hours exit at the side of the building and morphed into the shadows of the courtyard and alley. This was the routine now, my new familiar. Rolling up the collar of my jacket, I puckered my lips and steeled myself with all the purposefulness of a pull-yourself-together outbreath. The anxiety and warm air swirling around inside me collided with the spirited coolness of the night, transforming into a third thing that couldn't have existed without the collision – a puff of magic that made the unseen visible, if only for a second. I loved the coldness at night. It reminded me of the joy I could feel in being alive. Tonight it just made me realise that since Gordon had gone into hospital, my connection to the natural world had been reduced to these times of getting in and out of the car to drive to and from this building. I made my way over to the parking bays that sat waiting to release their last occupant. Despite scanning for it every night, there had so far been no reappearance of the rabbit. I fiddled with my keys, fingers clumsy with cold under the darkness of a sky that shared only the light of its stars with the street tonight. *New Moon. Of course. And Winter Solstice too, hadn't someone said?*

Eventually, with windows wound down to the chill, I made my way on autopilot back to the house. A house that for some reason, and now more than ever, I feared returning to tonight.

It was cavern-cold when I stepped inside, and the steel of the staircase echoed out an empty welcome as my feet trudged up to the lounge. The eyes of the stone Buddha remained closed upon my arrival at the top of the steps, indifferent to the yawning sprawl of space to be found there. Dropping my bags, I squatted down by the wall and fumbled with the knob on the gas heater. It didn't respond. *Shit. No bloody gas.* Cursing, I went and grabbed the blanket in our bedroom and came back out, throwing it on top of the sofa's dishevelled bedding. I clicked the switch on the wall. Two long rows of spotlights sprang into interrogation on the ceiling, dragging my eyes and legs down to the shambles in the kitchen. One look at the clutter in the sink, there since the day we had gone to hospital, and I sighed. Elsewhere, cups of cold, half-drunken tea dotted the bench-tops, each with a shrivelled yet protective skin against the apparent rejection. I knew I should clean up, that such an act would correlate with the "normal world". But I didn't live in that world now. That world would be Gordon out of hospital, or at least out of coma. Returning all the mess back to darkness, I migrated to the sofa at the other end of the floor.

Snuggling under the covers, I turned the laptop on and began to read the Journey Page. The consensus there seemed to be one of joy to see the nurses embracing and supporting our group healings. I agreed, noting in particular the development Sarah had undergone with this and how she was now including – even enlisting – all of us in the work that needed to be done. I admired her willingness to be open and wondered what she would feel about the way in which our community had responded to her request today. The more I read, the more I welled up with appreciation and gratitude.

Francesca: For the 2 p.m. healing, I found myself beating out a heartbeat on my crystal bowl. I had the strongest vision of entrainment. Usually associated with sound, entrainment is when one instrument adjusts its pitch to match another nearby. It is not impossible that with our group focus we could envision Gordon's heart "entraining" with our healthy hearts. This is symbolic and literal, despite how whacky it sounds. I also saw that scene in the last Harry Potter movie, where Harry and Dumbledore are talking about Harry's choice to return to life or continue with his journey.

Linda: A gentle play on my doumbek for Gordon tonight because it's softer & the rhythm reminds me of a heartbeat. Imagined Gordon's heart while I played, sometimes soft beats, sometimes strong beats, but tried to keep it consistent.

Jessica: Yes me too, I tapped on the heart meridian rhythmically and calmly, and it felt gentle tonight. Love to you both. Xxx

Pam: Had the privilege of spending this afternoon and

early evening with Caroline and Gordon. My intuitive guidance for the day was all about grounding . . . about being Earth Angels and setting Gordon and Caroline's roots in Mother Earth again. I spent nearly two hours with Gordon alone and talked to him and used my reiki skills, especially on his heart and lungs. It was amazing to feel how open his base and crown chakras were. I spent a lot of time on his heart, throat and third eye chakras. I received messages from Gordon all day and, like Caroline has found too, I could feel when others were sending healing to him from afar, even outside the healing times. It is a miracle he is with us right now.

Sherry: I want to say, to each person involved in Gordon's healing, you are so very awesome, your love and commitment to this man's healing is to be admired, if everyone could think and love like each one of you, this world would be healed. It has been so amazing to watch.

It helped me a lot to feel that I was not alone. Yet by the time I had finished reading the comments each night, I returned to my sense of isolation. As I saw it, I *was* alone here in this house. I hunched over the pillows in my lap. I could count on both hands the number of hours I had slept since Gordon's crash. It had been five harrowing days of being caught up in the destruction and relentlessness of the flood that had ensued from the tsunami that had hit my life and changed its terrain forever. Days of being dragged under the torrent of the main event only to cling with anguish and frenzy to whatever I could grab in those waters. Days of resistance to the flow of the flood because it felt like there were too many things in it that could take me out, and because I didn't know where the waters were going to dump me.

It was a blessing and miracle that Gordon was still here, yet tonight I felt I had to face the reality that his overall status and prognosis still hadn't really changed. The monitors still beeped and their numbers still went up and down. The nurses still came and went around the clock. He was still flat on his back when I left him, eyelids still shut. The thick plastic tube was still sticking its way down his throat, the ventilator pump still hissed and puffed, and his body was still swollen beyond recognition. I had no idea how long we were all going to have to do this or whether I even had the fortitude.

The irony was that it was Gordon who was the fan of endurance challenges. At least that fact was a drop of comfort that could perhaps massage its way into my heart. If anyone could have the stamina to handle the gruelling nature of coma, Gordon would have that fighting chance. With his mountain bike, he had cycled the steep Picos Mountains in 40 degree heat, for days on end. He had trekked long distance bushwalks. What was his experience like now? Was it as arduous for him as it was for me? Intuition would have been my bridge to tune in to his energy and find out but my exhaustion and shell-shock was such that I couldn't clear my mind to receive. And anyway, part of me was too spooked with fear of what I might discover.

The moon was going through its phase of diminished gravitational pull, correlating with what I was experiencing in my own body. My motivation and optimism were ebbing and tonight felt like the heaviness of the long exhale. I felt a tugging within, a sinking into my core, and a sense of being unable to avoid dropping into the terror of the vastness of space opening up inside me. Like the early Australian pearl divers who had been forced to dive without breathing apparatus, I could sense my resistance between the pull to plunge deeper and the fear of losing the air and light at the surface of my world. Plumbing the depths may well lead to connections that liberate and transform, but I felt daunted by any further journeying required to do that, especially if it had to happen tonight without anyone here with me. I felt a foreboding, a sense that in these wee small hours a date with something awaited. I didn't want to turn up. Instead, my thoughts tumbled back to Gordon. Was he also at the next stage of his date with something, wherever he was? It struck me that just as I felt bogged down in all the heaviness of the physical plane, he was being stretched farther into the lightness of the astral planes, a cord connecting to his body in hospital while his soul engrossed in a flight of discovery, testing to see how far it could extend up and out without leaving altogether.

I twiddled his ring on my finger, a quirk of mine now. Looking down at it made me wonder if we were not only doing our own journeys in all this but that a joint one might be taking place too. The groove around the middle of the ring answered my touch and responded to my musings. *I am Rainbow Serpent Dreaming.* I pondered, trying to recall what the indigenous Australians had said about this Dreaming and what it might have to do with our marriage. Was I to take it that Gordon and I were being called to reshape our inner landscapes? To die to fears and limitations, transmuting them into the sorts of gifts of empowerment and strength that, like the serpent, would then refashion the outer landscape of our marriage? After all, both of us had now let go of living the life we had been living together. Now that we found ourselves cut adrift from that way, perhaps this chain of events was taking place to force a review and to gain insights, to help us learn and decide what we still wanted to energise as a couple, and maybe to discern whether both of us still wanted to even *be* in this relationship.

I stared at the band again. For a second I felt dizziness generating words in me which didn't seem to be thought. How could we have never seen a serpent in this ring when we designed it all those years ago? And yet, like the serpent in the Dreaming, it had been there the whole time, slumbering underground until its mission of transformation had become activated. Had the ring been a prophecy of the marital journey we now found ourselves on? My mind wanted to banish this as nonsense. Yet what of the unusualness too of my engagement ring? Any other shape would never have been able to hold his band in place on my finger. Had we *always* been coming *here*, to this stage of our sacred work together? And if so, how would the story continue? Fear answered with a whisper and shiver of misgiving.

In the crashing stillness of the house, I was aware of the lub-dub of my heart as it drummed up the tempest of my inner reality. I exhaled, realising I didn't like being on my own in this monster of a building we had called home. I dimmed the lights and lit the candles that were sitting on the unit. But the candles offered no comfort. I tensed as their flickers cast an in-between-worlds graffiti on the wall, shaping an ominous story. Before I knew it, the reminder fanned into my awareness again of the shadow that both Mum and Carolyn had experienced, independent of one another, passing across their wall on the night Gordon had been put into coma – a shadow the size and height of an actual person that had instinctively felt like Gordon visiting them. I felt the jitters flittering through me and tried to push out the thought that had already been thought about. But with much sneakiness another one popped up, taking me back to a childhood habit of checking under the bed and in the wardrobe before sleep, for fear of something sinister lying in wait for me. I never forgot the night when Mum, responding to my anxious calls, brought the comforting waft of her perfume with her as she arrived at my door and turned on the bedroom light to show me how the shadow that I feared was nothing more than one of my brother's farmyard animals perched on top of the cupboard. It had taken a while after she'd gone but I did manage to fall asleep. Sitting on the couch now though, I felt gripped by terror again. The impulse to call out was quicker than my rationale to stop it.

"Guides . . . God . . . Universe . . . help me! Are you there?"

I paused, waiting for something, a sign, anything. But there was no reply. My words ricocheted off the wall, off windows blackened by the inkiness of night and by the turning away from earth of the moon's illuminated face. I stared into their obsidian panes, forced to confront myself in the reflection, compelled to confirm my greatest fear. *I am alone.* There was nothing. Just silence. And much as I felt desolate in the presence of such silence, I also didn't feel any inclination to put a stop to it with music or to go downstairs and turn on the TV. Silence seemed to be holding court for some reason. It was as if, courtesy of its energy, all I could do was sit with and uncover the truth of how I ever ended up here in this place of fear.

I squinted at the time on my laptop, head throbbing with fatigue. It was 2.37 a.m. My eyes were struggling with their burden of having to put up the good fight, a warped version perhaps of times as a youngster when I hadn't wanted to be "awake alone" if my brother ever drifted off to sleep before I did. I used to wonder where he went when he left me with just the quietness of his inhales and exhales. Sometimes, in my fretfulness, I had nudged him or resorted to making noises just to wake him up. Anything to not have to bear the panic and lonesomeness of being the only one left outside of sleep. Such angst! I had even experienced it when I couldn't hear any sounds from downstairs. I would creep to the top of the staircase and crane my ears to hear Mum or Dad talking or even the sound of the TV. But the door to the lounge would be shut and I'd hear nothing. That "nothing" had deafened me. What was it I had feared, I wonder? Did I think they had left the house? One night, I lost my footing and to rebalance I'd had to stand on the second step, causing it to creak. That's when the door downstairs had flung open, releasing all the warmth and rainbows of canned laughter from the TV, and the fury of Mum railing at me to get back to bed. It had been such a relief to hear her shouting like that. That somebody was there after all! I frowned. Isn't that what we all yearn for – to know that we are not alone?

Still I could not surrender to sleep right now. Perhaps it *was* the shadows. I had always said to Gordon in jest, and in seriousness, that if he ever transitioned before I did, he was not to appear to me at the end of the bed in the middle of the night, or to brush my cheek so that I would feel the sensation. He had laughed at me, but I had insisted that he only connect in ways that reassured. Since he had been in hospital, I'd spent every night fighting off sleep, out of terror that he might pass his shadow across my wall or appear to me as an apparition. Worse, that he would use the opportunity presented by my falling asleep, to tell me in my dreams that he was going. Maybe it was Peter Pan who had put that idea in my head all those years ago. I had always remembered the quote. "*You know that place between sleep and awake, the place where you can still remember dreaming? That's where I will always love you, that's where I'll be waiting.*" I was convinced that if I didn't sleep, or only allowed myself to fall asleep an hour or so before daybreak, I could stop him from coming to tell me he was leaving me. I could see now that this was also the reason I never wanted to connect to my intuition about Gordon whilst I was at the house.

The candle flame flickered higher for a second, throwing darkness under the frame of the mirror. In that moment, I knew it wasn't so much the shadows on the wall that I feared tonight but more the meeting of my own – my fear of abandonment.

By about 3 a.m. the full force of a thought I had been suppressing all day and all night – because I believed it to be the truth – finally triggered the floodgates to open within me, releasing a dam so pent up with angst and remorse and grief, that I thought I would drown in its torrential cascading.

A. W.O.L.

It struck right to the core. The short-cut phrase I'd used over the past five years to describe the times after an argument when Gordon would disappear from the house for hours on end without contacting me. He loathed my loose borrowing of the term, feeling that I was trying to shame him with it. Only now did it occur to me that it could have stood for Abandoned With Out Love. I was sure he wouldn't like that interpretation either, since he never believed or felt he was ever "abandoning" me.

There was a pattern that would play out: a heated argument earlier in the day, me saying something barbed to tip things over the edge, him exiting the house in a traumatic way, and us experiencing physical separation. More often than not, if he did not return by 6 p.m. it was pretty much a guarantee he would pull an all-nighter or arrive back nearer to daybreak. To me it was an act of cruelty that he should disappear for hours and not let me know where he was, or take my calls, or allow him or us to be helped to come back to a place of love. Later on he would tell me that it was because he was simply hurting. At the time, I felt his absence as a controlling passive–aggressiveness on his part, an unconscious behaviour and strategy impelled by feeling emotionally unsafe, yet wrapped up in fury and unjustness, and designed to achieve the safety he so needed through the certainty of withdrawing. For him it was a case of doing the abandoning before he was abandoned by me. In the solitude he created for himself by leaving, he could calm his anger down, lick his wounds, blame me, rationalise about the hopelessness of the marriage, go to the pub for a drink alone, and go walking to derive pleasure in nature. For hours, these acts buffered him from having to open up to self-examination, to enquire into the truth of his thoughts, or to actually feel the pain that arose from believing he was un-loveable and unwanted. The trouble was that the longer he perpetuated his absence the more he became lost to his story, disconnecting from the truth in his heart.

All of a sudden, as if energised and animated, the flame on one of the candles shot up higher. *Fire and air, just like our star signs.* It made me think. We were indeed different the way we went into our "funks". I would explode. In the past couple of years I had been learning to hasten my simmering down again, and to try and regain consciousness and respond with appropriateness rather than react. It had been a work in progress and had never excused the blowing up in the first place, of course. Yet I hated it when he could not hasten *his* bouncing back. I would experience this as the ultimate abandonment. Despite recognising that I had caused it by losing control and saying things I shouldn't have, I felt it was him who had continued it, had continued to *do* the abandoning *to* me. That was how I invariably internalised it. Even though I would go all day giving him his space, there was something about the night that got to me. The night was when I most felt my vulnerability to being left like that, and when my pattern rolled out its next stage.

At first I would be angry at the persistence of his unconsciousness, frustrated that he could not hurry up and come back to a place of love, or return home or contact me. By the time 4 p.m. passed and

6 p.m. arrived and there was still no word or sign, my anxiety would rise. Hysteria would jangle in my throat and because I couldn't just sit with the sensation, I'd find myself pacing up and down the room. I hated the vulnerability that rose in me and what I believed it said about me. I struggled to get past my perception that he was cruel to not receive the love I wanted to give. I felt that he had exiled me, even though he was the one who had removed himself from the house. Why did I feel like that? A throwback perhaps, to the punishments meted out by parents who were only trying to do their best? I could only think of the usual things like being sent to my room, or being made to stay in the kitchen till I had eaten the dinner I didn't like whilst everyone else peeled off into the lounge-room and shut the door. Later on it had been about my father making me stand in the corner of the lounge and face the wall for hours on end, while the rest of the family watched TV. In these instances, I had felt an abject separation, a feeling that I had been cut off, deliberately, from love. So it was too, on the nights when Gordon went AWOL.

Thinking about it again, a sense of remorse seeped into my being. Remorse for the fight we had both had the night before this crash, remorse for every argument over the past five years. For all the times I had tunnel-visioned and coloured my world a raging red, for the times I had disconnected from the truth and slid into conditioning instead. If only I had been able to get to a place of honesty in the heat of things, or even before things had become heated! If only I had been able to say "I'm scared" instead of ranting and raging or venting and projecting. Those acts had concealed rather than revealed what was really going on inside me. An acid wash, guilt now blistered the softest parts of my core as I contemplated my past and my behaviours and all the times I had chosen anger over vulnerability, over the nakedness and rawness of levelling with him down to the bone. What on earth had I thought I would lose each of those times that I believed anger would safeguard me? My smoke and mirrors bluster?

I could see that when I had lost control prior to his leaving, I had used anger like a riot shield, buffering me from the depth of pain that *I* was un-loveable enough to warrant *being* abandoned. Yet the protection that the outer surface of that armour had offered had also brought me face to face with the separation presented by the inner surface. It is, after all, an impossibility to guard and connect in openness at the same time. The two are mutually exclusive, so why had I wasted all that time and energy? Emotional riot shields: masters at creating the illusion of separation. As long as we hold them up, the "toughness" they offer leads to a guarantee of pain, isolation, coldness, fear and disconnection. A lot more than if we dare to let in vulnerability. With every argument that had gone this way, and during the moments in which each of them had played out, we had missed connecting with something of beauty and preciousness. They were moments that we couldn't get back and, as I feared now and was being forced to face, new moments that we might never get to share.

This thought ratcheted up my anxiety. *Oh my God, please come back! Please come home!* I couldn't tell if I was in a frantic memory from the past or right here in this moment. There were no boundaries in this oceanic world I was now drowning in. Pounding through the veins in my body was the notion that, via his coma, Gordon was doing the ultimate AWOL. He was here, but not here. Yes, possibly receiving my love and my "messages" just like when I had sent all those texts in desperation. Yet rather than exhibiting an *unwillingness* to reply, he was now *unable* to. He had "gone off" to who knew where, leaving me here on my own.

It felt too much to bear as the pain of all the times I believed I had been left by the masculine rose up in me like cruel demons dressed in black and carrying hanging lanterns. Abandoned by my father even before I was out of the womb! Sure, he didn't leave the home but he had not wanted me to come along when I did and I believe I had felt that. Abandoned by my first love! Yes, Kevin had dumped me one night by not turning up at my home to meet me. Abandoned by Gordon! Given the past, and now with his coma, would this be an AWOL from which he would never return? For a second my fear of abandonment felt like a plunge into icy water, knowing after the first lung-aching gasp that I should breathe out yet the reflexes in my body freezing up. Survival instincts kicked in. Returning my attention to my laptop, I allowed the vulnerable, tentative trail of my fingers to cross the keyboard in an attempt to connect with the outside world:

I'm scared. Is anybody there?

I squirmed as I pressed the send button but I knew my heartfelt desire for connection exceeded, in that moment, my likely embarrassment at looking pathetic to others. I waited a few minutes. There was no reply. Of course there wasn't. After all, it was 4 a.m. and everybody was sleeping. Perhaps too, I still expected abandonment. My face crumpled, as silent sobs took me by surprise, spilling over and down into the ravines and crevices of my isolation.

A sound stopped me mid sob. I held my breath, straining my ear. It was the Boobook owl. It hooted again and I realised that I had been aware of it at a subliminal level for a while. I got up, slid open the doors and stepped onto the balcony, joining in with the shivering of the bare-branched trees in the stillness and crispness of the night's thin air. The sky had pulled its covers up, obscuring the stars by putting them to bed. I looked down to see the waters below transformed into a void of harboured secrets. The owl hooted again. Unease curled itself around me. I hadn't wanted to think the thought but it was already too late. *Didn't shamans view owls as the souls of the recently deceased, messengers of the underworld, and carriers of spirits into the afterlife?* I gripped onto the slab-cold railing, entertaining the notion that the owl was here to tell me that the mortality Gordon was facing had indeed come to pass. Was I going to get a phone call? *Breathe! Caroline, breathe into that sensation in your body, yes, the one you call fear. Breathe. Yes, you are alone on this deck. Accept that. Breathe into that sensation in your body, the one you call aloneness. Meet it. Accept the sensation. Breathe.*

I filled my lungs, used the release to soften into my churning and trembling and thudding. It took many cycles. Somehow, I felt a nudge to retrain my ear back on the hooting. The owl was far away yet still close enough to echo across the bay, to energetically wrap his wings around me with the softness and the haunting, the rise and the fall, of his cuckoo-like call. Bu-book! Bu-book! Bu-Book! I knew he was hunting in the darkness, bringing back nourishment for himself and maybe his family. I kept listening. Bu-Book! His call soothed and hypnotised, beckoning me as I gave myself to it and focussed only on that sound. The more I did so, a warmth and peacefulness descended upon me and the less awareness of thoughts I had, until it was as if I had soared above them, breathing yet also not in my body, here but beyond here, the owl hooting in me and me as the owl hooting. Pure Aliveness. Spaciousness. Oneness.

Maybe a couple of minutes passed, though in truth I didn't know. When I opened my eyes again, the sense was one of acceptance – acceptance of my physical aloneness and yet, paradox that it was, also acceptance of my utter connectedness. Of knowing the truth that I had never, ever, really been alone, even in times of feeling on my own. The owl had somehow reconnected me to a depth of knowing blocked out for eons, to the truth of something which trumped my fear of what could be lost to me in the physical world, and which surpassed my belief in abandonment: *Separation is an illusion. And you are never "not held".*

By lighting up my blind side, the Boobook had helped me to squeeze through the chink of a door I had slammed long before I could even remember. He had led me back to an experience of Love, of what others might call God, or Source. In the moment of it, there were no words to describe it, nor any sense of a "Caroline". Afterwards, however, I was left with the most alive feeling that I had just immersed in the *real* me: the "I" that filled up "owl" and "Caroline"; the "I" that was the environs in which they both sat; the "I" that was the ever-presence of space and silence – that which was never inherently alone, nor abandoned, nor separate, nor ending, nor beginning. It was as if in meeting "aloneness" head on and with acceptance, I had been able to meet with or be this "All of Love".

For a second or two the balcony brightened as a car sleepily purred down the corridor of road with headlights on low beam. I listened to it disappear and closed my eyes again. A memory projected itself on the screen of my mind. A time when Gordon had been out for hours after an argument, his phone switched off. Finally, in the witching hours, when I knew that my pushing would not bring him back and that I should move into accepting what was, I had just let go. I let go of chasing him with calls and instead had left a message with love, saying that when he was ready there was a hug waiting for him at home. I let go of powering the story that I was alone and abandoned and that I needed to do something about that to fix it, and instead, I chose to look after myself, put myself to bed, tell my inner child that I was taking care of her and she need not fear. Thirty minutes later and with an hour to go before dawn, Gordon had turned up exhausted on the doorstep.

I had always imagined that he had returned because of my part in letting go. After all, aren't we told that if we just let go, things will come to us and with more ease and speed? But standing here now in the freshness of night, I questioned whether I had, in the deepest sense, let go that night. Yes, I had stopped fighting with the facts and had engaged in self-care in the end. And yes, it did appear that I had "allowed" Gordon his freedom to stay out if that was what he was going to choose. In many regards, I could argue I had chosen to act from a higher vibration. But what I could see now that was hiding from me back then, was that I still hadn't shown the willingness or the capacity to journey into fully meeting my sense of aloneness that night. I had been "doing" the letting go. It had still been a means to a desired outcome of things getting back to normality and of Gordon returning home. A letting go that smacked of positivity on the surface and in many ways *was* a lot more aware than the dysfunctional way I had been behaving up until then, but still was not true surrender. More a game I played with myself so that I might avoid having to face the farthest reaches of that fear in me.

Tonight's experience, including with the owl, had shown me something about back then: that in not meeting my sense of aloneness, I hadn't been free to be All of Love and to love with the freedom that Love does, or is. I hadn't known in my bones and in my soul that if Gordon had finished our relationship that night then I would still be this Aliveness, this Spaciousness, this Love that "I" really am. If I had, I would have realised these qualities are innate and so could never be "given" by anyone and nor, therefore, ever taken away. So, had I known these things or even had an experience of them on that night two years ago? I didn't feel that I had. And yet wasn't this the "larger truth" that the owl had led me to, that the breath had expanded in me and beyond me, that the darkness had cossetted tonight with love, and that naked and raw aloneness itself had bared? I stood for a few moments, staring out at the white boats huddling together below, a dot to dot picture, like the one in my heart that my lines of enquiry and insights were only now starting to join up.

There was, I realised, another irony to that day and night when I had felt such a sense of separation, and it was this: how much Gordon and I had still been connected, even within the disconnection of his pain and anger and absence, and even within my frustration and anxiety! It felt like provocation to consider it, yet my clarity now told me it was so. Though not the most resourceful way to experience connection, I had to admit that it *had* been there in the interplay of cause and effect within the dynamics of our relationship and our individual stories. It had pointed to itself in the compassion and remembering – once we got around to it – that everyone has a "heart" and Greatness. It had revealed itself through the thread of an abiding love for one another that had still been held by both of us somewhere underneath the flurry of comings and goings from our conditioned, fearful and "false" selves. And in spite of the physical disconnection at the time, connection had been our truth, not least because as souls we are always connected to all things through all time and space dimensions, we are not just our physical incarnations but also that boundless spirit which inhabits them.

We must meet aloneness in order to be the wisdom that we are never, and can never, be alone. We may experience the illusion of disconnection but as humans we are always powering the connection to something, whether it is to the direct moment of Now or to our concepts, to the heart or to the mind, to our innocence or our assumptions, to infinite Love and truth or to the story and behaviours that drive the dysfunction of our patterns. From a place of consciousness we can ask "what do we choose?" And though we may experience the illusion of disconnection, our "inherent" connection will stand firm and be so, regardless of circumstances.

Such paradoxes! Just like the fact that my mind was spinning and yet standing still in its alignment with my heart. I shivered. The temperature had dropped, the way it does when night and dawn meet and merge, arrive and take leave. Bringing out the blanket from inside the house, I pulled up one of the chairs and sat down, cocooning myself for warmth. Somehow, I needed to stay out here even though my bones ached with cold. I remembered the winter solstice, and that I had just experienced the longest night after the shortest day. It had felt like it too. Winter solstice: marking the point at which the sun reached the furthest it would go from the equator after so much ebbing presence, and the point before it turned back, when the days would become longer and the night times shorter. *This too shall pass.* Was there a possibility that yesterday Gordon had now gone as far out as he could and that he would also start turning back now? I twirled his ring around on my finger, allowing myself to open to the wondering and the potential. In silence, I prayed to the Universe and for the highest good of all, that if this included Gordon's return, of course I would be overjoyed to have him back in my arms, back in this life!

And then, I surrendered.

I don't know how long I sat there like that with eyes closed: my prayer riding out and away on the hint of the breeze; my stories and fears acknowledged and allowed to be without resistance; my vulnerability watched over with love by the trees and the darkness and the clouds and the water and the spirit I was that ran through it all; my humanity held in strength by the ever-presence and stillness. A message rose and fell from somewhere into nowhere: *We are all on the way Home. We are the Home we are returning to.*

When I finally reopened my eyes, it was to discover the hint of first light at the edge of the sky, rebirthing itself into the fading and tawny darkness that held it safe and secure. My feet were like blocks of ice as I listened across the bay. When had the Boobook stopped its calling? I had no idea. Hopping on feet of pins and needles, I let myself back into the house, snuggling down on the couch under the bedding again. Aching, nauseous tiredness called. The laptop showed 5.05 a.m. Although I was fragile from the huge journey the night had taken me on, I realised I was okay.

Sleep wasted no time and grabbed me.

Chapter Twenty-three

Day 6

6.00 a.m. – Home

I AWOKE AN HOUR OR SO LATER. There were messages waiting for me on the Journey Page. A sob made it up as far as my throat as I witnessed peoples' generosity of spirit and their acceptance of my vulnerability. Rather than my honesty being subjected to ridicule or rejection, I could see that it had been safe for me to express in the way I did. I realised too, that *I* had made it safe for me to express in that way, by giving myself permission to do so in the first place. Despite now emerging from that darkness and carrying the gold of my experience and insights, it still warmed my heart to see that people had been a phone-call away and they would have been there for me regardless of the time, even those whom I barely knew. Filled with appreciation, I read the last replies up to the end of the page.

> Eva: "scared" . . . when you said it just like that I got how honest it is. Where you've been would have scared an automaton. You are welcome to call me anytime I will message you my number. Xx

Donald: yes beautiful, I'm here, just on my way to the airport for 0600 flight. Will message you my number. Call me after 5 if you want to.

Sharon: Hey Caroline, I keep my phone by the bed. You know you can call me any time if you want talk and process. It is ok to be scared. That is just an emotion. It is guiding you back to love and surrender. Much love. Xx

Linda: Don't be afraid to call – we are here for you. Is there a pattern now of the time that you have trouble sleeping? We could probably create a list of people set to be available around 1 or 2 a.m. to call . . .

Bruce: I'm up but as I'm in the UK it is a few hours now since you wrote. You are both in my thoughts.

Rubbing the gratitude and bleariness from my eyes, I made a cup of tea and returned to the laptop to write a note of thanks before showering.

Update from me: Last night was like a long dark night of the soul, such a challenge. From 7 p.m. I felt my energy and spirit sag and I latched onto fear and hopelessness. I think I hit a wall. I have been in this bubble of intensity since Saturday. And I guess I just wanted to see some proof that we were heading somewhere better with things. Yesterday, I was attaching to the "Caroline" outcome, to the outcome of me needing Gordon to show more signs or evidence that he intends to come back even if it does take some days for him to do that return. But attaching to the lower outcome will always lead to suffering. I experience the suffering that results when I cannot control the outcome but want to. And I feel the suffering that arises when I believe I "need" the outcome to happen for me to be alright. Of course, I know that I am human and that I am having that experience here too, not just a spiritual one and so, yeah, I do need my man back! I long to see him open his eyes so that I can look into them again and so that he can look into mine and we can have that particular connection. I acknowledge that. The only way to transcend the suffering though, is to go for the higher outcome, choose whatever will serve the highest good of his soul, and look fear in the face and say, yes, he could pass, yes . . . and then sit in that pain and not fight that idea but accept it in my heart. But I struggled with that one for the majority of the night, having a powerful breakthrough only as dawn itself started to break through. For most of the night I felt such grief and aloneness. The fear of Gordon not wanting to come back and that I will be alone, without him. My sense is that before getting sick, his life had felt to him to be in a state of hopelessness and that he just didn't know how he could turn things around.

One of Gordon's patterns during times of stress between us was to go what I called "AWOL" for hours and not get in touch. It was everything I felt I could do just to get him to come back. I would ask and reason with him by text (the only way he would permit communication) and try to help him get out of his pattern that my pattern beforehand had tripped in him into. He would often say it all felt hopeless. That was the spiral he entered. Last night it felt like he was doing the ultimate and longest AWOL ever and that there was nothing I could do to get him to come back or to get him to say he is coming back. Of course the situation makes that an impossibility. Also, my pattern cannot play out like that anymore. It is easy for me to feel that there would be much for him to come back for. Truth is I don't know if he wants to do the journey. The invitation now, is for me to meet my aloneness and to stop powering the need for him to come home. Yes, acknowledge the need, but don't power from need. I had insight into this last night, about true allowing and surrender, and that I can sit in that now if I choose. I'm still processing that.

Patience. Gordon is my teacher again, on this and so many things. He has always been my most remarkable teacher, showing me another way of being, showing me who it is I really am, how it is I choose, and how I can re-choose to be in any given moment. This "showing" is what Love is, what Love does.

I have to keep acknowledging that I do not know the ultimate plan for Gordon or me. I cannot see the Big Picture. There is an irony to ICU in all this too. It appears as if the place is set up for the detail and the smaller picture in a way, what with all the machines and their readings. At any time I go in there I can have it in my face via a number on a screen, whether his blood pressure or his heart rate has gone in a direction that is wanted or unwanted. If the figure for blood pressure drops to 70, I consider it bad because someone had told me that they wanted to see it around 80 and above which was their need at the time. I went in there late last night and saw the lower number and asked if Gordon was struggling or not doing so well in the past hour. Dave, the nurse, asked me whether my question arose because of the lower number for blood pressure, to which I replied yes. He explained how not half an hour before he had experimented with lowering the dosage of Gordon's adrenalin to see how he might react to that . . . and that this will bring about a drop in blood pressure temporarily. His point to me was that I have to try to not fixate too much on the numbers on the screen even though the specialists do talk about those numbers a lot during the day. He said I must pull back a bit and focus on knowing that as far as their treatment is concerned, there is the bigger picture. It was so clear to me in that moment how we think we can know something based on what we are seeing and yet often, we only "see" something in its apparent separation or isolation. The truth is we cannot know everything about what we see and also, that nothing really exists in isolation or separation. It exists and is experienced in relationship to someone or something else. There is always a bigger picture, in this case what Dave was doing as part of the attempts to wean Gordon off support. But of course, the biggest picture of all is the Divine Plan that is rolling out, of which I nor any of us can ever know everything about, and for which even trying to come up with a "story" of what it might be, is madness.

I want to finish this post by thanking you for all your overwhelming support, care, love and generosity of spirit. You have touched me beyond measure with your offers of phone calls in the night and it buoys me to know you are so focused on healings. Can I please ask that any support you have for me, moving forwards, continue to be positive support. Please do not send me private messages or post comments to do with things about Gordon that you may have sensed from healings or tune-ins and that relate to how fearful you believe he is right now, or what he is going through right now or is musing at this time. I am feeling so raw at this juncture, and want to thank you for your understanding. With love. Xx

Though the tiredness from the night had set into my bones, I hurried with getting ready for the day. It had been like this every morning since it all began, wanting to be at the hospital for every minute I was allowed to be there. My shower had been more of a cat lick and now, in the kitchen, I put the last of my pots in soak, and snatched the remaining forkful of scrambled egg into my mouth. I hadn't wanted breakfast but I knew I must eat something. Eggs were the only thing in the fridge, the two this morning being the last of the carton Gordon had opened on Saturday. It was protein at least, and would keep me going.

I returned to the lounge, pausing to slump back down onto the couch and read the messages that had arrived in response to my post. Being able to take people's words with me into my heart as I returned to the hospital was something that helped to nourish my fortitude and courage, supported me in my refocusing. They were a gift and worth taking the minute or so to receive before I left the house for another day of the unknown.

> Kate: Caroline, reading your posts has been amazing. I knew you would be suffering but this makes it more real to me and so makes me look at my life and give Daz that extra hug and tell him I love him. We're both with you in spirit. Take care of you. Our love goes out to you both xx

> Claire: I can't even imagine how you are getting through all this. Every morning I eagerly get on here to see if you're ok and how Gordon is doing. You're an inspiration. Xx

> Grace: Remember, he allowed the text messages while he retreated to his dark space. He is still receiving your presence Caroline but allowing you to trust your heart. Sharing your angst and pain with us is freeing you for the heart work you and Gordon are doing together. Xx

> Nadia: Wow that is the journey I have been on in my loving relationship. I know I need to be different in this and to not "try."

Lindy: I was encouraged to read Pam's post that she could feel the healings even outside the healing times. It is gratifying to know that whenever I have a quiet moment to just hold both Gordon and Caroline in my heart that it is not in vain.

Francesca: When the 10 a.m. healing began I was whacking a balloon around the house with two of my kids and a furiously yapping dog. It was crazy, spontaneous and joyful. I saw this quote by Rumi this morning: "Dance, when you're broken open. Dance, if you've torn the bandage off. Dance in the middle of the fighting. Dance in your blood. Dance when you're perfectly free." I felt the dance in my blood, the dance and the song in my heart. So I danced round the bend, danced life. I saw Gordon smile and felt the great fortitude that lives within him. May we all remember to dance this life wherever we're at with it. Xx

Nicole: Today on a walk thru Noosa National park to honour Gordon's journey I saw something: when the whole expanse of the view – the ocean, rocks, and waves – is uninterrupted, it is somehow less beautiful than when it is obstructed and you catch glimpses of it through the trees – that's when I see the awe and beauty of all that it is. Kevin has often spoken about this but today I got it. I see that the obstructions in our lives allow us to see the great beauty in the world and that without it, it is too much to truly grasp, and not so appreciated. X

Ruth: Hi folks. Thought I would say a big thank you: for all the love, care and "wiggle room" you are all giving Caroline; for honouring Gordon's choice, no matter which path he chooses; for lending your energy to the highest good, rather than trying to force an outcome;

for the awareness and understanding of Caroline's space and not predicting anything; for being loving beings and a community with a massive heart; For being you . . . .and for showing up. Thank you.

Holly: As I joined in the 10 p.m. healing last night and allowed love to flow through me, I felt my own heart healing and wondered "who is this really for?" Though my conscious intention was to be part of Gordon's supporting team, I saw that I couldn't help but be healed by this action too. There is a deep truth in this about giving and receiving. All of us are learning it and all of us are learning to choose love.

Charlotte: At the 6 a.m. healing this morning I saw a huge masculine sun shining with fierceness onto Gordon and telling him that it is safe for him to step up and be that masculine warrior that he has in his heart. Whichever way he chooses, that sun is fierce within him.

CHAPTER TWENTY-FOUR

Day 6

7.40 a.m. – En route to hospital

DRIVING PAST THE BAY, I realised that today was the first time I had taken notice of it since Gordon had been in the car with me. Across the water, the sun yawned, stretching its arms out of slumber while the line-up of cars for the day had yet to come and park along the waterfront. A smattering of latte-drinking, newspaper-straightening locals were already toasting the day, while dog walkers re-enacted the lobbing of tennis balls for their pooches. It was the same old, same old. Except for me. I was no longer the same. Five days had changed me inside and out, the results catching me by surprise when I had glanced at the reddened eyes and pallor of the stranger in the mirror after my shower. Last night had been off the charts. There was no denying that the extraordinary continued to take place in my world and that it was something I could not back out of even if I had wanted to or had been offered the chance. More than this, I sensed that it was something that now asked for my total *awake-ness*, my complete participation, and my willingness to contribute my insights and experiences for the benefit of the whole.

The car struggled and protested under my acceleration. I eased off, allowing the engine to take the effort and pull me up the hill and out of the shire. Although I didn't know what the day would have in store, compared to Saturday I was at least much savvier about the world into which I was now returning. No longer the one who didn't have a clue and had held her husband's hand during a "routine-procedure", I was now something of a veteran of ICU, a battle-scarred wife who had been forced to witness traumas involving the love of her life that no person would ever want to see. And as for the events of the night, they had gifted me with a conviction about two things: it is in the darkest seeing that our eyes open the widest, and it is in the facing of our biggest fear that our heart expands beyond all previous limitations.

The recall that had jumped in the car with me this morning was that of waking up within a strange "dream". There was a sense that there was no need to put my efforts into fixing the "dream" – the "reality" that I perceived and interpreted through my fear – or into bettering it as such, or even into trying to outrun the dream from within it in a bid for avoidance. Rather, all I had to do was wake up inside the dream, know it as a dream, and stay awake to that. That had been the message in the void and the owl had led me to a profound experience of it. I didn't have to fix or suppress or try to run away from the fears. I only had to acknowledge them and meet them fully. In doing so, I could bring heaven to earth and experience who I really am, *be* that awake-ness. What irony that every night so far, I had fought to literally stay awake on my couch, not allowing myself to close my eyes and snooze for fear of what I might meet in my dreams, and yet all the while not computing that by powering that fear and taking action from the place of believing it to be the truth, I was *already* asleep within the biggest "dream" of all: the dream of my fear. It was the dream of all the perceptions I held about my world that caused me to experience separation, and of what I believed these perceptions meant for me about my viability, safety, security and survival, with or without Gordon's return. Perhaps it's the case that we are here to open our eyes through opening our hearts, and to open our hearts through opening our eyes. My experience seemed to be bearing out the theory.

In the minute it took for the car to zip right past them, the shimmer of the yellow wattle bushes that edged the National Park flashed and grabbed my attention, their burst of radiance and aliveness trailblazing a message across the windscreen and my heart. Fear had not been able to see them these last mornings but, in an instant, I realised that the life force that ran through them as bushes, and through the bird as owl, was the same life force running through "me" as Caroline. It was the force from last night, the one that is always there, always holding, always connecting form. And what of the flames in today's sunrise, such similarity with the skies from the morning before! They had been the only dawns like it that I had been aware of since my world had changed. It made me realise that after the events of the night, I could either consume myself with trying to seek Gordon in his body on the bed, or I could accept instead that his ultimate essence *is* what flows through all manifested things, even that it *is* the space from which these all come and to which they return to. I could connect with the truth of him in these wattles, or in the sunrise from this morning, or even in myself as Caroline driving the car. In fact, these other manifestations and expressions of his ultimate essence were perhaps easier places in which to discover and connect with his truth than a puffed-up body had been, a body that was punctured by drips and drains, obscured by a scramble of wires, and overlaid by the mechanics of bips and beeps.

My gut clamped again and the moment of illumination in my heart was snuffed out. I sighed. Somehow there had been an ease with all this during the window of grace that had seemed to open with the owl. Darkening my mood now, though, was the understanding that whilst ultimate essence was Gordon's truth, I just wanted the man. After all, as "the man" was how I had mostly experienced and related to him during our lives together – Gordon as his body, his set of preferences, loves and dislikes, and passions and gifts. *That* had been Gordon to me. I wasn't used to communing with him as ultimate essence that had formed itself into his character and then flowed through that manifestation, animating and enlivening it every day. I wondered who, of any of us, related with our loved ones in this way all the time or at all. Perhaps none of us do until we are opened up to it and invited to do just that.

Time for the zigzag down. Not long now. I had reached the first of four hairpin bends that would see me exit my boundaries and set me onto the road towards the hospital. The car hugged the tarmac into the swerves as a notion veered across my mind. There was something about Gordon hanging on for all this time that seemed to be taking us into a new phase. Each day that he remained with us was a vote for his chances of recovery, yet each day that his condition remained critical or unchanged raised the stakes that he could transition. Whatever it had taken me to get to this point, I did sense that from now on I would need to be bolder in my courage. Courage the way the French understood it by their word for it: *le coeur*, heart, taking action from an open-heart. It was as if those sweeps in the sunrise had been there today to summons me into actions and stances that were needing that temerity and that degree of fearlessness through Love, to wake up from within the "dream" and be an embodiment of that courage and open-heartedness I had drawn upon within myself last night.

Already I was on the third bend. It had been right here, on Saturday, where I'd had that rush of desire to make love to Gordon. What was it that I had "known" then but that I hadn't been consciously able or allowed to see? Even now I remembered the "oddness" of that moment. Were we always going on this ride? All I knew was that by being on it, I had been learning so much about unconditional Love, the Love that exists before and outside of the agendas of personality. Love as life force, and Love as true creative power.

After the insights during the night, I had convinced myself that I must now take the gold from it with me into the hospital and be this change. A doubt in my head nagged that I wouldn't succeed. How could one night combat over forty years of conditioning of being asleep within my dream and asleep to my fear and perceptions? Not to mention while I was still here on earth as a *woman*, a wife who yearned for the return of her man, who pined for him, and who bore an ache for him in her belly and womb and breasts as hot as the earth's molten core? *It's okay. You are allowed to feel desire, you know! You are allowed to fear. But the fearful thoughts say nothing true about your real capacity. Remember: le couer.* I exhaled. Negotiating the last bend of the hill, I wound my window down. Life rushed in to greet me with its swirl of coolness, echoes of birdsong, dankness of forest, and succession of whooshing engines encased in metal – all of it a marvel, all of it enlivened and animated by the same force.

Fifteen minutes later I was making my way down the corridors to my man and to the news that lay waiting for me.

CHAPTER TWENTY-FIVE

Day 6

8.15 a.m. – Hospital

IT HAD BEEN TEN MINUTES NOW. My alarm bells were still ringing. *What did she mean by "attending"? What's wrong with him?* I kept replaying the scene with the new nurse, the way she had stood at the entrance to ICU when I had arrived, her tone as she had announced that I couldn't come in to see Gordon yet because they were "attending to some things with him." To my frustration, she had displayed no willingness to provide details and had sent me back here, to wait. It hadn't seemed to take much to set me off again. I'd allowed the appearance of this stranger and my rampant mind to unnerve me.

The facts, for Pete's sake! Caroline, stay with the facts. Drop the telling of anything that is not a fact. I began the recap. When I had left Gordon last night, Dave had rejoiced at the improvements since the previous nightshift. Gordon had been taken off of two medications and his body was now doing its job, plus there had been a reduction in the dosage of another drug whilst he made up for the deficit himself. There was a hint of an upswing with his kidneys and with the sepsis. It was, as Dave had said, a process of edging forwards and though Gordon was critical and it was going to take time to get to the point of being able to wake him up, we were at least crawling and in the right direction. All Gordon had to do was hang on in there.

I exhaled. Facts aside, I wondered if the gains were a hint that Gordon's will maybe *was* in this now, that he or his soul was leaning towards choosing to return to his body. The thought delivered me right into wanting him back and into wanting to control any flashes of hope in case they led to tears about an opposite scenario being the truth. I still felt daunted, aware of my terror. But there was gratitude too, since each day was another day I had been gifted to encourage his heart, to kiss him, touch him, smell him and talk to him, and sometimes see him "respond" in some way.

Further down the corridor, footsteps hurried on the squeaky floor and disappeared. A man cheerfully shouted out that he would return the file when he came back. A door slammed, releasing its jailhouse echo all the way up to me as I shifted in my chair. The noises vanished into the silence from which they had emerged. I swallowed, the sound reverberating in my ears.

I never imagined that my life circumstances would find themselves here: enmeshed in this hospital; tied up in my coming here day after day, pushing the boundaries of when I could arrive and leave; dividing my time between the confines of the room in which Gordon lay and this room here, the size of a handkerchief where I sat and waited, fed by a few friends who brought vats of homemade soup and loaves of sourdough. Here we were, both Gordon and I, in our cocoons – mine with a clock on the wall marking white-rabbit, earthly time and Gordon's room without one at all, inviting the timelessness of Spirit.

"See my face?"

I was snapped back to the here and now by the tone of somebody who sounded like they would burst if they didn't share their secret. It was Christine, the hospital manager, balancing a box of heavy files in in the crook of one arm while her thumb and finger on the other hand secured a cardboard holder of takeaway coffees.

"See my face?" she said again, beaming. "There's been a turning point overnight. We're thrilled!"

"Seriously?"

"Yes! Seriously! Now, not to worry, Dr Brentwood is coming to brief you, okay?"

And with that, she clipped away down the corridor, leaving me with a fluttering in my chest.

As if his ears had been burning at the mention of his name, Dr Brentwood breezed into the room, parking himself up against the sink. Brentwood, the Grim Reaper. Brentwood, the intense Intensivist, who hadn't smiled once in the unravelling of this whole ordeal. Brentwood, the bearer of news you invariably didn't want to hear. Brentwood, now standing there before me with a spirited flush to his cheeks and a smile so wide that it invited me to smile too, as a whirling dervish of excitement and anticipation took to the floor inside my chest.

"Well, there's been a significant boost in Gordon overnight, Caroline. I'm starting to think your husband could actually make it. He could well pull through this!"

YES! YES! YES! I pressed my fingertips against one another as if I were in a strength contest of my own making, bringing them to my mouth, my breath backed up in my throat because I didn't want to release it into the space he had left at the end of his proclamation, willing that he should fill it with more positivity, more hope, more boldness, more reasons for us to smile.

As if he understood me, Brentwood continued, "Yes well, this department has only ever had one person on maximum life support. That person died, didn't make it through the night. And when we raced Gordon from Coronary Care to ICU, he had a 0.5% chance of survival. He could have died at any point in that first hour it took us to stabilise him. Once we did steady him, he had around a 1% chance of getting through the night. He's remained at a 1% chance of survival. Then, 48 hours ago, he went up to a 2 to 4% chance of survival. This morning though, I'm pleased to say that he's now sitting at around a 30% chance of coming out of this with his life. So he needs to keep hanging in there and then, yes, if things continue to resolve at a good rate . . . Yes, he could just pull through."

"Oh my God! I don't . . . I can't believe it. How does . . . ? I mean, what you are saying, is it true? I mean, Oh my God! That's incredible!"

"You have cause to smile, Caroline. This is now what we would call positive news! Your husband is on ten times less medication in 24 hours than he has ever been, and on a third of the drugs he was on 48 hours ago. Of course, the amounts would kill you or me, but it is keeping *him* alive at this stage."

"I don't know what to say!"

"Now, you need to keep the physical touch going with him, and keep talking to him. These things are of huge importance and it has been fantastic to see that Gordon has had so much of this from you and others. So please keep it up. What else . . . ? Yes, the sepsis. We have seen improvement with it but we still haven't managed to figure out what strain of bacteria is causing the ongoing pneumonia, if indeed it's not viral. That is delaying our understanding of the way to treat it I'm afraid, which is still a concern. Despite the gains today, Gordon is still hanging by a thread. I must stress that. He remains on a massive amount of life support and we are still only creeping forwards on our bellies here. The gains simply point to the fact there *is* movement and it is *forward.*"

He paused, and I watched his lips moving again but this time the words weren't filtering through to me. As he departed, my inner world was reeling, somersaulting with sheer joy at the news of hope; spinning from the learning that Gordon had already defied the odds of death; teetering from hearing those statistics for the first time; and revolving as if I were caught inside a boat that had barrel-rolled, with everything it once housed in shelves and cupboards now spewed out in chaos and confusion. The numbers had disoriented me the most. It was one thing all this time to have known that Gordon was "hanging by a thread" and "critically ill" and yet another entirely to put percentages to those phrases. The statistics sounded so much more horrifying than the vernacular. At least with hanging by a thread, I'd thought at the time that there was still a slither of a chance, and that there was at least a thread and he was at least dangling from it. Yet with "0.5%", all I could hear now was how much likelihood there had been that he would have died. It drove home to me, like never before, where we had been and from where we had journeyed. And yet hadn't the truth been that the language of love hadn't cared for numbers, nor had been swayed by them?

Gordon could just make it. That's what he said. I sighed, long and loud. The initial shock over, my boat had come to rest. I was humbled by the enormity of how far Gordon had come, how far we had *all* come. Feeling for his ring on my finger I twiddled it around again. Had he – or his soul – chosen to return to the Gordon experience? Had he learned things where he had been during these past few days? If there was a "review" taking place in some other realm, had it reached completion now and was it time to bring those learnings back into this world? I couldn't be sure. But the signs pointed to Gordon coming back to earth.

With excitement propelling my legs down to the entrance of the hospital, I went to ring through an update to Ruth for the Journey Page, and to call the boys, who would be in later.

I had calmed myself by the afternoon. Back in Gordon's room, I put on a Gurrumul CD and sat stroking Gordon's hand. I wondered if he was listening. I felt sure he had responded the moment the song had started, his head inclining a centimetre in the direction of the stereo. All I knew was that it flung my heart wide open to hear this man's voice. Over the hours that I had been playing it, it had steadied me and helped me to ground after the excitement of the news from the morning. A gentleness emanating from the end of the bed now brought me out of my trance.

"May I ask, what is this music?"

I looked up. It was Sarah, her eyes glistening. She smiled and repeated the question, pointing to the stereo.

"The music? It's by someone called Gurrumul. You like it?"

"I do, it's . . . I don't know . . . beautiful."

"I know, I think so too. I'm playing it for Gordon, he loves it. This always took him right back to his heart, to his connection with the land and the indigenous people, and to what he loves. The artist is an Aboriginal man. He was born blind but has the most extraordinary gift in his vocals, don't you think? There's something about him and his spirit, something about Aboriginal language for me and how it sounds. The softness, you know? Although there are words being sung, they bypass the mind that can't understand them, and so all that's left is the energy and vibration of the harmony. For me, his voice is pure love."

She nodded, clearly moved by the music. I observed her for a second, surprised to see that on her robust finger she was wearing a wedding band, a simple and honest one at that. It struck me that I had never noticed the woman underneath the nurse. I felt drawn to connect with her as a person. I continued chatting, bursting into the importance of living our truth day to day, about being who we came here to be, about my and Gordon's journey to date – where we had powered that truth and where we had sabotaged it. As the boundaries between her and I slipped away, she revealed she had a huge family that she loved and lived for and grandchildren who filled up her heart with blessings and joy. She showed me their faces and I took Gordon's phone out of my pocket and shared the photos of his art. She marvelled at them, and stared at Gordon.

"You know I have to admit we are trained to see him as an ICU patient. But it's wonderful to have this window into the 'man' and his 'other' heart. Thank you."

Tears of gratitude brimmed in my eyes as I received the gift of our exchange. The message was clear: feeling another through the heart-space dissolves the barriers that prevent deeper connection, and breaks down the labels and definitions that dictate how we must see and therefore behave. It fired my heart that Sarah had connected anew with Gordon, and with a deeper sense of shared humanity. In a moment of epiphany, I understood. We had just experienced another case of "I see you" happening in ICU! I shivered at the magic of it.

Ed greeted me with an unusually warm smile when I returned about an hour later. Like Sarah, he commented on the beauty of the music and enquired after the artist. Though I couldn't put my finger on it, it felt like there was more of Ed in the room, more of his energy than I had experienced to date. I told him about the connection between Gurrumul and Gordon. He lingered, engaging me in more conversation. Sharing with him as I had with Sarah, I felt moved to ask about his own heart and what it loved. With just Gordon and me in the room, he began to talk of his fears and self-doubt around whether he could make a living out of his passion for photography. He even revealed an idea he was incubating – a message he had for humanity concerning the preciousness of life, one that he wanted to express using black and white photos from ICU, without the people's faces. I was humbled by the tales he told of what working in ICU had shown him about life over the years, and by the depth of his wisdom. And all the while, Gurrumul sang, a sound so expressive of the highest vibration, that it was capable of being the bridge that could connect us to this shared humanity and divinity.

"Life is short," Ed murmured, looking at Gordon. "It is a treasure, a gift in every moment. And if we could truly come from that place of knowing this, we would argue less with each other and create all manner of second chances for ourselves."

"You speak the truth, Ed."

"Caroline, my work in ICU calls for the preservation and sanctity of life. It calls for calmness and presence. Because of this I find those same qualities spilling over into my life away from ICU, and in my connections with other people too. So you see it's a challenge for me to get angry with others. Not only that, I am constantly aware that when faced with a problem, there is always a solution that can be sought, a possibility, a chance. You know why I say that? Because that is the attitude we take on a daily basis here in ICU."

Now I comprehended why Ed had spoken so little during that day when Gordon's temperature had been raging. It had been as hard for him to get flustered or join me in the space of my spiral, as it was for him to get angry or stressed. Instead, he had been searching in silence for a possibility, holding open the chance, being calm in service to the solution. I looked at him with renewed respect.

We continued to share and as Ed contemplated how to claim his heart out in the world, he asked me – with my background in coaching – tentative questions about how to do that, and how to manage the fear that arose in him about it. In a moment of heightened awareness, I saw the perfection that was the co-creation of all of us in that room. The way that Gordon was serving as he lay there in coma, providing the perfect opportunity for Ed to see himself, just as we had all seen ourselves; the way I was serving as I asked the questions that took Ed more into his heart and into what he would love to create in the world; the way that Ed and I were serving Gordon, should a part of him have been listening to the nature of our conversation at the foot of his bed; and the way that Gurrumul and his music was serving the whole, with no conscious awareness of the effect his heart was having on all of ours in this moment. We were all inter-connected. Blown away by the obviousness and is-ness of it all, I was deeply moved. I realised that in every moment Life gives us the people and the opportunities and the ability to claim our truth wherever we are. And that sometimes, "wherever we are" can turn out to be a "cocoon", a tiny ICU room in which these alignments and transformations take place.

Later, the nurses noticed after washing Gordon that despite his body responding with the usual stress signals of a drop in oxygen and blood pressure, the response hadn't endured. Ed wondered if the music had been part of the reason for that change. Instinct told me it was, and that maybe it was also as a result of what we had been speaking about. Maybe Gordon was listening, taking it in, and receiving a droplet of life-saving elixir.

Charles left after the 10 p.m. healing. He had taken time away from his family again, just as he had most nights so far to participate in person. Seeing him stride off had been a wrench. The last of all the visitors for the day. He was like the big brother I had never had. I sat back into the quietness of Gordon's room.

It had been a busy evening. Jim, Steve and their girlfriends had left for the airport. There was uncertainty as to when they could come back and so we hugged and I wished them a safe trip, promising to call them if anything major happened. Christine had dropped in again and noted that the changes with Gordon were "fascinating". Dr Brentwood also reappeared, declaring that today had seen a "remarkable improvement". The murmurs of excitement from them both did much to raise my spirits, though Dr Brentwood had also balanced his comment with, "We're not out of the woods yet. I've seen patients do little rallies like this before but it still doesn't mean anything." At around 6.30 p.m., Ruth and Larry had visited. Ruth looked drawn, her blonde hair strained into a ponytail, and a black baseball cap pulled down over her forehead. I knew that to have arrived by the time she did would have required a quick change out of corporate gear and into jeans and jumper, and I appreciated her effort. Like Charles and Rebecca, she had family that needed her too. I felt gratitude for the friendship and love I was receiving, but also happiness that they had picked such a magical night to visit. Standing and looking at Gordon, we were all in agreement that it felt like a miracle was taking place. There was a peacefulness and even aliveness to his appearance. His toes were pink again, life force inhabited his cheeks, and his hair was fluffy and soft. All the stress seemed to have gone from his face. There was something unexpected in these changes and when Ruth and Larry went home, it was with a smile.

"Time to get everything shipshape!"

I looked up to see Dave, all trimmed goatee and bright eyes as he came in to change Gordon's drip, his neat fingernails and smooth hands swapping over the bags. He had been on every nightshift for Gordon. I felt a confidence when he was at the helm and it helped me to leave and go back to the house when my time was up.

"I'm trying Gordon tonight without the ventilator on full. So, he has to instigate the breath himself and then the machine helps give that breath a good push out."

"Right, okay."

"It's something we like to get coma patients doing as soon as possible, because like any muscle, the lungs can get lazy if not used. He's managing it okay so far."

"Well I'll take that as good news."

"I'll tell you something else, if you like." He turned to look me in the eye, lowering his voice. "In all my years in ICU, I have never seen a patient being given as much adrenalin as Gordon has been given. I mean, he needs it, to maintain blood pressure. But it has a very negative and dangerous consequence in that it creates acidosis. It makes the body too acidic. What I'm trying to say, is that the levels of acidosis in Gordon's body should be through the roof right now, dangerously high. But Gordon has no acidosis."

"*None?*"

"None at all."

"But . . . what does that mean?"

"It means that it defies explanation. That it makes no sense at all."

CHAPTER TWENTY-SIX

Day 6

11.55 p.m. – Home

ALL I COULD THINK OF on the way home was that Gordon must have unseen help. Dave had not gone as far as to say that, yet what other conclusion could there be when something was said to defy explanation? By the time I landed back on my couch, it was all I could do to try to remain in the not knowing. The flood of excitement from those on the Journey Page who had been following my updates on Gordon's increased chances of surviving now pumped my own adrenalin further. Reading through the shares was like a celebration in itself, an acknowledgement of how far we had come, a willingness to embrace the notion of magic. I rolled the cursor down the page. It was going to be a while again before I slept tonight.

> Holly: Gordon, you are amazing! Caroline, you are also amazing also! I am overjoyed to hear this. I continue to send my love regularly throughout the day and during the healing times.

Owen: Love is the Greatest.

Margaret: Such proof of the power of Gordon's healing capabilities and the power of magic and of our connection to each other and to Source. Modern medicine is of course playing its huge part but we are witnessing miracles, thank you Gordon!

Ruth: I am aware of something greater, in a large way right now. And I'm acutely aware of the power of love and that saying YES to what is true (no matter what), is all that we need to do. In my heart I am grateful, in awe, and experiencing such love for the nature of being human. Caroline, I love you, I love your heart and I love your courage. And Gordon is one brave and delicious man. No wonder you two are taking this journey together. Xx

Cindy: I have tears of joy as I read your words Caroline. It is honouring to walk alongside you both on this part of your journeys. We are witnessing a higher force at play with two beautiful souls reminding us that possibilities are endless when unconditional love vibrates en masse. I am with you constantly. Time to wake up Gordy!

Lauren: Who can ever be the same after a journey such as this Caroline! Even though we are on the sidelines we hold our breath and sigh with relief with each new update, let's hope for more good news like this. X

Jessica: Small steps breath by breath, wow! It's such positive news. I feel like we can breathe a little easier too now. Hugs Xxx

Lorraine: I read the messages being posted daily and I think, with all this love and support, there's no way Gordon could NOT be improving!

Chapter Twenty-seven

Day 7

6.00 a.m. – Home

STANDING UNDER THE SHOWER, I tried to let the hot water pummel and steam away my tension. It had been another night of restlessness. Still spinning from the news about the lack of acidosis, I only teetered on the edges of trusting that Gordon could pull through. The news whooped at me that all was not as I thought or feared, and that much good was happening here. But still, I was jittery. I had woken this morning recalling Dr Brentwood's caution that "we're not out of the woods yet" and that, inevitably, this ride was going to be a rollercoaster with more ups and downs before we reached any finish-line. Last night I had been able to keep a distance from his view and tell myself that past performances of other patients were not an indication of what will happen for Gordon. Yet my experiences had taught me not to assume anything and that all I did know was I had to continue to choose the highest good, remain in the not-knowing, and keep a dash of hope.

I lathered up the sponge and slowly washed. If all went well today, there would be much stroking of Gordon again from me. I'd spent an incredible amount of time sitting at his left side since his coma, cupping his hand, stroking his forehead, smoothing my fingers over the blankets covering his legs. Through that, I had come to learn what intensity there could be when stroking someone, when you were so focused on "being" the stroking. From that space, it wasn't about me or what I received out of it because at that moment of being the stroking itself, there never felt like there was any "me" – there was no "stroker" or even "one who was being stroked", there was just "the stroking". Yes, it always started off with a sense of me and my concerns and my worries, but then I would switch my focus to Gordon, and there would be an incredible desire to be in presence with him. Yet the more I immersed myself in becoming the simplicity of stroking and lost myself to the rhythm of that, somehow the more the sense of "me" and of "him" would disappear. That would be when stroking became the bridge, where "we" would seem to meet as "one". If you could become "touch" itself, rather than stay identified with yourself as "the one who touches", then you would have slipped through a crack in the wall, slipped beyond form, merged with the limitlessness of Love. Gordon understood this, he had known this. Only now did I realise that he became "one" with the stroking when stroking *me*. He had desired touch from me – that was his language in love, far more than being told he was loved. He knew the "portal" of touch. What a wise man. He was continuing to teach me, it seemed.

Still mulling things over, I turned off the tap and grabbed my towel to rub down. For the past couple of days there had been more of that "sensation" happening in the space over Gordon's feet again, a sense of him wriggling his toes. It struck me now, how much time I had spent standing or sitting at his feet since he was in coma too. I had either found myself being of service there and massaging them; being in shame there and weeping; being in sorrow there and aching; being in surrender there and aware; or being in song there and humming. But the more I had stood there and been present to all of him, the more I had re-experienced and discovered the gorgeousness of him on a new level. What a profound journey it had been! Especially for those first days when he had been pumped up like a sumo wrestler and his face and hands were hardly recognisable as Gordon. It hadn't mattered. I had somehow still been able to see right past all of that, past all the tubes and the ugliness of how it is to be in coma and hanging by a thread, to see his gorgeousness inside and out.

In a rush of understanding I realised these breakthroughs had come about because I was *seeing* Gordon, not just looking at him. To look at him was to only view the carnage. I had wasted so much time just looking at him in recent years. Looking at him (and us) through the carnage of what had transpired between us, through the drama and chaos and trauma of what unfolded - the "filter" through which I had viewed everything. Too busy, during that time, with looking at him through my hurt and grief and anger, through my story of me as the wife who had suffered betrayal and deceit and denial and who had been thwarted. Too busy looking at him through my pain of the husband who had broken trust and who had failed to protect and keep safe the person he loved and cared for. Far too much preoccupation with spending the last three years looking at him through my deepest fears, viewing him as too old, too spineless, too stressed, too unhealthy – whatever it was, it was always "less this" or "more that" or too much of something else undesirable. On top of this, I had spent too much time being in fear of those definitions I had assigned him. I was only able to receive the experience of him that these labels and blinkers had inevitably led me to.

The irony – and the wonder – wasn't lost on me, that despite all the tubes, drips, pumps and ugliness, he appeared more gorgeous to me now than he had done in ages – back to the attractiveness even, of our first years together. During the healings so far in the hospital, he even seemed to radiate. I was sure that he was absorbing the love and light coming his way and that the excess was bouncing off him. But it was something else too. It was because I was seeing his Greatness. Sometimes it had been evoked by the music that played or by what he was "showing me" when I closed my eyes, and at other times it was because I had simply chosen to see him from that perspective. *Greatness is Truth.* Yes. It's not some mushy romantic way of looking at someone. It is a way of seeing them so that you see what is true about them. And it is grounded in the ability to also see, accept and embrace that person's "story" and childhood wounds, as well as their heart or their essence. To see all of that is to see and be able to "receive" all of that wondrous Being who is laid out before you. There is enormous beauty to behold when you do that. There is freedom when you are Love like that.

I had seen Gordon from his Greatness before. But the busyness, the worries and concerns and survival tendencies of the day-to-day, and the habits and patterns of being on auto-pilot and wanting to come from addictive stories and ideas about who a person was, well, they do take over. I had *let* them take over, allowed them to stop me from seeing with awareness more of the time. His coma was gifting me more time to not just look at him, but see him. And what I saw was a Divine Human and the Human Divine. I saw a peaceful warrior, a man of ancient wisdom, a man of the land whose feet were rooted in the core of Mother Earth. I saw his wounds and frailties, I saw the gentleness and humility of his soul, and it was something I wanted to celebrate and appreciate, not change! I saw everything and he was transforming before my eyes.

I smiled. I had fallen in love again, the romance and attachment and wonderful ordinariness of human love. At the same time, I felt like I was being opened to the grace of what unconditional, infinite Love is like – something transcending attachment, beyond words and over and above the expression of bodies. It expanded my heart in incalculable ways.

I arrived at the hospital to more blessings. There had been momentum overnight and Robert began shooting off the list of changes. Gordon had come off the third of five medications he had been on for blood pressure. His oxygen needs were down to just 30% instead of the range of between 60% and 100%. The pneumonia had nudged again in the direction of clearing, helped by the general antibiotics he had been on, though they had not yet been able to grow a culture in the lab to know if there could be a more specific antibiotic to give him. His sepsis had cleared slightly. His sedative was also down from the level of 24 just 48 hours before, to a level now of 4.

Overjoyed and with tears brimming as I clutched at my throat, I walked over to Gordon. A slither of iris peeked through the watery slit of his eyelids. Robert told me Gordon wasn't seeing anything much but I didn't care.

"Oh my God, Gordon, I love you so much! You are one strong man!"

"He has been coughing, so try not to startle when you hear it." I looked up, hadn't clocked the other nurse when I'd entered. "It's an indicator that he has awareness of the tube and that he is not tolerating it. It's a good sign. But please, you have to understand, he is still critically unwell. We have a long way to go."

I nodded. I felt like that phrase had been branded in my psyche. But for the rest of the day, it didn't drag me down.

CHAPTER TWENTY-EIGHT

Day 8

3.00 a.m. – Home and hospital

SOMEBODY, PLEASE HELP ME! My heart pounded. Panic coursed through my veins. To my horror, my teeth continued to crumble and fall out of their gum sockets, bit by bit, one by one. I was powerless to stop it happening. There was no pain, only a spongy mass of crimson gunk. All I could do was continue to spit out the lot, while hysteria and anxiety wrangled with each other in my throat.

I woke with a start, listening to the sound of my own panting, T-shirt drenched in sweat. *Oh my God – the dream. It came back. Where am I? Home. I'm at home.* I checked my teeth, a force of habit. They were all there. I switched the light on and leaned back in the couch. It was 3 a.m.

Now and again during my life, I had experienced vivid dreams about my teeth, nightmares to do with losing my teeth in a way that was out of my control. This one was as grotesque as all the others but I felt spooked it had chosen now to put in an appearance.

I knew only too well that these dreams denoted one thing for me and one thing only: they occurred just before I would learn of a hefty decision I would have to make or one that I would feel out of my depth to make. The dream left me swallowing the jittery bile back down my throat. I had a sense of foreboding that something colossal lay ahead, a decision I'd need to make that would require boldness. *What decision?* The thought nagged at me, hooking its claws into my skin, a mighty bird of prey descended for the kill. In being only too willing to let it drag me away, I had now rendered myself unavailable to my intuition, intuition that may have been able to inform me further.

I couldn't get back to sleep. I knew something was coming. I just didn't know what or when. By 6 a.m. I was up and showered for the day, feeling as if a truck had run me over. God-light shafted through the windows and landed across the amber floorboards, illuminating dust and stray hairs, and transmuting chaos into golden, mystical glitter. I played the video clip that Rebecca had posted for me online – The Beatles, "Love is All You Need". Someone else had posted the clip for "Stand by Me". So many comments and well-wishes were written underneath. It took half an hour to read them all before switching off the computer and leaving for the day, my cheeks wet as once again I allowed myself to receive the love and support here for us both.

I slowed my pace to something just shy of a tiptoe as I crossed the threshold of Gordon's room. In an instant, my breath locked in. There had been a change, I could sense and see it in the busyness of Sarah's movements and those of her assistant as they hemmed in close to Gordon. Blocking my view from the door as they worked, all I could experience was the sound of his coughing, a dreadful hacking, the volume of which seemed to increase as the sputum shunted back into the tube coming out of his mouth.

"What's happening?" I made it over to my usual spot at the left side of the bed. Gordon's eyes were a slit. He did not and could not register me as yet.

"Gordon, we're going to have to clear out your lungs and tube again, okay? It will make you more comfortable."

I cringed, unable to control my reaction. I had seen them do this for a couple of days now but still hated to see it. To clear out the sputum in his chest, they fed another, thinner tube through the existing one going down his throat. By the time this arrived into the lungs, it agitated the area, causing the cough to bring up the sputum, which they would then suck out by pulling back the inner tube. Gordon scrunched his forehead and rolled his head away on the pillow as the noise of the sluicing soon followed, a wet and loose rattling not too dissimilar to the death rattles I had heard minutes before he had crashed. Every muscle in my body tensed up. Sarah turned to me.

"Gordon had difficulties in the night." She knew I didn't want bullshitting though somehow she managed to never sound like Brentwood. The unwavering hold of her eyes on me gave cause for concern. "Well actually, to be more precise, he had a bit of a setback."

Setback. My back went rigid, my pulse jumped into my throat. For a crazy moment I hoped I didn't look like a frog. Before I could speak, Sarah cut in.

"Well, okay, so here's the thing. We brought him out of coma in the early hours, but he wasn't awake enough to be able to comply with our instructions about his tube. There was some agitation from him, then lots of panic and distress. So we had to sedate him again, take him back under – not as much as when we first put him in coma, as you can see, but still, not as light as what he had been. The coughing, which is normal, has been unhelpful because each time he is agitated by the tube and coughs it affects his situation with the dialysis machine and it drops his blood pressure, neither of which we want." She paused, as the younger nurse read out a figure to which she nodded, turned back to me, and continued. "Our issue with this setback is that we do need to remove the tube from his mouth. He's had it in for a long time now. We don't like to keep them in for more than ten days or so as it increases the risk of pneumonia, and we don't need his existing pneumonia to worsen. The tube also makes his body a magnet for other infections too. So what this all means is that we are going to perform a tracheostomy on him in the next hour."

"A tracheostomy? What's that?" This was a change I wasn't ready for and the idea of them "performing" anything on Gordon at this stage made the battalion of hairs on my arm stand in line, braced for conflict.

"It's where we remove the tube going into his mouth. We'll make a small incision at the base of his throat near his voice box and use that opening to direct the ventilator tube and its oxygen right down into his lungs. There is risk, as there is with anything we do at this stage, but we believe the rewards outweigh all of that. And the opening gets covered of course, with plastic. It also means we will be able to try bringing him out of coma again, only this time he won't have the intrusion in his mouth and down his windpipe that freaked him out. The tracheostomy will be an improvement for him. He'll experience more comfort and we will be able to move him onto his side and manage him better on the bed than we've been able to up until now. And down the track, when we end up taking it out, the incision will heal over and only leaves a small scar."

"Right . . ."

"Other than that, there have been no gains with the kidneys and so he's still going to need to remain on dialysis. He did move his bowels in the night and I want to stimulate this more, it's crucial. So this morning, I want you to massage that acupressure point I showed you yesterday, okay? And we will get things ready for the procedure." She paused, looking me straight in the eye again. "Hey, in cases like your husband's, progress is never an upwards trajectory, there will be setbacks and plateaus before advancement begins again. Last night was a setback but he has been responding well these past three days so we can't ignore that – it's a positive. And *you* need to keep the positivity going too." With that she smiled and walked out, leaving me to watch Gordon through a briny film that threatened to come between us.

Life is change. I knew this. They were trying to bring him out of coma, Sarah had said. At least he was more conscious than when they first induced him. Isn't this what I wanted? Gordon out of coma? *Of course it was.* But nothing had prepared me for what this journey out of coma would be like and the shock of how unsettled I felt by it. It wasn't like they depicted it in the movies. My man was in discomfort and fear, as anybody would be in not understanding or knowing what was going on. The only gifts I had to give for the next hour were massages to his feet and his acupressure points, stroking his forehead and cheeks and arms, and speaking words that soothed, close to his ear. Love in action.

I waited in the place I always waited, back in the Relatives' Room. Time seemed an inhale on hold. I noted with intrigue that the magazines on the table had changed as of that morning. Travel and outback themes were now replaced with publications to do with house, home and garden. Again, their titles jumped off the page at me as a strange curling sensation flowed through my body. I wondered if I was being messaged once more, the suggestion being that he was going to come home. Stomach fluttering, I twiddled his ring around on my finger only to be distracted by a voice at the door.

"Caroline, we've done the tracheostomy."

I looked up to see Brentwood. He had somebody else with him whom I hadn't yet met – a man dressed in light blue scrubs over his trousers. I sensed something else was coming.

"Caroline, this is Rick. He is the senior cardiologist here to replace Dr Karl who is now on leave for his holiday." Rick flashed a smile and offered an assured and good-natured hello as he flicked his fingers through the wave of brown hair across his forehead. Brentwood continued. "Now, as we took care of the tracheostomy, we saw from his X-ray that we needed to give Gordon another chest drain. We were concerned about this build-up of fluid still in his left lung. It's a large mass on the X-ray. You can see for yourself when you go in later. Anyway, we fitted the drain but found a couple of other things which are a bit of a worry. He has bleeding in his abdomen. We aren't sure where it is coming from. It could be perfectly innocent, like a small blood vessel that has ruptured, for instance. Or it could be something more serious. We need to take him for a CAT scan straight away. To rule things in or rule things out."

"A *bleed*? Jesus. Will he be okay?" I searched the creases and folds of his face, looking for what he really thought but might not be willing to say. I should have realised this was Brentwood and he didn't hold back.

"Look, we often see things like this in ICU. We get a patient over the hump or near to over the hump and then a curve ball can appear and often kill them. Like I said before, the last and only time we had a patient on maximum life support here they died. Even patients who seem to be advancing . . . Well you know, things can just come out of left field and kill them. So anyway, we're getting him ready for the scan now. It's going to take us a while to prepare him. We haven't moved him since he came here and the CAT scan is a trip down the corridor . . ."

"Is it okay to move him?"

"It's not the best. But we do need to do the scan. We just have to make sure that he is stable and secure in his position when we transport him. Okay, right, I need to get back in there. We'll let you know afterwards how it went."

My boat seemed to be capsizing again, everything flying out of cupboards and drawers, water starting to force its way through cracks that were yielding under the pressure. The shakes had arrived in my body, shivers from my blood running cold at Brentwood's seeming unfeelingness. As I stared at the emptiness their departure had left in the doorway, my eyes widened, a necessary reflex for seeing into the darkness that his words had cast. *Oh my God. No. Please, no. How can he be so blunt?* But the chairs kept their silence over the matter and the tap dripped, indifferent. It was time to wait.

The hands on the clock may have been there but I didn't see them move. I hadn't been coping well since the moment the team had wheeled Gordon past the door and I had let myself get triggered after snatching only a glimpse of his left hand and part of the thick blanket that insinuated his legs. Tammy and Rebecca, who had rushed to my side after my S.O.S. phone call, were doing their best to console me, as were two other friends who had appeared courtesy of synchronicity. But I wasn't making it easy for them or me, unwilling to take my power of focus away from the brusqueness and message behind Brentwood's words. I clutched onto his worst-case scenario under the misapprehension that if I didn't, I would be guilty of energising a utopian outcome. Had there been the space, I would have paced. Instead, I sat rocking slightly in my seat and jigging my legs, the only way to allow the energy inside me to move through. *Please, please, please, please, please.* I thought about Dorothy and Brenda leaving me to have to deal with all this on the front line. *Not one single phone call of support to me, not one since Gordon landed here.* Molar-grinding and jaw-twitching anger pulsed, only to blast its way out of my nostrils as invisible toxic clouds.

Now and again I looked to one or the other of my friends and declared "he's going to go, isn't he?" No sooner were the words out and named, than my tears would spill over yet again and the rocking would return. All the while, Tammy sat stroking my hair, talking to me with soothing but firm tones while everyone else did their best to reassure me or hold the space. I told myself to stay with the facts, the "this-is-just-what-is-happening" part, and to be here now. When I could do it, I calmed down. But fear, like any addiction, kept needing its fix and felt stronger than my will to transcend it or my remembering about the highest good. I wanted to escape, leave the video game I felt trapped in, and bolt down the corridor as fast as my legs would take me.

"I can't do any more of this. I can't do it. I can't do it. I can't do it. Please God, you have to help him! Help me! Help us!"

My cheeks seared with shame, shame for wanting out when so far my man had chosen "in" in a body that, right now, was so assaulted. The edge. It was an excruciating spot to have to perch on, at a time when I believed there was even an edge at all and when I had convinced myself there was no alternative other than perching.

After what seemed like an eternity, Rick appeared at the doorway, grinning.

"Cheer up! It's all *good!*"

I burst into tears, relief and anxiety rolled into one big spongy ball now being wrung out with gratitude.

"C'mon! I said it's *good* news! We didn't find anything sinister. Just a little blood vessel we think he may have ruptured somehow from coughing or something," he reassured.

Seeing the state I was in, he came in and plonked himself down in the seat next to me. His smile warmed the room again and he gave me a brotherly pinch on the arm.

"Hey, I understand that was a bit of a rollercoaster for you. ICU is like that, y'know? And I'll warn you, there'll likely be more rollercoasters to come yet. Your husband is still critically ill even if he is stable. He's not out of the woods yet. But there are some promising shifts."

He slouched back in the chair, resting the ankle of his foot on his knee as he went on to fill me in on things the staff had not mentioned that morning. For the life of me, I didn't know why they could not have told me earlier but then that was ICU – it was a challenge to get an overview from one person. I brought my attention back to him, thankful that he was willing to elaborate like this. The most wondrous news of all was that they had at last managed to grow a culture for the bacteria taken some days ago from Gordon's swab of sputum. Identification of the specific strain of bacteria causing the pneumonia meant that they could replace the broad spectrum antibiotics with targeted ones that would best support eradicating the condition. Rick relayed how Gordon's liver function continued to improve and reiterated that the proof his heart was now pumping with more efficiency and strength lay in the number of blood pressure drips they had removed. To end, he confirmed they had now removed Gordon's dialysis machine.

"Just for tonight to see how he goes and whether he outputs

urine by himself. I suspect we'll have to resume with dialysis in the morning for a couple of reasons but we're happy to run the trial later on tonight. That's a first since he came in here, too. Now, don't worry, he'll be safe without it for that short period. We're going to let him rest now after all the changes today, maybe do a little bit of physio on his leg but otherwise, yeah, let him rest. Give us a few more minutes, yeah? Somebody will come and let you know when you can come back in with him." He pinched my arm again, winked, and scuffed out of the room.

I slumped back into my chair, flattened by the juggernaut that had just run me over, yet also roused to an exhausted daze thanks to the kiss of life that had been the good news following that truck. Tammy, taking one look at me, suggested I let her give me some energy healing to soothe my frayed nerves. I accepted her offer, choosing to close my eyes and receive. Within seconds I felt the tingling of heat above my head and a spontaneous relaxation taking place in the fibres of my body, as if the heat were the sun and I was on a sandy beach with nothing I need do or not do. Drifting, I had no idea at what point I was no longer conscious of Tammy, the others or the room, or for how long this non-awareness continued. The experience was broken only by my "coming to" with an enormous frightened gasp, as if I had been underwater or holding my breath. Tammy rubbed my shoulder and stooped down to look into my eyes.

"Hey honey, welcome back. You're okay. You just went deep. You needed it. That was good for you."

A minute later, Rick reappeared at the doorway to let me know I could go back in. The others, preparing to let me have my time with Gordon, said their goodbyes and departed, promising to return soon. Last to leave, Tammy was on her way out when her left hand made a fast, awkward and exaggerated movement out to the side as her fingers tucked in and her thumb poked out, her arm oddly bent.

"What the? Um, well, I don't know what *that* was! *And* I'm right handed too, not left, ha-ha!"

But the hairs on my neck pulled me to attention and into the knowing that what she had just done had been a half-cocked effort at a thumbs-up sign. She couldn't have known this was the very symbol that had come up in conversation with other friends the night before at Gordon's bedside, when they had suggested I could perhaps think of a sign by which Gordon could let me know everything was okay. I had mentioned to them how his sign for that had been a big thumbs-up. It had been his way of saying "hey, it's all good y'know!" How often he had given me that signal over the years to reassure me! Sometimes it worked but when I wanted to stay addicted to my fear I would get cross with him for doing it and snap at him to quit already with his over-optimism. Having watched the clumsiness of Tammy's manoeuvre, I felt in no doubt whatsoever about what had taken place. With clarity and simplicity I had the most striking sense that in that bungled gesture, she had *been moved*. That her thumb had been moved into that thumbs-up sign and that something was moving through her, as her, for the purposes of a sign.

The evening spent by Gordon's side was another quiet one. In a bizarre way, I had grown to like the nights here with him when Dave came on shift, and especially after those 10 p.m. healings when our friends and their support would wind their way home and the room was back to Gordon and me. It felt like the part of the day when I could most enjoy quality time with him. This evening it provided the space in which I could "come down" from the high tension of earlier. I felt safe in here at night, with Gordon and with Dave, in the cocoon. Once visiting hours were over it was as if not just the heartbeat of ICU but also the heartbeat of the whole hospital became gentler, the way hearts do when they sleep peacefully. Even the air from the ceiling vent hushed. And with Dave at the helm, things seemed soothed. I watched as he went about his business: giving Gordon a meticulous shave; scrutinising the handover stats and assessing what he felt needed to be done for Gordon's medications for the next hour; wrapping him in a special insulating blanket "because he felt a touch cold"; adjusting the position of Gordon's arm to one he felt would be of more comfort; and telling Gordon at each point what it was he was doing and why. He finished by lowering the lighting and putting on his mellow music for us all. It was the same every night. I had taken to calling it The Dave Touch. Checks all done, he began chatting to me – something else I liked.

"Caroline, he's fortunate you know. To get admitted to this specific hospital, I mean." He directed his gaze straight at me and for a moment the words that followed sounded peculiar as if they were being delivered directly to my eardrum through earphones. "See, unlike the larger ones, this hospital will persist and persist with coma patients, they won't give up if the patient hasn't done anything in 24 to 48 hours."

A shiver flitted over me. I felt I was being messaged again. There had been so many comments and synchronicities now that if I hadn't known better, I would have said they pointed to grace having been with us right from the start, cushioning us on the journey we hadn't wanted but needed. Scenes and conversations now flashed on the screen of my mind. The earlier doctor's appointment I had been able to get for Gordon; the "luck" she had referenced regarding our choice of her clinic, given she had the exact piece of testing equipment Gordon had needed, and that had shown he must get to a hospital and pronto; the voice of the general registrar telling me how lucky it was that we had come when we did or Gordon would likely be dead; the receptionist telling me how lucky we were that he came in the day that he did, given that ICU had only just been closed down the night before and therefore was still able to reopen quickly for Gordon's emergency; the same receptionist telling me how fortunate we were that we had landed Robert in Gordon's crash team – Robert, who was "an angel" and who "luckily" could double-up as an ICU specialist too, in fact the only ICU specialist there when Gordon crashed.

Dave, as if tuning in to my thoughts, continued. His words sent another involuntary quiver fluttering through me in the way that can happen when magic is afoot.

"Caroline, what can I say, Gordon was so *lucky*, so unbelievably lucky to have the team that he had on that afternoon he crashed in Coronary Care. You know, they worked exceptionally hard to do a lot of things to save his life. A *lot* of things, in a tight space of time." He whistled a sigh of awe, turning to look at Gordon. "Yup. A herculean effort. Anyway, I'll leave you two to it. You know where I am if you need me."

And with that, he left. It was 11 p.m. Could I indeed trust in more of the grace and ease Dave had pointed to?

CHAPTER TWENTY-NINE

Day 9

8.00 a.m. – Hospital

ARRIVING IN THE RELATIVES' LOUNGE for the day, I dumped my bags only to see Dr Brentwood walk in, wearing a grin such as I had not seen on him to date.

"We're starting the day with positivity, I am pleased to say. Still critical and stable but there have been wins! I'm encouraged by Gordon's heart and the strengthening of its pumping. I know I have said this before but in all seriousness, anyone with severe heart failure like his has been, dies upon admission into hospital. I mean, cardiologists and people like me rarely get to even *manage* them as a patient, before they're dead. That's why this has all been such unchartered territory for the team. But, I have to admit, I'm warming more to the idea that we may well be witnessing the unfolding of a miracle!"

"Wow."

"We're even talking about a different treatment path opening up to us here, one that could see him leaving ICU at some point and going onto a general ward and then back out into the community. It's astonishing for me to be even *suggesting* that fresh possibility. Amazing business!" He stood shaking his head in wonderment.

Yes! Yes! Yes! My eyes smarted, this time from joy. A smile teased its way across my face, as if invisible fingers had taken both corners of my mouth and dragged them upwards to make sure I received the message.

"So do you mean you're not trying to get him onto a helicopter anymore, or have him transferred to St Mary's hospital? Are we no longer talking about inserting heart pumps?"

"That's right. Days ago we were saying that if he makes it then he will need a transplant. Now though, no, not if he carries on making headway like he is. I don't think one is going to be needed."

It was a fleeting visit from Brentwood but as he left, I could have sworn there was a spring in his step, fuelled, I imagined, by his awe and wonder and enthusiasm and hope. He hadn't even ended the discussion on his usual brooding, grim note. Of course, he didn't need to. I knew the rhetoric, realised that Gordon's criticality hadn't changed. But I also knew the train tracks had switched yet again, or we had jumped tracks, arriving at another one of those "parallel-reality" possibilities. A rippling expanded throughout my being – the convergence of shivers, goose-bumps and pure awareness.

Advancement continued to be the theme for the rest of the morning and the mood remained upbeat. Right in the middle of the 10 a.m. healing I was interrupted by a buoyant Ed. He announced that Gordon had just done his first pee down the tube since being temporarily taken off dialysis. Oh the irony, the thrill, of being able to see my man making his own urine, even if it was a trickle! We laughed and I returned to the group healing, still chuckling.

I'd had the hit to change the music again today, this time to a CD of bush-ballads from our time travelling in outback Queensland. I kept the songs playing throughout the day. Friends who joined me in the room during healings smiled to hear it, Ed hummed along as he did his duties and even the physio commented during her visit about how happy and carefree the tunes were. It was starting to feel like Gordon was in the next phase of his epic journey. Rebecca had felt it too, intuition calling her to bring in a rainbow-coloured piece of cloth for its qualities of energy vibration. Ed accommodated us, giving his permission to tape it on the window beside Gordon, so that the daylight lit it up and emanated joy into the room.

For the rest of the day Gordon was back to initiating his own breaths, with the machine adding a touch of oxygen and helping to squeeze that breath out a little. This too, was progress, although he still laboured. Not yet at the level where he initiated every breath, the machine would finally kick in for the ones he missed. It made for an irregular pattern and a strange sound overall, hard for me to listen to with ease at first. In fact it took me a little while to centre myself and my own breathing, to realise that holding my breath wouldn't help change anything, and to trust – or know – that the machine would activate on auto-pilot if it needed to.

By about lunchtime I was able to allow his breathing to be as it was, without needing for it to be a certain way for me and my internal comfort. Only then, and for the rest of the day, did I finally receive how humbling it was to be in the presence of breath, especially breath coming from a loved one fighting for their life. When at last I brought presence and awareness to it, I recognised it to be the most sacred of sounds. How often did we, as humans, not even hear our own sacredness, our own pureness of breath, the sound of spirit animating and enlivening our bodies? I looked over at Gordon. Seeing and listening to him in that moment, I could distinguish his breath as something else too. It was the sound of one man using will and choice to come back to this debilitated body, to come back to this life, to have life and to claim life. There I had been, breathing, without thinking anything of the miracle that my own breaths were. And there was Gordon, teaching me otherwise.

My skin prickled. Life was conversing with me again.

It was 8 p.m. when Christine, the General Manager, appeared in the doorframe of the Relatives' Room. I had been sitting alone whilst waiting for nurses to do whatever they needed to do with Gordon. Good reader of faces that I was, my stomach lurched the second I clapped eyes on her hovering there. The smile was present but not the broad beam she had been flashing these past couple of days, more a painted-on front. Instinct told me she was uncomfortable – but what about?

"Caroline, I need to speak with you. Can we go into the other room, just out here?"

Shit. She spoke with a more clipped and professional tone than usual, a wall to protect herself perhaps. Without speaking I followed her, my radars sweeping through a fog of tension and confusion and energy that, had it been visible to the eye, would have been as choking as black smoke. We sat down at the empty table. I watched as she rested her elbows and placed her fingertips together and up to her mouth, pure symmetry, as if to sanctify what she needed to say. I remained mute, my feet burning up in my boots, hands clammy. She locked eyes on me, pursed her lips together the way people do when they are chewing the inside of their lip, and after a sigh, dropped her bombshell.

"Caroline, I have a big problem. I'm sorry but Gordon has to leave this hospital by Friday."

"Huh?" It was the only sound I could make because I was holding my breath, winded in the blast of the explosion.

"I have to move him from here. We don't have the staff for him after Friday."

"I don't understand . . ."

"I'm sorry."

"I don't understand!"

"Yes. I know. Let me explain. We closed our doors to ICU the day before Gordon arrived here, an official decision by the Board to no longer have an ICU at this hospital. Of course, when Gordon arrived and crashed the way he did, we re-opened the unit for him. As luck would have it, Robert was on duty that day and in attendance with Gordon at the time. That was how we were even able to reopen in such a dire emergency. You see, Robert is trained in ICU and in working the ventilator, extremely specialised skills that Gordon needed."

"But . . . I still . . . I don't understand. Gordon *is* here now. ICU has been open for him all that time."

"Yes, but . . ."

"No. The nurses *are* here. It *is* working here. Why move him?"

"Because, Caroline, I have tweaked the staff rostering as much as I could during this time but I've reached a dead end. I did warn Dr Brentwood over a week ago that we would be in this position if Gordon hung in there. My issue is that from Friday, I will not have the staff to either oversee the ventilator for Gordon or to be in ICU. Both Robert and Dave will be on holiday with their families, time off which they booked a while ago."

"Yes, but there must be other staff elsewhere. That's just ridiculous!"

"There are no agency nurses available, Caroline. ICU is niche. And not many nurses choose to come to this hospital to work, they prefer the larger ones. It is difficult for us to get the staff these days, even though those of us who do work here are a close-knit family. Yes. This hospital *is* a family – all of us who work here feel like that about it. And that's why you won't know this, but both Dave and Robert have been agreeing to do extra shifts. They have surpassed what has been reasonable to ask for. Just for Gordon, just to continue his care, just to give him and you the best possible chance to pull a miracle. If it wasn't for them agreeing to work that overtime, Gordon would have had no specialised team to look after him and in all probability . . . Well, not probability, he *would* have died because up until a couple of days ago, if we hadn't had staff he would not have survived the transfer to another hospital!"

The shrapnel now rained down around my ears. My throat felt thick and gluggy, it was hard to swallow anything she was saying. Still, Christine continued.

"But it ends on Friday, Caroline. Robert and Dave can't be here for him after Friday. So I need to find him a bed somewhere else, in another hospital."

"Where?"

"My preference will be for Hawksford Private as it is only down the road and would mean that Gordon could keep the same cardiologist. Plus Dr Brentwood could also keep track and pop in." She paused, taking a sip of water without moving her lips. "Also, *you* are a huge factor in your husband's recovery and getting him in down the road would mean that you get to still be in the area you know, which will make it easy for you to visit and of course would mean that your friends could still come and support you. Like I said, I will try my best to get Gordon into Hawksford. But if there is nothing available for him there, I will need to get him into the Prince of Wales . . ."

"The Prince of Wales? But that's over two hours from here!"

"Yes, I realise that, and if we couldn't get him in there, then it would have to be somewhere further away still, which I understand would then mean you would be looking at a residential stay yourself. Caroline, I understand none of this is ideal. I know that you are comfortable being here with us, that you are used to it, and that your friends can come here and be with you too, which may be difficult if we can only get Gordon into another hospital further away, but . . ." She offered me a box of tissues.

Shit, shit, shit. The teeth dream. This is it. This is what it was telling me was coming.

"But how is there no danger in moving him now? We've been saying all this time that it is treacherous to move him!" I tried to compose myself, rubbing the tears away so they wouldn't drag down my face.

"With the improvements that Gordon has pulled today, he would be safe to move by Friday. It's not the best, but . . ."

"Please, I want a straight answer. Is there a risk in moving him?"

"Well, look, there is always a risk when a patient is in a coma. However we do feel the risk is the least it has been to date and his wins have been such that we feel it *will* be safe to transfer him now."

"Well, it seems to me as if you have guilt, as if you have something else you are hiding! What is it? I'm intuitive, there's something else you are not telling me here. I want to know what it is. Why do you seem sheepish?"

Now it was my turn to lock eyes with her, not letting her get away with a second of dropped gaze. No longer dissembling her motives, her eyes reddened as a film of tears - not enough to escape anywhere - washed across.

"Obviously Caroline, this is not what any General Manager of a hospital would want. I have a duty of care to all my patients. Yet I can't extend that care for Gordon after Friday. Yes, I feel terrible and I have been flagging it up to Dr Brentwood for some days now. I have tried to get agency staff but there is a shortage at the moment. Since Hawksford Private built their brand new Cardiac Unit we can't get the specialists here. And . . . Yes, there are other things in that ICU is meant to be officially closed here now – it was a decision made by the Board. These developments – Hawksford Private's new Cardiac Unit and the closure of our ICU . . . Well, they are part of even deeper changes here at the hospital. It saddens me greatly because I love this hospital, we are family here, and yet things are changing. I am in a tricky position right now. I have to balance the needs of the Board and the needs of Gordon and you, and all amidst a climate of structural change."

"So what are you saying?"

"There is nothing else I can do that I haven't already tried to do for you. My preference would be to keep him here but I can't. Tomorrow morning, with your consent, I have to tell Dr Brentwood and start making arrangements."

Her lips pressed together and she stood up. According to her, our meeting was over. I goggled at her, aware of a clamouring fear that everyone's efforts to support Gordon this far could be dashed on the mere moving of him into an ambulance and driving him someplace else. That, in spite of his gains, he could die because of this imposed transfer. She politely said goodnight, encouraging me to go home and get some sleep. Dumbfounded, and with queasiness rising from my stomach into my throat, I watched her exit, leaving me only with the top notes of her perfume to sweeten the sour.

CHAPTER THIRTY

Day 10

2.05 a.m. – Home

I HAD LEFT AT 1.30 A.M., having to peel myself away yet knowing I would have stayed all night if they had let me. It reminded me of my childhood when I would try to delay the inevitable bedtime in exchange for more of the reassurance from the lights and the sounds, the company, and the safety and security of the living room – of what was known.

Since Christine had dropped her bombshell, I had felt exhaustion from all the responsibility. With changes now being thrust upon me, I had gone into my default mode of resistance and of not accepting what was so. My life seemed to have gone to a new level of madness, as if I were trapped back in the video game where the only way to get to the next screen was to get through to the end of this one, yet the "reward" waiting for me was just more complexity – either worse things to come, or me being incapacitated in some way so that the things that did present themselves became too intricate to navigate.

Feeling uprooted at the prospect of a transfer, I realised the swiftness with which my adaptation to life in this hospital had taken place. It was my pattern to at first baulk at enforced change but to then adjust and try to swim with the tide. Unconsciously, I had always made my life be about survival – habituating so that I could recreate stability and familiarity, cope and be safe. Tonight it was revealing to see the extent to which I had merged with my new world of ICU: the tramline to and from the house that my car took every day; the hospital itself; the ICU ward; the language this world spoke; the "family" of nurses and specialists with whom I had come to feel a degree of comfort, to know their personalities, and from whom I took my direction; the Relatives' Room that no other member of the public used and which seemed to be just for me and my friends, and for Jim and Steve while they'd been here; the ability to come and go pretty much as I pleased; the bending of the rules for how late into the night I could stay and for the number of people who could be around Gordon; the allowances made by staff for our group healings, crystals round the bed, fabric up at the window. I felt *held* here. It was a place of protection. In an odd way, it was as if I had created home here. I felt connected to it but hadn't grasped that until this moment. And now, I was being kicked out, as my father had tried to do to me on a number of occasions all those years ago.

I howled in the car all the way home, a mouth-wide-open bawling, with tears and snot streaking down my cold cheeks as the windscreen wipers lashed the rain away in haste. Other than releasing and letting energy move up and out, my crying managed to reduce my world of circumstances to something a little less stimulating and overwhelming: blurred blobs of red, green and white that lit my path back to the house.

By the time morning came, I was resolute that no matter what, I would focus on steering myself and everyone else towards opening as a channel of Love for Gordon. As for his body, I knew his kidneys still needed to recover but his heart was strengthening, the pneumonia was diminishing, the sepsis still clearing, and he was weaning off the remainder of medications for blood pressure. We had two days to make any headway that could offset the risks involved with moving him. I wanted to make those days count. In the shower, it didn't escape my attention that I was now feeling he could *survive* those two days. Afterwards, I messaged with both Ruth and Charles. We agreed I would request a meeting with Christine and Dr Brentwood for that morning, and that Charles would come to the hospital to hear the facts with me once again, so that I could make a decision. No sooner had I ended the call than the phone rang.

I stepped out onto the deck to get better reception. It was a wrong number but in the moment that I hung up, I became aware of what was right in front of me and had been waiting with patience all along, for me to come outside and notice it. My heart skipped a beat. The dainty face of a deep-blue, star-shaped flower looked back at me. Radiating outwards and upwards towards the overcast sky, it had all the hallmarks of having just been born. I gaped at it. My borage plant! I had planted it not two months before, checking on it day after day in the anticipation of buds while Gordon joked with me that a watched pot never boiled. True to his prediction, the flowers showed no sign of emerging. Since his coma, both this plant and my herbs had appeared to all but die or pull back in response to my neglect or the encroaching winter. And yet now, today of all days, there it was – my borage had produced its first exquisite bloom.

A peculiar flutter in my chest came and went. *Borage is the "Healer of Hearts", remember? Yes. How fitting!* I recalled how the plant was associated with courage, for those times when a person might have uncertainty as to whether they can face the task ahead. I had even read some time ago about its link to the easing of grief and sadness, to the removal of heaviness of heart, and to the bestowing of joy and lightness of spirit – a plant to fill you with optimism. What delight I'd enjoyed at the discovery of this back then! I had even rushed out to procure myself a healthy specimen to bring back home and nurture.

As I stood bearing witness to this remarkable event and timing, the fine hairs prickled on the back of my neck and tops of my forearms. Likewise, and perhaps in response to seeing *me*, the feathery hairs of the borage plant seemed to be sending prickles of excitement up its own stem and across its leaves. I shook my head in wonderment. *Today of all days!* There was a significance here I could not deny, my intuitive radar screamed it. Borage also went by the name of Star Flower. Now, on the deck, its celestial blue re-imprinted onto my heart that we are all comprised of the same matter as the stars of the sky, we are the same energy that animates them and gives rise to them. No matter what circumstances may come along to shake us up or bring us to our knees, we are more than those circumstances and the real "we" can never come and go, can never be born or die. A tingle swept up the back of my neck again. *Gordon. This is from Gordon. He is using the flower – being the flower – to message me!* I was convinced. *Courage. Le couer: action from an open heart.*

Whatever happened in Christine's office today, I knew my decision had to come from an open heart, not from shadow agendas. A decision guided by my infinite self, rather than my limited nature.

Though her conclave accommodated the four of us it still felt as if the walls were nosey-parkers, crowding in to eavesdrop and spy on a verdict for the sheer voyeuristic thrill of watching it all happen. I fidgeted with my tissue in my lap. Christine's assistant clattered teapot and teacups while Dr Brentwood cleared an awkward space for her to set them down. I looked to Charles next to me, clean shaven, and as bolt upright as his favourite spearfishing speargun. He had set his brown leather folder square in front of him on the desk and now opened it out, clicking his pen on and laying it down on the clean white page, ready to take notes. Watching Christine pour the tea as her tapered red fingernail kept the lid in place, Brentwood kicked things off by announcing that it was good we were all meeting today. He only had a small window for that so we were to get started right away. It transpired that "getting started" involved Brentwood declaring he was not in favour of the move but that he understood there were no other options. Both he and Christine went on to discuss some of the inner politics they were dealing with both at the hospital and within the region, and which only served to complicate the precariousness of Gordon's position. But all Charles and I wanted to know was whether it was safe to move him.

"Well look, here's the thing. It is with delight that I can say that this morning there have continued to be small but significant breakthroughs with Gordon," Brentwood began. "That reassures me in the light of his transfer out of here. He is now almost off those last drips for blood pressure and his heart is compensating for that itself. Bear in mind, Gordon's heart *had* needed *all five* of those medications for blood pressure, just to enable his heart to work at a mere one third of output!" He paused, nodding with excitement as he saw my eyes widen. "Yes, that's right! One third. We gave him the maximum drugs we could for his heart and despite that and his heart being unable to do any of the work for itself, all those drugs were *still* only getting it to work at a third of its function! That is how shot your husband's heart was, Caroline. At full dosage, this was all the chemicals were able to achieve. His heart had all but completely failed. And *now* – well he is almost off those two medications, as I've said, and not only that, but his heart is nearing the 'almost normal' category."

"Hang on. I need to back us up a moment. This is my husband and I need to understand. What does that mean?"

"You're saying *almost normal*?" Charles pierced the phrase in an instant. "You mean he has no heart condition anymore?" He cocked his head an inch as if to make sense of what he was hearing.

"It means that Gordon is not likely to need a heart transplant anymore but instead, well, *instead* the probability is that his heart will revert back to normal. It's not far off that right now."

"Hmm, yes, it is an exceptional development!" Christine was almost purring as she topped up her own teacup, while Dr Brentwood beamed at me like a young boy on Christmas morning.

"Caroline! I have never seen this before in someone who has been as sick as Gordon! It's looking like an absolute miracle! This morning he is not only initiating breaths with greater ease but he is also starting to breathe them out by himself too. Now look, I'll grant you, the machine is still helping him with oxygen, but nevertheless, this is another step that we needed to see. Not to mention that he has emptied his bowels twice overnight."

As the truth sunk in about where we were now at with Gordon, my body trembled with the thrill of the news. I quizzed them on the dangers of moving Gordon. Brentwood spent a few minutes going over the risk/reward overview, answering me or Charles each time we didn't understand. His summary contained words that could have catapulted me to the moon and back in joy.

"Caroline, there are always going to be risks in moving Gordon but I need to reiterate: with the progress from yesterday and the strides made overnight, we almost have Gordon approaching the '*recovery*' stage of his journey, rather than being in the 'survival' stage!" At the word "recovery" he had smiled and clapped his hands once in jubilation, sending a wave of excitement around the room. "There are uncertainties with the move but it's the least perilous it has ever been!"

"Oh my God. Honestly?" I checked in with Charles to make sure he was nodding in agreement. "Really? Wow! That is astonishing. I don't know what to say. Other than that my man is an absolute spunk to have got himself this far!"

"Spunk indeed!"

"So I think the consensus of opinion is that we will book Gordon's transfer for Friday at noon. Now, throughout today, as we continue to wean him off the drugs that were keeping him unconscious, he will be getting the 'lightest' in awareness that he has ever been. The next stage for us will be to check that he hasn't suffered damage to his brain from any lack of oxygen when he crashed. Over the course of today we'll be asking basic requests of him to monitor that – to see if he can do what we ask. But for right now . . . let's continue to hope that the only way is *up!*"

CHAPTER THIRTY-ONE

Day 11

7.30 a.m. – Hospital

STOP RINGING, GODDAMMIT. Gordon's mobile phone refused to comply, vibrating on the passenger seat as I made my way to the hospital, and flashing the words "private number" on the screen like an invasion of my privacy. In my resistance to it I felt the familiarity of that knot of gnarled old rope tightening inside my stomach. They would have to wait. Yes, they would. But deep down I knew my words were mere bolshy defiance. I had to sort things. Time was running out. *Stop ringing.* I sighed in exasperation. For nearly two weeks I had lived at the hospital and within the intensity of its bubble, the only real world I could relate to or have time and energy for. But more and more, there were other worlds demanding my attention. *Stop ringing, for Pete's sake!* In recent days I'd had to deal with calls regarding pressing and complex matters of finance that were putting our house and car at risk. The funds I needed so that I could attend to these affairs lay in a bank account I could not access, one in Gordon's name. It was an admin error he had never got around to changing but which was now having devastating consequences. As a result of being hospitalised – and one day before payday at that – he had not been able to transfer the necessary funds into our joint account like he would have usually done.

I knew that today was going to need some concrete action on this, even though I still did not know what that looked like. Yesterday I had been slugged with overwhelm. Aside from dealing with the decision to move Gordon, throughout the day I had to take calls on his phone from people who didn't seem to show much understanding, and had to try and figure the way forward to sorting our finances. Today it looked once again like the "other world" was still threatening to storm in on my life here at ICU. The thought clamped the muscles of my neck and shoulders. In frustration I yelled at the phone to shut up. It continued for another few seconds and then silence fell.

It wasn't just about the calls and the stuff to do with money. Today was Gordon's last full day at this hospital – *our* last day here. The nurses would be doing tests on him to see if his brain had sustained any loss of oxygen during his crash. *Brain damage.* Even the term brought shudders. Not once, up until Dr Brentwood had inferred it yesterday, had that concern crossed my mind as a potentiality. I knew I had to accept that there might indeed have been damage. *You can't just accept it at the level of "thinking" the acceptance, Caroline. You know that. You need to feel it.* I sucked in the air, shunted it out, and allowed the thought. *It's true, there might have been damage. He might have brain damage.* It took a few minutes but once I let in that thought with acceptance, the squirms in my body calmed down. *And by the same token, all other things are possible too, including a healthy brain.* That was truth as well, I couldn't deny it.

Approaching the intersection I motioned to the mother with her child that she could cross, flicked the indicator on and turned right, choosing to align myself for the day ahead in favour of outcomes that would serve the highest good for all of us. I knew this was my only seat of power and I was learning to sit in it. Five minutes later, the most vivid rainbow I'd seen for ages appeared in the sky in front of me, its arch touching down behind the houses to my left and spanning over the hospital to my right. For a moment I was in awe, a smile spreading across my face.

On my way into Gordon, Dr Brentwood almost ran me down as he strode out of the doors of ICU.

"Oops! Caroline, well good morning, good morning! Are you ready for a boost? Try this on for size: Gordon has achieved some more increments overnight!" He smiled, his eyes brighter than they had been for days. My heart quickened at the cheer of his tone as well as at his update. "We've been able to get him off the last med for blood pressure and he is managing to maintain it all by himself!"

"Oh God! That's fantastic!"

"It sure is. His kidney function has also advanced. And he needs less help now from the ventilator to exhale, and less oxygen to be given to him. This is incredible, Caroline. I don't know what else to say other than that. Last Monday, I still didn't think your husband would make it." He nodded his head in wonderment again, then, sensing my eagerness, gave the go ahead. "Yes, yes, you can go in, he's more 'awake' now than when you left him last night but he's in and out, still coming out of the coma. It'll take a few days. Well anyway, enjoy saying hello. I'll say goodbye!"

And with that, he sauntered off down the corridor, leaving me to catch my breath while I typed out a text message to Ruth for the

Journey Page, knowing that she and everyone else would be elated to hear the news.

For the rest of the day, in-between being with Gordon, I tried to take the next steps for our finances. We were going to require Gordon to be deemed by a lawyer to be of "sound enough mental faculty" to sign a power of attorney permitting me access to his funds in the bank. I was also confronted with the reality of what it was like for someone to start "coming out of coma".

When I first walked in, Gordon's eyes, though drowsy were at least more open. It was both inconceivable and thrilling for me to behold after so much desperation and yearning, to be able to look into his eyes and see life there. Yet although his gaze lingered on me, there seemed no recognition of who he was looking at. I felt a jab in my heart but in truth I had braced myself for this after Dr Brentwood's parting words. *Coming out of coma takes time. Coming down from all those drugs takes time.* I smiled in Gordon's direction and told him I loved him, as I moved around the bed to brush a gentle kiss on his forehead. He rolled his head toward me, some sense of acknowledgement at having been touched there. I could see that his mental faculties were not back. What I didn't know was whether this was temporary – or not.

In the hours that followed, I watched as my man grimaced and frowned, writhing his torso in discomfort. Sarah, noticing me wincing at seeing him like that, gently explained that they needed him to feel a degree of his pain and that it was a part of him "awakening", adding, that if it appeared to get too much for him, they would give him Paracetamol. It vexed me to be thrust into this presentation of Gordon after days of him lying immobile with eyes shut and unconscious. In coma he gave no grimaces and whereas I had been able to talk away and "know" that somehow he could hear me, it occurred to me now that he might not want to hear

me and whatever I blabbered on about, might not want anything
I did. I couldn't work out if the frown from him came because
he didn't like the music I had chosen, or for some other reason. I
was clueless whether he even wanted music or not, or desired my
stroking or not, or needed me to be in silence or not. All I wanted
was to be of service to him but I didn't know how to do that in
practice. In his new condition, in this incapacity to speak or fix his
gaze, and in this situation of his mental faculties being not fully
back, he felt a bit like a stranger to me. It was startling to say the
least and yet so exciting that he was even at this point of coming to
full consciousness.

The group healings continued at their usual times, only now I
asked the visitors who arrived not to come to his bedside. He was
becoming "lighter" in his awareness and I didn't want to disorient
him or overstimulate him. I wanted to show respect for his space
and consider the need for his dignity – he may not want people
seeing him wake up like this. But that wasn't the only difference
about the feel of the sessions now. Given that his consciousness
was returning, it was a challenge for me to sit there in presence
during the sessions in the way I had before. He coughed almost
continuously, a dreadful chesty hacking that took effort and which
often shunted liquid – sometimes pink-coloured from blood – into
the tube leading out of his windpipe. I cringed to look at it. His
coughing triggered the ventilator to chime out with its bing-bing-
bing-bing-bing-bing, and the stats on the monitor to flash. That
was the point at which he delayed inhaling for a few seconds. Even
though I knew there was no urgency and that one of the nurses
would come in straight away to turn the chiming off, with every
incident I couldn't help but angle on the edge of my seat, scrunch
my fingernails down into the bed-sheet and hold my own breath

until it was over. It was unthinkable to now experience the healings in this way but what I had lost in my own sense of peace to be able to sit there and be aware of healing coming through me, I more than made up for with the knowing that all the kerfuffle was only occurring as a result of my man making his return back into his body, back into this world.

Watching it, I somehow felt like a child exposed to the paradox of the colliding and sensory world that was the miracle of its first fireworks display. Excitement rocketed in me and glee whizzed around; fear cracked and banged in my head; overwhelm kept spinning and expanding upon itself, shooting sparks in all directions; while awe, wonder and Love showered down on us both in abundance – fountains of multi-coloured magic.

By about 2 p.m. the winds of change whipped up momentum. Christine informed me that they had managed to secure a bed for Gordon at Hawksford Private, thirty minutes down the road. It was such a lift to discover that Gordon and I would not have to be sent to the backwaters somewhere and I sighed with relief and gratitude. She carried on filling me in and I sensed that a lot had been going on behind the scenes to get us to this point with Hawksford, though what that had been I didn't know. She told me that the Heart Centre was so brand new that it wasn't even officially open yet, didn't even have a patient.

"In fact, they have agreed to open a few days earlier than they intended – just for Gordon!"

Again, as at other times, it sounded as if words were being filtered straight down into my eardrum. I licked my lip, feeling a certainty I was receiving a "message". We were being looked after again by the same visible and invisible strings that had seemed to be here for us all along. A shiver rippled over me.

Of course, Gordon still needed to be in the best possible shape he could be for the transfer. But sure enough – and as if a Grand Master Plan was unfolding – things continued to shift as the afternoon rolled on. His eyes began to reveal more of the man I knew in them, with more of his spirit animating their colour and energising their essence. There had also been further rallying in the strength of his coughs, harrowing as they were to have to listen to. On top of this he had given a nod for "yes" – a definitive and singular movement in response to a question Sarah had asked him. And he showed signs of increasing "presence" in his behaviour towards her each time she tried to suction his mouth when he coughed, pursing his lips almost in defiance and jerking his head away from her hand. Sarah laughed. It was as if he sensed this was the only bit of power that he had and therefore was sure as hell going to use it!

Change was in the air alright. Since I'd set foot inside ICU that morning, there had been nothing but rowdiness in the ward outside Gordon's room. Two patients had arrived during the night but unlike him, they were not on life support and so, with their visitors coming and going, there had been much banter around their bedsides. It was the most populated and liveliest I'd seen ICU since Gordon had been admitted. Even a bird had messaged us by raining down pecks on the window in the 2 p.m. healing. Gordon was being called to *rise*. He now had to move on – to a new hospital, and, we all prayed, to the next stage of his recovery. It seemed so fitting that there was literally more life in ICU today. Yet in a rather unexpected way, it was taking me some getting used to.

An ear-splitting whirring and growling revved up outside Gordon's window, jerking my attention away from him and over to the source of the intrusion. Speechless, I computed what was about to take place as a workman approached one of the three trees, his chainsaw poised and angled for action, about to cut down the beauty and majesty and very existence of a tree that had been a friendly onlooker since the day Gordon had moved in here. There I'd been all morning, celebrating the signs of Gordon's return to life and the land of the living, and now here stood another human being outside, about to snuff out life.

"It's preparations for the building site they have to put in there." One of the nurses obviously felt the need to apologise, had seen the look on my face. "These are the last of the trees to go, I'm afraid."

I didn't answer. I felt a lump mushrooming in my throat, unshed tears from who knew how long plus new ones for the tree. I watched as the worker launched into hewing and savaging the branches. He may as well have been cleaving my own heart.

"I can pull the blind down if you like."

But I declined the offer. If ICU had taught me anything about humanity during my time here, it was the importance of bearing witness. Somebody had to bear witness to this beauty, this living expression of Nature – a nature we all were – and to thank it for its Greatness and all that it had gifted during its life. Still the workman butchered away. It was another stark reminder of mortality, a raw wound for me. By the time three limbs had crashed to the ground faster than they had taken to grow, my heart felt like it was bleeding out – for me, for this tree, for all trees being destroyed by man, for those who had lost loved ones in ICU wards up and down the country. I availed myself to feeling all of it, crying in silence. I understood that nothing infinitely real could ever be lost, and also that there was a human plane of experience which demanded to be felt and honoured. Somehow, in accessing my humanity about the situation, I realigned with its divinity. As I had experienced through Gordon's coma, so too was I seeing that in bearing witness and in feeling, we can appreciate how fleeting physical life is in all its presentations. In doing so, we come more alive to our own true nature, remembering the sacredness of our connection to everything and everyone, remembering ourselves as sacredness itself . . . even the worker, with his chainsaw.

Dave was chatting more than usual during the final evening. Perhaps it was due to feeling buoyed by all the winking that Gordon had been doing earlier. It was a new behaviour that had emerged from my man and was not in character for him. Neither Dave nor I had been able to explain it but we had laughed whenever he had done it, grateful also for the sense that his cognition may well be returning.

As the night wore on in peace and exhaustion, I invited him to share more about his passion for flying, noting the irony that Gordon, himself a private pilot, should have scored an ICU nurse who had the same determination to get their own licence. I listened as with gestured animations he told me of his desire to finish building his plane and then fly it around the world. Again I was struck by just how magical this room in ICU was – a space in which Gordon, through his near-death, had gathered everyone together. Not only had it been the incubator for me "seeing" my husband's true essence – his heart and his Greatness – but it had also been where I had opened the nurses up to seeing that in him too. It was the place where I had "seen" and learned about Love in all its expressions. The space where friends and Gordon's sons had "seen" him and had held the space for his healing, been channels for it and loving guardians at the gates that welcomed him back to earth. This room was where we had "seen" Gordon's physical heart rally, and where we believed we were now "seeing" his human will triumph. And of course, it had been inside these four walls, where I had "seen" the hearts and Greatness of Ed, Sarah and Dave.

This container had held the energy for them to open up to me about their passions and in turn had allowed me to open them to the magic of where their passions could lead them and "see" that if Gordon's journey was anything to go by, they were to make actioning those passions a must. This "I See You"/I.C.U room truly *had* been a portal to profound seeing and connection. A room for bringing all aspects of "the heart" back to life for everyone who had been a party to being in there. In a way, we had all been on life support.

"Gordon, can you squeeze my hand?" Dave was not letting his eyes leave the end of Gordon's arm.

No response. I waited with baited breath. It had taken much will all day on my part to acknowledge both the possibility of recovery and also my fears around brain damage – and then to refocus on the now. Other than a singular nod of the head, none of the nurses so far had been able to get Gordon to respond to the request to squeeze their hand. Testing for neurological functioning required patience it seemed, and yet there was a need from staff to know what we were dealing with, what we might have to rule in, or could rule out. I had felt increasing tension during the afternoon though Robert had reassured me it would take Gordon a few days yet to be fully conscious, something that everybody seemed to be telling me whenever they could.

"Gordon, I'm going to ask you again to give my hand a squeeze and I want you to let go when I tell you to let go, okay? So let's try that now. Can you give me a squeeze?"

There was a pause again, nothing from Gordon, his eyes closed. Dave repeated the question. As if in slow motion, he curled his fingers around Dave's hand, a faint clasp, but a squeeze nonetheless, letting go when asked. Dave congratulated Gordon, smiled at me.

"We have a breakthrough! I'm satisfied that what we witnessed there wasn't just a reflex action. We'll run more tests but it's looking probable that he doesn't have brain damage."

Relief billowed out of me in a sigh to end all sighs. It had been a long day, and a quantum leap. I kissed Gordon and, grinning, told him how much I loved him.

I knew better than to bring my money worries with me when I re-entered the room after having stepped out to take a necessary call from Gordon's HR department in Hong Kong. Gordon rolled his head. He fixed his groggy gaze onto me, appearing to recognise me. What joy! Pausing by his feet, I mouthed "I love you" and blew him a kiss off the palm of my hand. To my wonderment his eyes continued to lock onto me, electricity between us as he raised his eyebrows in an almost comical and child-like way and then, with pursed lips, attempted to blow me a kiss right back. In a rush of warm exhilaration I spun round to look at Dave.

"Oh my God! Dave! Did you . . . ? Did he . . . ? Did . . . *yes*, he bloody well *did!* Woohoo!" Dave gave a low whistle and nodded his head, just as floored as I was. Glued to the spot at Gordon's feet, and with tears streaming down my cheek, I blew him yet another kiss. "Oh Gordon, darling, I love you!" He raised his eyebrows further, closed his eyes and pursed his lips again, this time leaving them pursed. I frowned, laughing. "What on earth . . . ? He's asking for a proper kiss, isn't he? Dave, look! He's inviting me to kiss him!"

"I'll be buggered! Well don't keep the man waiting! It's bad enough we're going to have some explaining to do to Dr Brentwood in the morning about all this smooching in his ICU room!"

I rushed over to Gordon, leaned across his chest and kissed him with a puckering-up to match his own. Giddy with excitement, my heart soared to feel him push his chapped but warm lips back at me. Tears of exulted joy streamed down my face.

"It's a bloody miracle! Gordon, *you* are a miracle. I love you so much. That kiss my darling, has just surpassed the one you gave me on the day we were married. Oh, I'm sorry . . . I'm blubbering all over you. But I'm just so happy!"

Every cell in my body tingled and danced with aliveness, sung awake by the jubilation in my heart. Gordon smiled back at me but not the grin I was used to seeing him do, rather the beam that a developmentally-challenged child might gift. It was strange to witness it and yet there was such innocence to its radiance, something so unconditional and stripped back and magical about it, that I was deeply moved.

Walking out of the hospital just after 1 a.m., any sense of sadness at this being the last night I was ever going to do so was lost amidst the triumph at what had taken place. I waited until I was in the car before letting rip with the biggest whoop I'd ever done in my life. Back at the house, I shot off an update on the Journey Page. It was the best medium I had, given the lateness of the hour, but in truth I wanted to yell it from the rooftops, ring the bells, blast the trumpets, honk the horns, and get the loudspeaker out and deafen everyone: Hey everyone! My man kissed me! My man *kissed* me! I typed a few animated lines and pressed the send button. Within seconds, some of the night-owls at their computers replied, cheering and sharing in my joy. It was the beginning of a sweeping celebration that was to trigger phone calls and written well-wishes for some while yet into the night and ongoing into the next day.

For now, I was on cloud nine.

CHAPTER THIRTY-TWO

Day 12

8.30 a.m. – Hospital

GORDON'S SPECIAL AMBULANCE was scheduled for 10 a.m., and until then, it was to be all hands to the pump to sedate him and ready him for moving into the vehicle in a way that reduced his risks during transit. I popped into his room to say my last hello and goodbye to him there. He was tired, having been taken off the ventilator for a couple of hours as part of his first trial on what was a long road ahead to wean him off the machine. I quivered a kiss upon his lips, telling him how much I loved him.

Nerves were taking over now that we were facing his imminent removal from this, his cocoon, a room that had served its purpose as an extraordinary place of safety, healing, and transformation. As if it were a chrysalis, Gordon's body had barely moved the whole fortnight and yet so many fascinating and miraculous changes had taken place within it. I looked up at the clouds painted on the ceiling, saying farewell to them in my mind. In their own way they too had swaddled him, helping to create refuge for the changeling they had watched over.

I gathered up his things: the rose quartz crystal at the head of his bed and all the other crystals dotted around; the red cloth; the painting from a friend; the drumsticks from under the bed; the stereo and CDs. Taking down the rainbow cloth still taped to the window, I knew in my heart that all the signs affirmed it was time for this butterfly to emerge. The rebirthing journey from chrysalis to newly-awakening adult was well underway now. As if in agreement, Dr Brentwood came in and it was time for me to go back to the only place I knew to be in right now, the Relatives' Room, with my heart a mix of happiness and sadness, and my solar plexus whirring.

"So how are you doing, Caroline?"

"Oh, you know . . . good . . . happy that Gordon is still okay, but a bit of nervousness about the move."

"He's doing okay. We did have to put him back on one of his blood pressure medications by 5 p.m. yesterday, a low dosage. It happens sometimes – the patient has a dip and we help them get along again for a bit. It's all part of the process. Today at Hawksford, they'll continue carrying out the checks for whether he can respond to more of their simple commands. But so far his responses have been encouraging. He's even been puckering up to you, I'm told!"

"Dr Brentwood, I can't begin to tell you how much gratitude I have for you and your team. I feel you worked with Gordon from such a place of humility, not the arrogance that you often read about with doctors at your level. So thank you from the bottom of my heart."

"Well Caroline, there's no place for arrogance in my opinion, not in intensive care. Yes, we have machines in here, but the machines can only do so much. On the night Gordon crashed, I flung the maximum support I could at him but then I had to surrender, acknowledge there was not a single bit of extra help I could give him."

"Someone told me you are a man of religion, Dr Brentwood. You'd have to say this has been a miracle so far, wouldn't you?"

"I guess I would have to, yes. Gordon's progression out of coma has been nothing short of spectacular. I know I keep saying it but in all honesty he shouldn't have even survived last Monday let alone a fortnight in here."

"Even now, I shudder to hear you say that . . ."

"I know this may sound like arrogance and I want you to know it doesn't come from that place at all, but . . . well, I do still believe if it wasn't for getting me as his Intensivist, Gordon would in all likelihood be dead now. You see my treatment approach is, um, well somewhat . . . unorthodox. I don't believe solely in what conventional journals have to say about the human circulation in these kinds of circumstances, nor do I subscribe to their stipulation of how one should be treating it. My experience has shown me – with reliability – the opposite of what my peers agree is the truth surrounding best practice. I have over five hundred case studies to prove it. Your husband is the latest one and, I might add, my most compelling proof to date that my premise is no longer a theory but a working reality that needs to be taken notice of. It could *revolutionise* how we treat heart failure in this country, around the world!"

He went on to explain in more detail how his methods so contravened the usual practice. I listened spellbound, feeling once again the next pieces of this magical puzzle slotting into place. That everything should have come to pass in the way that it had, so that we ended up here together, in *this* hospital with *this* specialist!

"I can't help but feel you were meant to get Gordon as your patient. Maybe you were *always* meant to get him."

"Well, I must say, yes, since I have been getting more into my research it has been as if God has been sending me things to help me along – these notes here, that book there, this patient to cross my path, that patient to need my help, and then of course, the 'patient of all patients' in Gordon!"

"I knew it! I am in no doubt that you were sent to Gordon! You know, there are some folk who believe in soul contracts – that at the level of soul you agree to hook up with certain people in this lifetime, to go on a specific journey that will further evolve the soul. Maybe you don't subscribe to all that. But if I did base these events on that school of thought, I'd have to think that you two had a soul contract. That you were meant to witness this miracle with Gordon so that you can share the medical journey of it with your peers and students, to help others, maybe to get treatment plans changed forever or this one at least known and made available as an alternative!"

"Well, I do think there was at least luck at play in how Gordon even came to be here at our hospital – and on that particular day. Anyway time is pressing on and we have a miracle to transfer! Let's cross everything we have that the move goes without a hitch. I'll see you in a few days at Hawksford when I pop back in on Gordon."

Before he could go, I found myself flinging my arms around him and burying my head in his neck. "Thank you so very much!" I blubbered without shame, my tears dampening his shirt.

It took more than a few minutes to collect myself after that outpouring of affection and emotion. Before I could pull it off, Christine came to visit me. There were more tears, more hugs, more realisations of the presence of grace and synchronicities since having been here, more gratitude than I could bestow. Five minutes later, the scene repeated with another of the nurses. By the time Sarah popped her head round the door, I was already a choked-up wreck.

"Just to let you know, they are about to wheel Gordon out now. And he's fine, in case you are wondering. We've done the sedation. And it'll be me, Dr Brentwood and two other nurses who'll be travelling in the ambulance with him. So he will be attended to all the way."

"Well that's a relief to hear, thank you."

"You know, I was never a believer of what it was that you were doing with the crystals. I don't think I can say I ever understood what you actually did in your group healings either but I have come to the conclusion that it helped, it really did help. I know you can't quantify some things. Group healings and unconditional love don't come in the form of machines with beeps and colours and lines we can trace but if they did, I guess you would say it would be a very powerful machine to have in your arsenal."

"Yes!"

"I want to also thank you for your cooperation, Caroline. You never got in the *way*. You always had respect for our work and what we had to do, whenever we had to do it. That helped us enormously."

"Thank you for bending the rules with me Sarah, for letting us gather as small groups round his bed, and for humouring us with the things we wanted to place around the room. Thank you for telling me like it was – but with heart. That helped *me* enormously."

She nodded her head and turned to leave, only to pause again, her voice softening. "I expect it will be hard for you to leave here. We've become a little bit like family to you perhaps? It's different at Hawksford. But you will be okay. Take care of yourself, Caroline – that's going to be crucial moving forwards. Gordon's going to need you more than ever as he makes his recovery. I may well see you at ICU if they put me on shifts there. Anyway, I'm sure our paths will cross again. I'll be getting back to Gordon now. Drive safely."

Biting a trembling bottom lip, I watched her disappear, my eyes awash and stinging, chest heaving in silent sobs. *Family*. She'd hit the nail right on the head.

I stiffened as they wheeled Gordon past the door. *Shit. This is it.* The sheer presence of nurses and doctors meant that I could only glimpse Gordon's left hand – its third finger still waiting, I hoped, for the ring that was yet to be returned.

I didn't follow them down the corridor. With everybody else gone, I needed to calm myself, pull myself together. In a strange way, I also felt to say my goodbyes to this tiny Relatives' Room. For a fortnight it had housed everyone connected to Gordon; had acted as a container for mediation, a space for healing, and a kitchen and dining room for when people had come to feed me; been the host for "messages" of magic; the scene of bad and horrifying news as well as good and miraculous news; the receptacle for the ever-present-whooshing from the ceiling vent; and my place at night where I waited when nurses attended to Gordon. This room had been as much my home to me as Gordon's room had been. For a second I heard all the echoes of laughter and tears, the whispers of fear and the words of anger that had taken place in here. My heart twinged to be leaving. It was the same sadness I had experienced whenever something special came to an end but especially when something had drawn to a close that had involved experiences of closeness, bonding and connection. But now, it was time to leave.

My bags slowed me down as I walked along the corridor, a corridor that to my surprise began to come alive for me now in a way it never had before, as if the walls themselves intended to bid me farewell. It was, of course, a fanciful notion. And yet, for the first time I now spied an oar, mounted at eye level, and reminding me of the rowboats back in the bay. Further ahead were a selection of pelicans, plovers and seagulls painted directly onto the walls – the very birdlife that loved to surround us down by the water at home. My skin tingled as my mind tried to catch up with what was obvious. Since being at the hospital, I had felt separated from my old life and my normal world and everything in it. And yet the bay, our home, had been right here in spirit and on these walls with us the whole time! How on earth could I have missed it? For thirteen days and nights I had walked past these walls and yet had never once seen what had always been here. I gazed around in disbelief.

I managed only a couple of paces more before I stopped again, my feet glued to the spot in front of a painting that compelled me into its scene. I gaped at the details, my lips parting in amazement. I could have sworn it was a rendition of the dog-walking track that ran along a mangrove-lined section of the bay we happened to live near – part of the route by the water's edge that Gordon and I used to love walking to get to and from the house. Inside the painting, the trail cut through bush and silver gum trees that towered and arched towards each other, their canopies filtering light onto kookaburras in flight. At the centre was a boy with his back to me in jeans and a red fleece jacket, walking alongside water that sparkled like popping candy. *Gordon.* It was a weird thought to have zipped into my mind and yet, there it was. The boy did somehow cut a striking figure. There was purposefulness in the brushstrokes that had made him, yet he had an air of innocence too, even though I couldn't see his face. The scene looked uncannily identical to a photo I had once taken of Gordon on the dog-walking track in *his* red fleece, as he wound his way back home one winter's afternoon.

His hospital bed would have been wheeled straight past this painting, en route to the ambulance.

CHAPTER THIRTY-THREE

Day 12

1.00 p.m. – Hospital

FROM THE MINUTE I'd watched the ambulance inch away and disappear round the corner with its precious cargo, a thousand traps had pulled back taut all over my body, each ready to spring.

The first had caught me by surprise just seconds after a nurse had arrived with smiles in tow, to bring me to Gordon after the agony of a two hour wait in the new hospital. Punching a code in the door that then clicked open for us she led me down the plush carpet of the link-way. There were no PVC flaps to initiate me, grant entry, or refuse it, and no time to steel myself as I clapped eyes on my man just yards ahead. Dwarfed by the supersized bed he now lay in, stranded at the centre of a huge cubicle, one look at his frailness and vulnerability took my breath away. I scanned the ward only to discover the sprawl of other identical yet vacant cubicles extending either side of him and down to my left, in what was in effect an L-shaped, state-of-the-art ICU with five beds. Here in the dimness, the ward's stark walls bumped up against bare ceiling that wasn't painted as the sky. I took in the cavernous, vapid space before me and swallowed hard. The tears were pricking already and I wanted them to go back down. *Be strong Caroline.* Drawing closer and seeing the fever on Gordon's cheeks and the return of sweat on his brow, I felt a second trap fling itself shut inside my chest. The nurse began orientating me.

"He's raging a bit of a temperature. It was a major thing for him to be moved like that, as we suspected it would be, and so it's caused his heart rate to rise, which we are monitoring. It's some of the reason for the fever. The other, we think, is because he is still fighting the pneumonia." She paused, making a space for me to ask questions but no words seemed to want to come out of my mouth. "Well, he's sedated from the transfer but that will be wearing off soon. I expect you know it's going to take some days for him to be fully awake from the coma. So I guess today he's having a setback."

My heart thudded all the way up into my ears. He didn't look well. Not, at any rate, in comparison to yesterday nor to when I had told him I loved him just hours ago. This reversal was the first since the day of the bleed in his abdomen. It wasn't what I wanted to hear. I stroked his forehead, murmured that I was here. He didn't stir. Motioning to the soap at the end of his bed, the nurse instructed me to wash my hands. The stuff smelt even more sickly-sweet at this hospital, its ethanol vapours peeling the skin off in the back of my throat. I read the name on the label. Angel Blue. *Angel.* She said something else I didn't register and returned to her enormous nursing station with its down-lights, the only lights that were on in the ward other than the screaming brightness of Gordon's X-Ray on the lightbox behind her. I honed in on the scan, a freak exhibit that showcased the abnormality of his enlarged heart from the heart failure, and the denseness of white areas in his lungs from the pneumonia.

As the main hand on the clock next to the lightbox dragged itself not once but twice round the circumference of time, I sat in aching silence next to Gordon, jigging my legs, waiting it out for his temperature to drop and his sedative to wear off. The 2 p.m. healing came and went. Though its energy coursed through me it was a challenge to sit with focus. I hadn't yet told the nurses about what we were doing and in their oblivion, they had busied themselves around us both during that time, creating distraction after distraction. Half an hour later, I had asked if I could put some music on. Looking up, the nurse had advised it should be fine as long as the volume was kept low. I'd wondered who on earth it could possibly have bothered, but it didn't matter. The music just wasn't the same here anyway and I stashed the player away in the only nook I could find – the shelving behind his bed.

There was nowhere here to unpack the things from his other room – no ledge for his crystals, no spot on the wall to hang his painting. I didn't feel inclined to place the red cloth over his sheet, and the only window in this space (and indeed that I could see in the whole ward) was elevated and behind his bed. Staring up at it, all I could glimpse was a streak of gloom in the sky and a couple of tree tops. I doubted we would be allowed to hang the rainbow cloth from the glass and anyway, it wouldn't have fitted. Putting on my coat for extra warmth, my eyes smarted and metal filings jangled in my throat.

The calls on the mobile were coming in thick and fast too, sometimes coinciding with one of the visits from the nurse as she looked at Gordon, shook her head, and declared once again that we were nowhere near being out of the woods. Her pronouncements and the vibrations from inside my pocket were enough to threaten the snaps on all those invisible and strained traps set since leaving the first hospital. I knew, of course, who all the calls were from.

Nobody else would be ringing Gordon's mobile other than his workplace, the human resources department, his medical insurance, the leasing companies and the banks. I also knew I had to attend to them. At the same time, I wasn't game enough to leave Gordon's side to go and do it until he showed at least some sign of resurgence.

Suspended from the ceiling in the central walkway, digital black faces sought me out, branding-irons with glowing yellow numbers that burned 15:30 onto me, intent on marking me as belonging only to this physical world and subject therefore to the illusion of its timeframes and all the meanings of time and the way in which these wanted to dictate how I should feel. The more I checked the clocks and let myself be hypnotized by their spell, the less I inhabited Spirit time where all potentialities existed at once. I knew this and yet still I couldn't seem to stop my behaviour. The monitor by Gordon's side vied for my attention too. Its coloured numbers were chopping and changing, two of the squiggly lines tracing a new pattern. I knew enough to understand that it meant he had reverted to less stability, to his heart being back out of normal rhythm, to his blood pressure dropping below the level that Burleigh Fields had been keeping it at. Uneasiness was starting to extend its thick and sinewy roots into my core. I didn't *trust* this hospital, didn't trust they had it *right*. Hadn't Dr Brentwood himself said that his methods had played a vital role in Gordon even making it this far? That if Gordon had gone to any other hospital he could have ended up dying? I wanted Dr Brentwood to be here now but instead all I got were shift changes, and more strangers who didn't know us and who hadn't followed Gordon's journey nor experienced how far he had already come.

Sitting beside my man in marooned silence, I clung to the life raft he now found himself on, feeling the exposure not only to this sea of space in the cubicle but also to the vast ocean of ward around us. All the while the nurses didn't engage much. That wasn't their fault, of course. After all, what could they say? And they had their jobs to do – checking on Gordon from time to time and frowning, answering the phone with hushed voices, wordlessly collecting the paper that flicked out of the fax machine whenever it hummed into life, and then leaving the ward in noiseless shoes while I rocked on the edge of my chair.

In the end, the smiling nurse pulled rank after scrutinising me for a few seconds and told me I looked dreadful. She ordered me to go and get something to eat and I attempted a joke with her about it having been an insane fortnight and that I had been averaging three hours sleep a night. But as the tears slid over my bottom lids, I found myself confiding in her about all the financial issues that were starting to come in on me. She softened, asking if anybody had sent a counsellor to me at the other hospital. I shook my head, assuring her that I had the help and support of many friends. I tried to impress upon her that the one thing I most needed help with was in accessing Gordon's salary. That by being here at the hospital every day, I myself wasn't able to earn any money – not that I had the space, the time, or the finances to even resurrect the clinic business I'd pretty much closed down some months beforehand. I confessed there were bills outstanding, some of them – for reasons I did not yet understand – going back two months now and some of them, if not resolved, about to desecrate my life. Grasping the situation, the nurse declared she would page the social worker in the building and see if they could meet with me when I returned from having something to eat. Though I wasn't hungry, I headed out of ICU and downstairs to the café. I had calls to return, outcomes I hoped to secure – and all without wanting to spend a second more away from my man than these tasks required.

An hour later I was back, my body wired yet aching from the bruising and viciousness of yet more invisible traps springing shut and clamping down. The calls hadn't gone entirely well. Soul-destroying, they had yielded nothing but confusion, frustration, blocks and complications. I had felt thwarted at every turn, astounded at the heartlessness and insensitivity of the people on the other end of the line. To make matters worse, new information had come to light that threw into question the eligibility of Gordon for salary continuation within his company. The car and house were still under threat as they had been all week and the only saving grace in the whole hour had been a few more days of waiver on having to make the payments outstanding on Gordon's two credit cards.

I stared across at him, avoiding blinking as I did so in a bid to fight back the tears. His eyelids had opened to a slit, the sedative from the transfer wearing off. There was more noise in the ward, more nurses behind the nursing station than before. As the chattering brought a new face in the form of a doctor over to the bed, I realised it must be yet another staffing handover. I fumed a singular breath through my nostrils, pursing my lips to contain the still boiling anger that had threatened to engulf me down in the hospital lobby not half an hour before where, sitting alone in the chair, I had watching all manner of people come and go through the doors, and felt the ache of no-one – of no family member – coming through them for *me*.

The thought badgered me again now as the doctor ran his checks. Neither of the boys had called since the day they'd left to go back to Melbourne. As for Dorothy and Brenda, they hadn't been in touch nor asked after me once since the night of my first calls to them and the subsequent couple of days I had sent updates by text. I did realise and accept that in reassuring my friend only that morning that I would be fine to make the trip here on my own to this new place, I had thereby made a statement to myself that I ought to be standing on my own two feet. After all, people had shown me incredible generosity with their love and support. I had felt it was time to act from the knowing that I did have the capacity to handle whatever showed up in Life from this point. Sitting here now however, the child in me – with all her overwhelm – was not so sure anymore.

In truth, many people had wanted to be with me today yet each of them for one reason or another had not been able to make it. I'd understood. This day was not like the one when Gordon had crashed. Dr Brentwood himself had said we were in a different phase now, moving away from survival and towards recovery. Hadn't this too, been the reason I had stopped people coming to see Gordon, now that he was emerging from coma with disorientation and maybe wanting to go through that process in privacy? It was all true. But the "me" who felt sorry for herself, still couldn't help but notice that of all the text messages asking after Gordon today, not one had included an enquiry as to how I was faring. It was silliness really. A little thing perhaps and yet it rubbed enough salt into a wound cracked open once again by the lack of contact from relatives.

The more I bought into my pain and the addiction of a story about the family's callousness in leaving me to deal with more than I felt I could handle, the more I seethed and the more I lumped everyone else in the same basket. Encapsulated in a bubble of distress of my own making, I sat in absence to the here and now, feeling separate from life itself. I ground my teeth, felt my chest heave with the force of unspent rage. When I'd been down in the lobby making those calls and seeing all those people entering through the door, it had been everything I could do to stay awake within the dream and to acknowledge my thoughts and feelings, and choose again with my behaviours. Back here on the ward, it was starting to feel like a losing battle. My story was in full swing: I was abandoned, Life was not supporting me, I was on my own, and nobody cared.

"Does Gordon have a will?"

I stared at the social worker's dark beady eyes as they fixated on me from behind the red-rimmed glasses dug into her puffy face. Though her lips were moving and I could hear the droning, I couldn't fathom why she was asking. She repeated the question. In a rush of understanding at what she was driving at, my eyes popped. How could she bring this up while he still fought for his life? Apology coloured her floury skin.

"*No,* he doesn't." I whacked the ball right out of court, hoping it wouldn't come back into play.

"What about a pension? If he has one of those, do you know what the policy states for if he is critically ill? Can you draw money down from it?"

"I have no idea. I know he has about three different pensions and I think two of them are still in the UK. He had been looking into getting them rolled over into the one he has here, but I don't think he actually did it. There was some red tape or something that put up a roadblock. I'm not sure about his pension, not sure who it is with. I don't know what it provides for . . ." I felt my stupidity at not knowing anything more concrete about it.

"Well, maybe when you get home you can have a check, see what paperwork you can find. In the meantime, do you have any family who could help or maybe give you some money?" I ground my back teeth as my lips drew a resolute line of "no" under that idea. She scratched into her perm and straightened up in the chair, clearing her throat. "Okay, so the other thing that you may well have to do is get a power of attorney. That would allow you to access Gordon's bank account. But also, given the critical nature of his illness, it would permit you to make significant decisions over his healthcare here at the hospital if need be . . . and, you know . . ."

"How do I get a power of attorney?"

A surge of heat rose inside my head, hundreds of pin pricks studding my scalp from the inside, while meaningless dots swam in front of my eyes. The small and soulless room felt like it was running out of air, as if the social worker had used almost all of it up by asking question after question. Perhaps it was a stroke of luck I hadn't known the answers to so many of them otherwise we both might have suffocated by now. *Please God, help me.* Taking her time, she began to unfold the details of how she could take care of that for me.

"Huh? He will need to be deemed in his mental faculties? What does that mean? He can't even talk. He can't lift his arm. He's not with it, not even out of coma . . ."

The room started to spin, words coming at me now as if from under general anaesthetic. Fearing I was about to faint I concentrated on slowing my breathing. I could make out enough of what she was saying to hear that she felt it would be unlikely over the next few hours or days that anything with a lawyer could take place between Gordon and me, but that this was where we would need to head. I recalled the car hire company's words, hard squash balls bouncing off walls that were closing in on me. *I'm sorry, you've got a week or we will have to recover the vehicles.* Other voices were joining in, other balls ricocheting. I tuned back in to the social worker. The phrase "post-traumatic stress" left her lips and hung in the heaviness. It was her label for me. I felt separate from it and didn't know what to do with it. She carried on speaking and briefed me that the lawyer would have to have conviction that Gordon had understood every question they would ask him – questions designed to explain why they had come to see him, whether he would give permission for me to act on his behalf with his finances, and to make and execute decisions that concerned him and his welfare. An image of Gordon filled my mind: critically ill, right in the middle of his setback, still with pneumonia, still with a temperature, still with a heart out of rhythm. Her words weren't matching reality.

In the end, all we could do was to agree upon the next steps we each would take, and to meet again over the next couple of days. I rubbed my cold and clammy hands on the knees of my jeans, mustering a smile of gratitude while somewhere inside of me I screamed for somebody to make this nightmare stop.

At around 7.30 p.m., my phone vibrated in my pocket. In a way, the interruption it provided was timely. Gordon had been coughing, his hacking echoing throughout the ward. No closeness of walls to absorb it, nor other patient to distract from it. He kept trying to resist the nurse suctioning the phlegm out through his tube. I gritted my teeth at the awfulness of it. Grabbing the phone out, I spied the text message.

> Have you thought what you are going to do about Africa? Probably the last thing you want to hear about right now. I just know you need to give an answer soon. Hope I haven't spoken out of turn. I'm here, if you want to chat.

It was my friend, Holly. Another trap snapped, grabbing my skin in its jaws. She was right of course. Our trip to Africa was only five weeks away now. Consumed with all the other financial affairs, I had been resisting thinking about it, not wanting to face what was looking like inevitability. Just like last year, it seemed we would have to pull out of this trip again, lose an opportunity hard won, and the money as well, since rightly or wrongly there would be no refunds. We'd had so much grace on our side since Gordon had crashed, grace that had kept him with us, and yet it seemed a push too far to believe there could be a miracle which would arrange for Gordon to be in the health needed to board a flight to a remote destination in just over a month and participate in a safari. Or for me to feel the assurance to go and leave him here by himself . . . if he even was still here. It felt wrong to feel it and yet I couldn't deny the swell of loss and grief in my chest. Before I had a chance to meet and acknowledge it in its fullness, a nurse was speaking to me. Oblivious to most of what she said, the only words that careered into my consciousness were a medical term that no one had mentioned until now.

"What was that you said? The syndrome, the thing you mentioned?"

"You mean the critical weakness syndrome? That's what Gordon has." She stood there, sturdy and unmoved, blinking back at me. Her short, strawberry-blond hair was thinning and revealing her scalp. "They didn't speak about that with you at the other hospital?" I shook my head, trying to stay calm and using her freckles as my anchor. "Okay. Well, critical weakness syndrome is what happens to a patient like Gordon when they have been on life support for as long as he has. He hasn't been using his muscles, so the muscles become weakened. They start to waste away a bit, and it can take a long time for them to get their strength back. That's why I said you need to prepare yourself."

"Prepare myself? I don't understand . . ." I could hear my voice spiralling, feel the slam of yet another trap in my body sending a wave of sickly fear into my system.

"His recovery. It's going to take weeks and weeks, more likely, months and months. You need to prepare yourself for that."

"What do you mean, months and months?"

"Well, whilst we still hope – and remain confident – that Gordon's kidneys will recover over time, his critical weakness syndrome is likely to endure many months. So there's a huge journey ahead of you before Gordon will be able to return to work, for example. He's going to need a lot of care and support if he pulls through." She flushed pink, her cheeks dimpling as she tried to offer her empathy.

"But how on earth will we *survive* in that time?" My brain whirred in a bid to process her meaning. "I wound up my business a few months ago to get ready for creating a new one. I'm not working right now! I don't have my own reliable income. And I don't understand what you are saying! How many months are we talking about? I mean, what is 'months and months'? How many are we talking about here? How would we pay our rent? How would we eat? We'd lose the house, the car! If we couldn't pay Gordon's credit cards, he would go bankrupt! Who would employ him ever again if that happened? How will we cope? How will *I* cope?"

"I understand."

"What do you mean, you *understand*? I don't think you do understand! I have spent the best part of this afternoon speaking to Gordon's HR, to his health insurance people, to credit card companies, to car leasing companies, to property managers, trying to sort out the mess that is our finances. I am five days away from the car we have and the means for being able to visit Gordon being taken away from me! I still can't access what funds we do have and I don't know when I will be able to and so I might lose the house before Gordon even makes it out of this place. Now you are telling me *this*? No!"

"Caroline, you're going to have to face it sooner or later, it's . . ."

"No! Not *now*! Please stop saying this. How does it help me right now, to know this? I can't *cope* with this!" I licked the salt of a tear that had splashed onto my lip. My heart hammered.

"Denying reality won't help you, or Gordon or anyone, Caroline, and you would be surprised at what you are able to cope with into the future. There are always resources, people who can help you. But for now, the facts are that he does have critical weakness syndrome, organ failures to still recover from, and right now, the pneumonia and temperature to overcome. Other things too that have destabilised him in the move. He is still incredibly sick. We still need to get him through the night. He's not out of the woods yet."

"Will you people stop saying that he's not out of the woods yet! I can't listen to that anymore! Not one of you has said a single positive thing about him today! I can't cope with this. Any of it! I can't cope. Don't you understand? I can't cope! I'm sorry. I have to get out of here!"

I heard the sob catch in my throat, felt bad for my rudeness but at the same time couldn't seem to help myself. In a blur I high-tailed it out of the ward, fleeing to the vacuousness of the waiting area where I'd first arrived. There, my eye caught one of the framed panoramic photographs on the wall behind the couch. I hadn't noticed it earlier. It was a scene of a beach, the photographer capturing the froth of the waves as they lavished over dark yellow sand. I wondered if I would ever get to walk the beach with Gordon again. Glancing down the picture, I spied the title: *Beautiful Day*. That has been the title of the tune the string quartet had played at our wedding as I walked up the aisle, and the soundtrack to the DVD of us snorkelling The Great Barrier Reef. Now it was the phrase that couldn't have been much more opposite to how I saw things. The sobs and the tears came flooding out, turning into howls loud enough to wake the dead. Two weeks of living through unprecedented degrees of trauma and terror; of trying to learn the art of gliding over the fast-shifting sands; of losses already sustained and the threat of more to be incurred; of fears for Gordon's future and survival and fears for my own; and on top of it all, my wretched aloneness. All were tributaries now, swelling an ocean of emotion. Blubbering, I rocked backwards and forwards, feeling like I was going mad, like I was losing control – needing to lose control perhaps, no longer wanting to be present to what was so because I no longer believed I could handle anything else Life was going to serve me.

You bloody COWARD! Shame seared my cheeks. The wisdom I had gained from the owl just nights before was lost to me amidst my own torrent of unconsciousness, and an unleashing of terror about whether Gordon was going to slide further backwards again and die, or pull through and lead us both into a daunting unknown. It was as if all our wins had been sacrificed, a devastating notion to consider, given the herculean effort it had taken to achieve those gains in the first place. Somewhere in all of my meltdown, I begged. *Please God! Help me! Help me align with the highest good!*

His name, I heard him tell me, was Dr Jordan. Mellifluous, his voice swaddled me. I looked up and saw a dark-skinned face punctuated by the bright whites of his eyes and teeth smiling in kindness.

"Caroline, I'm Dr Jordan. I'm in charge on the ward tonight. What's happening?" I tried to speak but was incoherent. "Caroline, you need to calm down. Gordon can hear you out here. Your breakdown isn't helping him. He needs you. And you need to be strong for him and for yourself right now. Talk to me. What is happening?"

I relayed my whole day, my fears, my anguish, my pain, and everything that was crashing in on me. He told me a story about how his parents had died when he was only a boy. His point was that he had survived it, was here now, helping others, and that life goes on whether people live or die. I heard him but I still wanted him to tell me – to give me some assurance – that Gordon was not in any danger right now, that he would make it, be okay, and live an okay life.

"All I can say is that we are doing the best for him that we can. Life is uncertainty, Caroline. We just don't know. We just don't *know*." He breathed these words again as I continued to cry and ask for reassurance of some kind. "Caroline! We. Just. Don't. Know. We don't know if you will go bankrupt, Caroline. You don't know that. We don't know if Gordon will be okay. We hope so but we just don't know. You just don't know what the future holds, Caroline. We just don't know."

I knew he was speaking about being in innocence, the space of "not knowing", where nothing makes sense and where judgements can be dropped to allow that which is true to come in and to happen next. In not knowing, a state of grace can be entered into, a place to receive what is rather than to block. I understood it. For two weeks now, I'd been doing that right at the coal face and as best I could. But the quantity of emotion to move up and out of my body – energy in motion that had been building not only today but since the crash – was enormous. Adding their weight had also been the meanings I had bought into about today's news. The result was a surge of feeling with so much power in its momentum that it wouldn't settle for anything less than its total release, irrevocably bursting the walls of a dam that over time had struggled to contain the burgeoning pressure.

When, after twenty minutes, I still couldn't pull myself together, Dr Jordan gave me an ultimatum: either I would agree to have him call one of my friends to be with me, or I would have to go home.

I understood but could not bring myself to leave the hospital, nor did I want to have a friend come out either. I had tried to stand on my own two feet all day, believing that I should be getting on with things by myself now, that "it was time" for that too, that I couldn't ask others for yet more support. I had to deal with this myself, I told him, not call in the help of others.

One look at me and he confirmed we would be ringing a friend.

Ruth and Larry arrived soon after with their sleepy, pyjama-clad daughter. I met them with my cheeks on fire, head hanging at not having been able to deal with things, and yet also a heart filled with gratitude for their love, support, and willingness to come out and be with me. We all hugged, sat together, and talked. They promised me that certain friends were ready to lend money for my immediate needs and bills, and that others were already talking about fundraising if need be. They shared with me all the support still coming in online, all the people still jumping on the healings, choosing the highest good and sending love to not only Gordon but to me too. Sitting with me, they held a space so that I could be held.

Two hours later, after they had gone and I was stroking Gordon's hand again, I realised something. Vulnerability is many things but it isn't just about asking for help once and then receiving it, or about being willing to ask for help and being open enough to receive it. It is also about staying open and asking for yet *more* help. That, precisely in the moment when our head screams at us that we shouldn't ask for any more support or receive any more of it, and when we try to convince ourselves that we have surely had our lot and must grow up, this is when vulnerability can take us deeper into its embrace as the Love that knows no bounds.

CHAPTER THIRTY-FOUR

Day 13

8.30 a.m. – Hospital

CONSCIOUS DECISIONS shape action from a place of power. They can set you on a different path, transform how you experience something. When I had greeted the day as it streamed in on me back at the house, I knew with clarity and conviction that I must refocus from the night before. Refocus and bring that freshness of attitude with me into the hospital. Refocus in favour of choosing the highest good for all, in favour of being of service to Gordon, in favour of being the Love that I was to myself and everyone else, in favour of doing what Love does. Another decision occurred to me too. From now on, given that Gordon was advancing out of coma and becoming more aware, I would ensure that he only saw smiles on my lips, strength in my face, love and compassion in my eyes. It was nothing to do with slushiness and everything to do with remembering that as "Love" itself, I could contribute much, be his rock, be the space in which he was able to experience his recovery. Although my energy had focused on "seeing" him during his coma, and bearing witness to him and connecting from my heart, I sensed that it was going to become critical that I add to this the choice to be his physical, emotional and mental strength too, until such time as he could be those things for himself. That in fact, this would serve us both. In truth, I couldn't think of any better antidote to my fears and self-doubt about whether I could cope with the road ahead, no better remedy for stopping the powering of my spiral-inducing stories.

As the day panned out, Gordon's alertness grew. It was a double-edged sword for him that brought with it a range of discomforts at landing squarely in the restrictions and pain of his body. Each time he hacked the most toe-curling of coughs and was suctioned, I stroked his leg with confidence, trying to offer at least one sensation that might gift pleasure in the face of so much that was not. In his bewilderment at not being able to move his hands and arms and legs, and in the inconvenience of sometimes having to be rolled onto the side of his pneumonia-ridden lung, there was power for me and for him in my being able to lock my gaze with his and talk through the eyes to soothe and calm him down. In tandem with the eyes and touch, I learned my voice and tone were a gift, demonstrating nothing but certitude about him being on the mend and about walking out of here and enjoying an active and fulfilling life. In truth, I didn't know for sure if he would be in a state to lead that life but I knew I had to say he would. With him showing confusion and fear about what was happening, it was not the time to express any negativity or doubt to him. The nurses, by virtue of the job they had to do, saw things differently. They steeped themselves in all the potentials for setbacks and downturns, were still conservative about any prognosis for the future, and were continuing to use medical names for what had happened to him.

By the 10 a.m. healing, I had asked them to stop using certain terms around his bedside. I explained that I had noticed him shutting his eyes whenever they told him what had happened. He was blocking, in denial, unable to absorb it or understand it. He was going to need to acknowledge what had happened to him and reach the point of acceptance for where he had been and where he was – but the truth in my heart said that there needed to be a gentler way at this stage. We needed to take baby steps, do nothing to scare him or cause him to feel hopelessness or terror or depression.

By around lunchtime and with Gordon still on the tail-end of exiting his coma, I watched in awe as he showed remarkable courage, focus and determination to participate in his recovery even though he was not yet lucid enough to fathom what on earth had happened to him. There was a shot at gripping a juggling ball, and his first two lots of twenty minute trials for breathing without the ventilator. My heart skipped for joy to observe that not only did he bring purposefulness to these endeavours but that with much resolve he attempted to lift his arms while doing them, as if this were extra "homework". He was not one to be an overachiever in life, so I could only put it down to his unwavering choice to be back in the land of the living, having taken what must have already been an epic return journey so far.

Both the nurses and I were able to comprehend his facial expressions towards early evening. He was able to nod yes or shake no to questions asked of him. It felt as if he had returned to us all with more humour, making me snort at one point with his exaggerated face of boredom, or the look that said "for Pete's sake!" that came with the comedy of rolling his eyes. He also played around with producing weird sounds through the tracheostomy in his throat, unable to speak of course, but wanting to make me smile. To see him display jocularity brought tears of joy to my eyes.

I couldn't believe the miracle I was witnessing, the spirited leaps that were taking place despite him not being fully out of coma.

At around 11 p.m. it happened.

Jim and Steve had arrived four hours earlier on a flight from Melbourne, to be with their dad for a couple of days. I had been nervous about seeing them again after what had transpired between us last time but there was no need for worry. We were all here for this man we had in common, here in a space of love, here to watch with humility an emergence like no other, here to pinch ourselves in excitement at what we were seeing. To his sons, Gordon was their hero. To me, he was the epitome of magic.

We were sitting around his bed, Jim and Steve to each side of him and me further down towards his feet. Glimmering in the dimness was a movie on the TV suspended from the ceiling above the end of the bed, its volume low. Gordon was the only one staring at the screen. Jim and Steve and I were still too preoccupied with stealing bashful glances at the man who was now sitting up in bed and the most alert he had been so far. For some reason, I looked up at the screen just in time to watch the main character, played by Stallone, emerging from his cryogenic freezing and stepping into a brand new world. As Stallone started to speak his lines, Dr Jordan appeared at the foot of the bed and cleared his throat.

"Just to say that as well as the temperature returning to normal a couple of hours ago, Gordon is now officially out of coma. It'll still take some days before he is able to experience that himself, but as far as we are concerned, yes, it is official."

Stunned, I sat there for a second before the widest smile spread over my face. Looking over to the boys I discovered a mirror image of myself, eyes shining so bright they lit up the universe held within them. A rush of warmth, then a starburst of energy exploded inside my chest, radiating outwards, electricity that activated every goose bump I owned. A wave of joy that filled the cubicle and advanced beyond it as a Love that knows no bounds, showering its magic and blessings upon everything it came into contact with. There were no loud cheers or clapping from any of us, but instead, the heightened presence and aliveness you experience when witnessing a miracle. Somewhere in amongst it all, sensations gave way to words that wanted to tumble and jumble themselves out in excitement.

"Oh my God, Babes, you are bloody unbelievable!" I grinned, squeezing his toes from where I stood, my eyes tearing up again.

"Dad, you're so amazing!" Steve muffled into his father's neck, hugging as much of him as tubes and drips would allow access to, while Jim joined in from the other side, beaming and shaking his head in wonderment, telling his dad that he loved him.

When they moved away, Gordon raised his eyebrows and managed one of his gorgeous new smiles of innocence. He was fighting back tiredness, soon to achieve its goal of drooping down his eyelids. It had indeed been a huge day for him. I doubted he had any real idea of what Dr Jordan was speaking. Deciding to leave him to get his rest, the boys left for their accommodation.

I sat for a while longer beside him. Soaking in the gift of what was now even more precious – one-on-one time with my man. Stroking his arms, his forehead, his face, and kissing him on the lips, I let him know how much I loved him, how proud of him I was. Fifteen minutes later, with coat on and bags ready to go, I bid him goodnight only to watch him mouth the words "I love you" and to see him blow me a kiss before finishing with another weary smile. My heart soared.

In the car park it was impossible to miss the beauty of thin clouds scudding across the magnificence of a giant white moon emanating magic with its aura of pastel rings. The moon was waxing, more than half-illuminated yet less than full size. Close, but not there yet, its re-emergence taking place after a period of withdrawal where it had seemed to have not even been there at all. Now it was expanding, increasing in illumination, ever-renewing itself in the realm of time and yet also showing me the regenerative power that was the timelessness of eternal life force. After what had happened on the ward today and this evening, we too were now a step closer with Gordon but not fully there yet. Still not "out of those woods", as the nurses so liked to say, but not as swallowed up by them either. He remained critical and stable, lungs clearing but still with pneumonia, breathing without the ventilator but only for short stints, and still on dialysis. I knew that there were many hurdles yet to overcome, hoops to have to get through for him and for me. Despite that, it was starting to feel that although there would be challenges in continuing to go forward, it would be perhaps less likely that we could slip back now. Like the moon, there was an increase in momentum it seemed. After all that had transpired, Gordon was still here now in this physical realm. I stood transfixed by the brilliance before me, and gave thanks.

CHAPTER THIRTY-FIVE

Seven weeks later

10.00 a.m. – Homecoming

DRIVING AWAY FROM THE HOSPITAL, the weather had gifted us a blessing after days of grey and rain. A clean slate of crisp blue skies, cool but moderate breeze and an abundance of sunshine were already adding up to the perfect late morning in winter. Though he was ecstatic during the trip home, Gordon was quieter than I thought he might have been. My intuition knew to let him be. Speaking only now and then through grins, I glanced over in his direction and squeezed his hand from time to time, sensing his overwhelm and myriad emotions about his release.

I was filled with appreciation to still have the car and be able to use it to drive him back. The much needed power of attorney had been granted just in time during a window of opportunity that presented itself three days after the official exit from coma. Gordon had completed his first ninety minute phase of breathing without the ventilator, and had shown brightness and alertness. No sooner had Dr Jordan given his approval I had rushed to get the lawyer in.

It was only much later, after Gordon's speech returned, that I had the chance to discover why it was my man had shaken his head with a "no" when the lawyer asked if he would agree to me being able to access his funds. Of course, I had stared at Gordon in disbelief and horror, not comprehending his objection, and explaining to him why I needed that money. I smiled now at the memory. To think he had actually been trying to crack a joke, trying to make himself understood that I should leave some dollars in there for his beers when he arrived home! It had been his first expression of lucidity and sophistication with humour but I had missed it because I was too busy identifying with my assumption that Life wasn't going to support me. The bloody bugger! That had been a tough day for me, a day of sliding back into stories, of a nail-biting wait for the doctor to give me the go-ahead for the lawyer, not to mention my formal cancellation of the trip to Africa and the anger and grief this had unleashed in me.

Emerging from the bend, I held my breath and gripped the wheel, my chest aflutter. The moment that had been dreamt of over weeks of longing, now drew level with the car and the top of the hill and the vista stretched out below us. I drank in the sapphire glitter of the bay, joyous to receive the welcoming committee of fishing boats and yachts, their masts standing tall and proud and their colourful hulls glinting.

"Wow!" I glanced across at Gordon as he spoke. His eyes shone as if they were discovering something for the first time. "It's more stunning than ever before! You have no idea how much I've fantasised about seeing this again!"

I held his hand and on behalf of us both, shrieked and whooped as I coasted the car down to the bottom with an air of ceremony, and then parked.

"Well that was worth the wait!"

"You liked that, eh?" I grinned, feeling the thrill of anticipation rising. "I have something special for you for lunch. I'm just going to nip in to the café and get it and I'll be right back, okay?"

Though it was midweek, the café was bustling and everybody seemed to be out celebrating, the break in the weather probably having something to do with it. As I waited at the counter for the owner to return from one of the tables, a kitchen server plonked two plates of scrambled eggs and green salad in front of me, calling out the number and a waitress's name. I smiled. The nutritionist at the hospital had pleaded with Gordon to eat eggs but he just couldn't, in fact, he'd had a reaction to even trying, feeling like he was going to vomit. I could only assume that it was one of those phenomena where the brain had created an association with the day he had crashed in terror and been intubated, that perhaps during that procedure he had vomited the last thing to have entered his stomach – the scrambled eggs and kale we had eaten before arriving.

"Hang on, Caroline. I'll be with you, just need to fix up these coffees." The owner Sarah was rushed, slamming her hand down on the bell again for the waitress.

I didn't mind the delay. I still had to pinch myself that I was even in here, fetching lunch for my man who, over nine weeks ago, hadn't known if he would ever open his eyes again. When he was back to full consciousness five weeks ago, I hadn't known if he would still be able to make it out of those woods that we were all so worried about.

It was still hard to take in, the colossal journey that had unfolded since then. Gordon had remained in ICU for another twelve days before being transferred to Critical Care and then, eventually, the Rehab Ward. I continued to visit him all day long and every night. A few friends still came to sit with me from time to time, others left the occasional bag of salad greens and eggs at my front door or brought in a lunch for me that they had prepared. And even yesterday another supporter of our cause had sent me a cleaner from her business in a touching gesture of help for me in the home in readiness for Gordon's arrival. As for the group healings, they continued four times a day up until he left for the Rehab Ward. Drummers drummed for him in their homes and groups, choir members dedicated songs for him in public performances, workshop attendees held energetic space for his recovery, and once he was in Critical Care there had even been a friend or two visiting him. It still staggered me, this level of unity in a community continuing to expand across four continents.

Those twelve days of wakefulness and of still being critical and stable, were the most intense of the post-coma journey. There were of course wins, setbacks, emotional rollercoasters and times of both of us having to dig deep. Yet there was also huge growth. I watched Gordon having to learn to apply will, to focus and refocus, take action when asked and even when not, and to marry it all with the acceptance for what was. I found myself opening even more to the gifts that acceptance, open-heartedness, presence and compassion could bring, as well as developing my resilience and courage in the face of post-traumatic stress and what was, in truth, a messy and painful recovery.

"My apologies, Caroline! Bit short staffed today. Be with you real soon! No matter how much I bang this jug up and down, the barista only goes so fast!"

"Hey, it's okay."

I watched her work the machine, listened to its frenzy of hissing and frothing and steaming. What a contrast to the softness of the "pooft" and sigh of the ventilator that had become such a part of my life and Gordon's! Weaning off that ventilator through incremental periods of unassisted breathing, was one of the toughest trials he'd had to meet. So too had been drying out his lungs; getting off dialysis; graduating from all his other machines and drips; progressing to the point where they could remove the tracheostomy; arriving at the stage where his swelling had reduced by as much as they wanted to see it dip to; and a plethora of other hurdles he'd had to jump. Thanks to his critical weakness syndrome and no food intake for a month, he had also lost 20kg in weight, emerging emaciated and malnourished and with tremors, so that he struggled to hold cups or write. To say we were both daunted at that time was an understatement and yet we had travelled through worse than this already.

In many ways recovery had been fraught with as much difficulty as survival. During those days immediately after he was pronounced officially out of coma, we had traversed an arduous terrain, and setbacks had peppered the route. Gordon's "ICU-psychosis" had presented itself within hours. The persistence of insomnia with no sense of night or day, the trippy cocktail of drugs yet to be excreted by organs that were diminished in their capacity for the job, and his not knowing or being able to grasp what had happened to him, meant that for two weeks he experienced paranoia, moodiness, irritability, anxiety, shut down and signs of darker depression. On day three of that period, both his compromised immune system and the plastic fitting of his tracheostomy had caused him to contract a hospital superbug, which increased his risk of further infections at a time when his vulnerability was already an issue. As the days passed, he developed nosebleeds that wouldn't stop running day or night due to the blood thinners he was on. The bleeds led him to undergo an emergency operation to cauterize and resolve the problem. On top of all this, he had suffered the agony of excoriated skin. The culprit: his prolific diarrhoea caused by the prolonging of high-dosage antibiotics and the choice to use a drip feed of chemicals in place of the solid food that, due to his condition, he was unable to swallow. The incontinence had humiliated him, humbled him, and stripped him of his last vestiges of dignity.

Scattered across this terrain were milestones aplenty, times when humour provided a welcome reprieve from the demands of recovery, and moments where wins and rites of passage and each "first" had been a boost and confirmation of the power of Love, of spirit and of Gordon's decision to fully claim being back here in this world.

Most of his advances had taken place in those first eight days out of coma. Day three had brought with it his qualifying victory in the exercises in bed with the D-ring above his head; then, the first machine that he was weaned off (dialysis – exciting and promising at the time); the completion of two hours of breathing without assistance from the ventilator; and experiments with speaking through the device in his tracheostomy. On day four, he ate two spoons of "starter" food (custard); hit the mark for breathing for four hours without the machine; enjoyed his inaugural trip of being wheeled onto the veranda for five minutes in gown, jacket, blanket, and sunglasses; and also claimed his win in being aided to stand for a minute and straighten his spine with all its protrusion of nodules. By day five, progress knocked in the form of the assertiveness we saw towards the staff, and via the gifts of his first sip of water and assisted shower – both declared by him to have been "sensational." From day seven he had managed to maintain a week off the dialysis machine, with the removal of a transfusion line also being a precursor for more to go, each one thereafter signalling that he was making it out of those woods. On the tenth day he initiated a shuffle around the ward with the walker. At eight metres, this was even more than he had been asked to do. He also celebrated standing another three times before evening came, and his milestone of breathing for a total of ten hours without the ventilator. And on the fifteenth day he completed a landmark twenty-four hours of breathing without that machine and his tracheostomy was removed. Finally, after a month spread across two ICU wards in two hospitals, he was no longer deemed to need "intensive care" and had been transferred into Critical Care. Only a couple of weeks after that they moved him to the rehab ward for the final leg of his grand tour.

"Hey Jess, it's to go to table four, with the dog!"

A voice, and a body bumping me, brought me right back to the café. The waitress had arrived for the plates of eggs. I looked down at the fluffy mass of sunshine on the plate and felt a wry smile spread across my face. In a flash, I *got* it. It was true what they said: rough though the way to get there may seem, you really can't make life's amazing omelette without first having to break a few eggs.

I exhaled.

A release.

We sat down on the bench on the grass. No-one else was around save a couple of fisherman on the end of the long jetty, their laughter travelling over on the fresh linen breeze that flapped across our cheeks, and fluttered and whooshed in our ears. Gordon was cold despite wearing four layers of clothing. He put his red fleece on. The sensitivity to the chill was a result of his dramatic loss of weight. So too, was his inability to sit for more than a minute without having to shift the weight on his buttocks over to the other side. I looked at him. He *was* Gordon and yet there was a change, the key to the difference intangible and yet somehow there in his eyes and in his smile, both of which emanated humility, gentleness, love, and innocence like never before. He had the essence of a newborn about him, or of a "reborn". It seemed outlandish to say it and yet, it was so. I knew that this sense of change was also because *my* eyes were the ones seeing him and that could see all this *in* him, eyes that had re-learned to receive him in a spirit of discovery and awe and with the same humility and gentleness. For a moment, unconditional Love was consciously aware of itself, as the one who was reflecting, as the reflecting itself, and also as the reflection.

"God I love you!" A romantic rush swept through my being. Remembering my gift, I reached under the table.

"I arranged a little treat for you, darling! I know how much you've wanted to eat one of these since coming out of coma, so I got you an extra special one!"

I pushed the white paper bag across the picnic table and towards him. Puzzled but smiling he took it, his hands shaking from the effects of his syndrome, while scrawny fingers fiddled with the opening. Dragging out the tray with difficulty, he united with his lunch: a large sausage roll. Not just any sausage roll this one had been handmade by our café and, at my request, with an extra layer of puff pastry "glued" on top. Cut out into that layer, letters spelt the word "HOME".

"That's bloody brilliant! Thanks, Babes. I *love* it!" His smile was gold. Priceless. I wrapped my arms around his neck, a small sob escaping from me as my heart burst once more and I told him again how much I loved him.

"I love you too, Babes. I absolutely adore you."

I sniffed back the tears, aware I needed to give him room to get to his sausage roll, and we laughed. As he picked at it and my hand rubbed his back, I gazed across at the water capping in front of us. No wave was any more or less discernible or definable than the other, nor could it be separated from the body of water that in truth it was. Lolling and licking and lapping, it butted up against the break-wall only to be absorbed back into itself. A sleek cormorant appeared from nowhere and skimmed across the water, heading for the shaft of dazzle playing upon the surface over to our right. So much light concentrated in one place that it seemed a solid body of blinding white. I squinted and honed in for a minute or so, mesmerized by the activity I discovered there. One spark of light appearing in a thousand places all at once – pure aliveness rearranging itself over and over, recreating itself again and again. I stayed with my awe and wonder as the spark – or sparks – transformed themselves into a trillion holy crosses, then spinning tops, and then stick figures stretching their arms out as they weaved in out of each other in a dance that knew no beginning and truly had no end. The movements were glittery and chaotic within the paradox of fundamental order, a spirited animation that suggested randomness and yet danced to the tune of synchronicity, thousands of potentials or individual "becomings" existing all at once. With all the flickering on and off, it was impossible to track the exact moment it went from one expression to the other, so perpetual was the underlying energy.

I thought about all the hearts that had helped us on our journey, diamonds that may have started out as rough as me, perhaps, yet likewise had been smoothed and polished by the ride we'd all been on. This week alone, stories had reached me of just how many strangers had been joining in on the healings. There were accounts of hairdressers eager to hear updates from their clients, and requesting of all who came into the salon that they help send love to this man in need; husbands returning home from work who didn't know us at all but whose first or second question to their wives upon coming through the door was, "Have you heard any news? How is he?", and couples reading my updates at night before switching on their TV shows. It was an ever-growing list of tales about how far and wide the request for help had gone out into the physical world, let alone to those realms invisible to us.

I breathed out, feeling warm inside. The creative force and quantum field of unconditional, infinite Love knows no boundaries of geography. It exists beyond the realm of time, outside of numerical limitations or grading, or definitions such as the statistics given to Gordon about his chances in those first hours. And, while it is true that as humans we are all connected as part of the singular body of humanity on this planet, we are also connected through the heart and its intelligence, a portal that opens us to experiencing our deepest, most profound interconnectedness of all: our connection as universal energy and infinite Love, as the One Animating Spark that we all are, that *lives* us as humans, and that conducts its mystery through us *as* "us" and *as* this body of people on earth. The spark that signals us and messages us and talks to us through all forms in life, ready to converse with us during the human experience if we would but open to its mystery, listen, and take the actions it guides us on. Connected in this way, we are never truly alone, who we are can never truly be separate, and so we can never truly be abandoned, even if our personality can forget or ignore this at times and believe in the illusions or stories that it creates to the contrary. To awaken within the dream is to know and experience ourselves as unconditional love, to know that from the perspective of ultimate truth, we are not our stories. We are not other people's projections onto us nor are they our projections; we are not our divisions; we are not our perceived limitations. We are not our fears or spirals or meltdowns or heartbreaks, nor are we our anger or guilt or non-forgiveness, even though these may all move through us or hold us hostage or terrorise us or stagnate in our body and cause *dis-ease,* as a part of what it can be to be human. We are not anything that can come and go or be born or die, even though our bodies and forms and personalities will be subject to this. Furthermore, if we only know ourselves as these things, it will cause us to want to hold on and to try to "control" life or outcomes, to close our heart down, to avoid the vulnerability of fully meeting our fears and pain and the truth that in fact we do not *absolutely* "know" anything.

I smiled as the realisation surfaced in my awareness again that today was the day we would have boarded our plane for the African adventure. But instead I was here, sitting beside a man who had, more than any other wonderful teachers to have crossed my path, taught my human heart about how to love with freedom and authenticity, and who had been an extraordinary catalyst for the deepest journey yet into my true nature.

I need not have been surprised. The intelligence and creative force of Love always knows what will bring us most alive as the Divine in this human experience. It knows what is most needed for each stage of that journey, what will most make sense of itself as "us" and of the vehicle of "our" body within this fascinating paradigm called Earth. And it is always lining it up beautifully, *even* when the beauty may appear as ugliness or arrives wearing the costume of something we have learned to fear and to believe we need to run away from or control.

The creative power of unconditional, infinite Love is the one and only constant. And as it moves through us in this human experience and we open our conscious awareness to this happening, we can experience this Love inspiring us to choose in favour of the highest good. We can realise that the creative power of Love and the highest good are one and the same thing. And so it might come to pass that we can experience Love stirring us to rearrange and receive ourselves in collaborative community; sense Love nudging us to remember that we *are* that One Animating Spark, expressing through the shared visions it invites within us; and feel Love steering us and *en-couraging* us to take action on that guidance. When we choose to live and express consciously as this Love – from the openhearted place of presence and awareness, acceptance and vulnerability – we can avail ourselves of the mystery and miracle that it is. That is when we might well discover that people can sometimes come back from the brink, that new paradigms can be born, exciting realities can open up, shining potentials can be realised, and a fresh awareness of the aliveness that always was and is now and always will be can be received. When we can acknowledge and accept it all within us, meet our shadow and our light, embrace our humanity and our divinity, then we can receive the wholeness that we are: heaven on earth, miracle of miracles.

From the tree behind us, a flock of raucous cockatoos let rip, their volume drowning out the "peep-peep" of the King Parrots in the distance.

"Bloody hell!" Gordon laughed. "That even beats the noise of the rehab ward!"

"You're not kidding me! And how fantastic is it that we can sit *here* away from *there* and be able to say that! Oh dear . . . Sorry . . . Here come the tears again! But I am so bloody grateful right now!"

"So am I, Babes. I feel overwhelmed to be here but so very, very grateful."

"You are phenomenal, do you know that?" I gazed into his eyes and shook my head in wonderment again. "You know what? I can't wait to pledge our new vows together! Can you believe it's only four months till our wedding anniversary? And so many people are saying they want to come, too."

"I can't wait either! I feel so incredibly loved right now."

"That's because you *are*." I hugged the bones of him. "Reckon

I'm going to have to fatten you up between now and then though. I mean, I don't want to give you your ring back if it's going to fall off your finger, right?"

"Fatten me up, eh? Well I like the sound of that!"

"Ha! I thought you might! Have to say though . . ." I smiled, wanting to tease him until he raised his eyebrows in that funny way again and quizzed me. "Okay, well I have to say that I've become somewhat used to having your ring on my finger. Not sure if I want to part with it. Such a *nice* ring, looks good on me, don't you think?" I gave him a wink.

"Yeah right, in your dreams!"

I looked back out across the water, tracing its meanderings all the way to the distance and the bridge that joined the two headlands rugged up in their woolly, green coats. The champagne-fizzy, Yellow Brick Road of light still played itself out on the surface of the water, winking at us, reminding us, beckoning us onwards to Gordon's recovery, our recovery, new growth, new adventures. I turned to Gordon.

"Shall we?" I nodded back over to the car.

"Sure thing, Babes!" He smiled at me, eyes shining as he stroked my arm.

Home.

The Continuing

Acknowledgements

Just as it took a dedicated group heart to support the miracle of Gordon's trajectory back into this life, so too, have there been many people to whom I am indebted for the creation of this book. Each has held the space for this project, raised its overall vibration by giving it their energy, and facilitated its passage out into the world.

I'd like to express gratitude to my editors Laurel Cohn and Siboney Duff at Laurel Cohn Manuscript and Editing Services. Their unafraid naming of what needed to be culled, insightful suggestions of what to add, and formidable copyediting and proofreading skills all helped my manuscript to develop strong wings.

I thank my beta readers and early reviewers for showing up and following through with reading my work, and for offering invaluable feedback which encouraged and fuelled me on the path.

All credit goes to Denise Williams at Six Degrees Publishing for urging me to add the rich layers of a Preface and Introduction, and for her unwavering dedication to quality and detail, which has helped shine and buff my work into a book that readers can treasure and immerse in.

Heartfelt appreciation also goes to James T. Eagen, my cover designer at Bookfly Design, for his masterful ability to translate my intricate brief, and to nail first time a stunning cover that both stands out from the crowd and draws in the reader.

To my friends, family members, clients, and fans who have been enthusiastic and encouraging cheerleaders for this book becoming a reality of "love in action" in the world – I hug you to the moon and back.

Last but by no means least I remain forever indebted to my husband: bringer of chocolate and hugs when needed, resident chef for the months upon months when my creative muse compelled me only to write and edit. My darling, you have walked every step of this journey with me. You deserve a medal.

About the Author

Caroline Cumming is an author and speaker, intuitive, mentor, and holistic therapist with over fourteen years of experience. She inspires and empowers people from all walks of life to live with an open heart. In this way they can be love in action for themselves, others, and the world. Often described as a "healer of the heart" she is most sought after for her talent in creating experiences that enable one to feel deeply alive again, live true, and plug back into a more natural flow of thriving. Her message is that we all have a heart and we need to marry it with our minds if we are to bring about the world in which we wish to live. Caroline teaches and empowers that union.

A lover of full moons and sunrise, sacred fire and dreams, her insatiable curiosity and relationship with both the natural world and the magical unseen informs all that she does. She lives with her husband on the beautiful coast of NSW, Australia. *The Love of One* is her first book.

For more information on mentoring with Caroline through her private programmes, visit **www.ccumming.com**. You can also sign up there for her free gift and engaging weekly editions of "Notes from the Eagles Nest", to feel more alive and connected in all that you do.

**Further information and event schedules,
visit Caroline's Author Page at
SixDegreesPublishing.com**